MORAL RESPONSIBILITY

BOOKS BY JOSEPH FLETCHER
Published by The Westminster Press

Moral Responsibility:
    Situation Ethics at Work

Situation Ethics:
    The New Morality

MORAL RESPONSIBILITY

SITUATION ETHICS AT WORK

by

Joseph Fletcher

THE WESTMINSTER PRESS

Philadelphia

LIBRARY OF CONGRESS CATALOG CARD No. 67–14515

Published by The Westminster Press ®
Philadelphia, Pennsylvania

PRINTED IN THE UNITED STATES OF AMERICA

Contents

Part Three: A STYLE OF LIFE

Foreword

SITUATION ETHICS puts such a high premium on freedom from prefabricated decisions and prescriptive rules that it constantly faces opposition from creatures of the conventional wisdom. Are people *capable* of making their own moral choices without being humbly subservient to moral principles? Are people, in fact, even *willing* to act and choose on behalf of their neighbors out of loving concern?

These questions are fairly raised. They point to the relevance and importance of "responsibility." Robert Greenleaf somewhere says that responsibility is a hard thing to talk about, that it is often seen as something others should have more of. I am sure that there are times when, for the sake of understanding, it is better to stop talking and simply point. In that spirit the following pages set out not only some theory or abstract talk about situation ethics but some practical treatments of concrete problems calling for moral decision. The only way we can be certain that we know what the other fellow is really saying is when he converts his statements and generalizations into their operational terms—who does what, when, in which circumstances.

The readers should be clear at the outset, however, about the relative or nonabsolute and variant or nonuniversal nature of the situational approach to ethical policy forming and decision making. The analyses of, and conclusions about, certain moral problems discussed in this book are *one* situationist's work. Others might, and do, come up with other results. The openness and nonlegalistic strategy of situationism allows for differences of judgment.

This book says a good deal indirectly about responsibility in the course of its wrestling with specific moral issues, but a final chapter turns pointedly to the subject, head on. Wisely or not, it was decided to make discussion of the concept itself a summary comment on what had been said rather than a prefatory theory about what was to be said. Situationists are chary about abstractions and generalizations, especially in the absence of concretion and circumstance.

Most people think of responsibility (conscientiousness?) as a matter of comforming to established practice and conventional morality, out of respect for or fear of familiar sanctions and reinforcements. What is smugly assumed in the establishmentarian's soul is that moral rules and reward-punishments are all set, and that people should come to heel and play the game that way. But not so. Responsibility means a free and critical "conformity" to the facts first of all—the shifting patterns of situations—and then to the unchanging single norm or boss principle of loving concern for persons and the social balance. As Bonhoeffer put it in his *Ethics* (p. 213, Eng. tr., 1955): "The conscience which has been set free is not timid like the conscience which is bound by the law, but it stands wide open for our neighbor and for his concrete distress." What a pity that Bonhoeffer was executed by the Hitlerites before he could put together his projected and outlined thesis on the "structure" of love and responsibility.

Grateful acknowledgment is due the publishers for permission to reproduce articles previously published. In some cases I have made minor revisions to bring these materials up to date. Sources are identified further on the first page of each chapter.

J. F.

Cambridge, Massachusetts

PART ONE

A NEW LOOK

PART FIVE

A NEW LOOK

I

The New Look in Christian Ethics

A RECONNOITERING of bedrock premises is always in order
for those of us who work mainly on casuistry, on actual
cases of conscience. We are called upon constantly to declare our "principles" when we wrestle with situations and
problems arising out of the ministry, the law, medicine,
diplomacy, industrial and business management, collective bargaining, public policy and government, family relations—anywhere in the whole range of human affairs.

In the language fashionable just now, "problem solving"
and "decision making" are the pragmatic dimensions of
Christian ethical analysis. But they desperately need the
discipline of "concept formation" too. True-life situations
are an endlessly rich and illuminating "field" in which
to hammer out a working theoretical apparatus, but the
foundations have to be laid in the various theological disciplines—Biblical, historical, moral, systematic, ascetical,
and philosophical. Yet it may be when the Christian problem solver in the middle of the twentieth century reviews
his presuppositions, the result will not seem to be in any
classical sense particularly Catholic or Anglican or Protestant or Orthodox.

Read before the Alumni Association of the Harvard Divinity School at its annual meeting in April, 1959, and published
in the *Harvard Divinity Bulletin,* October, 1959. It is often
cited as the "seed document" of situation ethics in recent
Christian ethical theory.

Six basic propositions emerge. Here, then, are terse and tight statements of these six propositions—in each case a distillation only, inelaborate. There are at least two reasons for such capsules or miniature constructions. For one thing, they are dictated by a lecture's time limits. But more important, they can, by being briefly drawn, silhouette the more sharply the vital issues at stake. Being so brief they may, of course, appear too stark or even alien to the Christian ethos, at least at first sight. Nevertheless they are, in actual and everyday fact, the "hidden persuaders" that lurk behind a great deal of both Christian ethics and contemporary culture. Now we shall set them out in plain sight.

However, before we can set them out there is one observation to be made about the nature of moral judgments, as we fashion them in Christian ethics. *Christian moral judgments are decisions, not conclusions.* From the point of view of "pure reason" it must be confessed that the "practical reason" (Kant's moral faculty) works in a style quite as arbitrary and absurd as the leap of faith. Just as we cannot by reason alone build a bridge philosophically from doubt to the side of faith, from hope to certainty, or from nature to grace, so we cannot build a logical bridge from facts to values, from is-ness to ought-ness. Indeed, this applies as much to aesthetics as to ethics, i.e., to art values as to moral values. Every kind of value proposition is a faith proposition. The leap of affirmation is essential. This is why William Temple said of value exactly what he said of revelation, that it "depends for its actuality upon the appreciating mind."[1]

There has always been this elementary truth to be dealt with, having its classical form in Hume's argument. It is the starting point used by our unbelieving contemporaries of the positivist persuasion, who remind us that we cannot except by a leap get across from descriptive to prescriptive propositions. To get from any hypothetical statement, such as, "If you believe in the Lordship of Christ, you will love your neighbors," to the normative statement, "You ought to love your neighbors," to say nothing of getting to the full imperative statement, "Love thy neighbors as thyself" —surely this is a question of a leap, not a step in logic or common sense! Anselm's *"Credo ut intelligam"* should always be paired with a *"Credo ut judiceam."*

In moral theology, or, if you prefer, theological morals or Christian ethics, there is no way to reach the key category of love, of *agape* as the primordial or axiomatic value, the *summum bonum,* except by an act of faith which says "yea" to the faith proposition that "God is love" and therefore to the value proposition that love is good. A sincere man, every whit as "decent" and intelligent as a committed Christian, can stand uncommitted to faith in the incarnation and atonement—and in the same way he can in all seriousness remain a doubter about the hope and the love which join that faith to form Paul's triad of theological virtues. Like the end product of the judicial process in civil law, the court's finding, Christian moral judgments are *decisions,* not conclusions. Both ethics and jurisprudence are evaluating and choosing; science and logic are only auxiliary. There is no way in the world, for example, to "prove" that the Supreme Court was "right" that the schools "ought" and "must" integrate across race lines.

The following six propositions are the fundamentals of Christian conscience. The first one points to the nature of value. The second reduces all values to love. The third equates love and justice. The fourth frees love from sentimentality. The fifth states the relation between means and ends. The sixth validates every judgment within its own context.

Proposition I

*Only one thing is intrinsically good, namely, love:
nothing else.*

The rock-bottom issue in all ethics is whether value is
inherent or contingent. Is the good or evil of a thing, the
right or wrong of an action, intrinsic or extrinsic? The
medieval nominalist-realist debate is still very much alive
in Christian ethics. Our whole present-day testimony is on
the nominalists' side. Brunner flatly asserts, "there are no
'intrinsic' values" and allows only that values "exist in
reference to persons."[2] This is the same "personalist" insight that we find in the existentialist Buber, who insists
that "value is always value for a person, rather than something with an absolute, independent existence."[3] It is held
even by a metaphysician such as Brightman, who found
that "in personality is the only true intrinsic value we
know or could conceive; all values are but forms of personal experience."[4]

Hence in such a Christian ethics nothing has any worth
except as it helps or hurts persons, either human or divine
—God or neighbor or self. Good and evil are extrinsic.
Right and wrong *depend upon the situation*. Apart from
helping or hurting persons, judgments—i.e., evaluations
—are meaningless. There is in Christian ethics with its
love norm only one thing which is intrinsically good,
always and everywhere, regardless of circumstances. That
one thing is love itself. On the reverse side, malice is,
therefore, the only thing intrinsically evil. Kant's second
maxim, to treat people as ends and never as means, parallels Paul's "law of love." And Kant's contention that the
only good thing is a good will, which is what the New
Testament means by love, goes necessarily with his second
maxim. Whatever is "benevolent" is right; whatever is
"malevolent" is wrong.

This proposition sets us over against any "intrinsicalist"

doctrines. For example, when John Bennett says "there are situations in which the best we can do is evil," we have to make a basic challenge.[5] Such statements divorce what is right from what is good, and this comes about because they rest upon the intrinsicalist assumption. On that basis if a merchant tells a lie to divert "protection" racketeers from their victim, no matter how compassionately and effectively, he has chosen to do what is evil. At the very best it can only be excused as a so-called "lesser evil." On the other hand, in the extrinsicalist world he has chosen to do the *good* rather than an evil! Since love is served according to the situation, good is done and righteousness prevails.

On the intrinsic theory Roman Catholic moralists deny that a captured soldier may commit suicide to avoid betraying his comrades to the enemy under torture.[6] This is because they find the evil of suicide *in the suicide itself*, intrinsically. But an extrinsic doctrine of value, such as the Christian love standard, finds the true evil in the multiple destruction which would follow if the prisoner's willing sacrifice is forbidden. Both Roman Catholic and many Protestant theologians often "reify" good and evil. For them, therefore, suicide and lying are always wrong regardless of circumstances, even though some of them may excuse such "evils" sometimes as relatively necessary. But this is all wrong, because *only one thing is intrinsically good, namely, love: nothing else.*

PROPOSITION II

The ultimate norm of Christian decisions is love: nothing else.

Love is a univalent or monolithic standard. It shoulders aside all codes. The Christian ethic reduces law from a statutory system of rules to the love canon alone. This is why Jesus was ready to ignore the Sabbath observance, why

Paul was plainly permissive about circumcision. They replaced the precepts of Torah with the living principle of *agape*—*agape* being good will at work in partnership with reason, seeking the neighbor's good radically, nonpreferentially. It is "no respecter of persons." The New Testament redeemed law from the letter back to its spirit, refined it from legalistic prescriptions to its core principle of love.

Consequently Christian ethics is not a scheme of codified conduct. It is a purposive effort to relate love to a world of relativities through a casuistry obedient to love. Moral theology seeks to work out love's strategy, and casuistry devises its tactics. This is no "antinomian" process, even though it *is* radically relativistic. Admittedly it separates creed from *code,* but not from conduct—as some Evangelical and Catholic critics charge.[7] What it does is to regard the "cardinal" and "theological" virtues as merely love's agents and subordinates, in the same way that the "capital vices" are pride's. Augustine was right to make love the source principle from which all else derives, not a virtue alongside other virtues. He was right to reduce the whole Christian ethic to the single maxim *dilige et quod vis, fac*—love and *then* what you will, do.[8] (It was not, by the way, *ama et fac quod vis*—love and do what you please!) The first question for ethics is not "How do we behave?" but "What do we want?"

What a difference it makes when love is the only norm! The "natural law" moralists are continually trapped into cheating or even altogether denying love's demands. For example, they prohibit surgeons from "tying off the tubes" of a cardiac mother in delivery, and sometimes even forbid a doctor to warn a girl innocently marrying one of his syphilitic patients.[9] This is done for the sake of alleged "natural" laws—of procreation in the first case and secrecy in the second. Given such nature legalism, it is no wonder that a Roman Catholic philosopher recently repudiated love's monopoly. He said, "While the motive of love is a noble one, it is not in Christian tradition to present it as the exclusive motive for moral action."[10] This succinctly challenges the love ethic.

But all the same, love *is* a "jealous" law to itself. It does not share its power with other kinds of law, either natural or supernatural. It is even capable of "desecrating" the Holy of Holies, the very tabernacle of the altar, if human (personal) hunger cries for help. Jesus left no doubt about love being the solitary commandment when he put his stamp of approval on the translegality of David's action, in the paradigm of the altar bread: "Have you not read what David did, when he was hungry, and those who were with him: how he entered the house of God and ate the bread of the Presence, which it was not lawful for him to eat nor for those who were with him, but only for the priests?" (Matt. 12:3–4.) Thus he left no doubt whatsoever that *the ultimate norm of Christian decisions is love: nothing else.*

PROPOSITION III

*Love and justice are the same,
for justice is love distributed.*

This proposition illuminates many of casuistry's shadows. Practically every problem of "perplexed" conscience, as distinguished from a "doubtful" conscience, can be reduced to the tension between love and justice. Augustine, let us remember, had to confess that love's rule needs "more than good will, and can be done only by a high degree of thoughtfulness and prudence."[11] Why, otherwise, would he have said *dilige*—i.e., be *carefully* concerned, be "diligent" about love? This is a point that businessmen fully appreciate when they try to balance quality and price in a low-income market, or by a personnel manager who has to choose between letting an illness-weakened supply clerk keep his job, on the one hand, and on the other, play-

ing fair with other workers whose output and piece rate
pay are being cut down by the clerk's delays. In this perspective we are forced to pull back from the single-minded
irrationalism of the Luther dictum, "Whoever wants to be
a Christian should tear out the eyes of reason" because
"reason is a whore."

Here is precisely the serious difficulty of love—how to
distribute its favors among so many beneficiaries, *how* to
love justice, how to be just about love. Granted that justice
is giving to each man what is his due, according to the
classical definition, how are we to calculate and distribute
love's benefits as between several claimants? Because as
persons we exist in community, love's outreach is pluralist,
not monist. Faced with the web of duties in our social existence, confronted by many neighbors, love is compelled to
be calculating. Even Paul Ramsey was finally forced, in his
exposition of the radical love ethic, to confess that love is,
so to speak, compelled to "figure the angles!"[12] Calculation or "prudence" keeps love's imagination sharpened and
at work, saves it from sentimental myopia as it seeks its
object. This is the operational or situational discipline of
the love ethic—finding absolute love's *relative* course.

In all humility, in spite of any pious hesitations, Christian ethics is under obligation from love itself to "tinker
with Scripture." We have to add an "s" to Jesus' Summary
of the Law, and to Paul's—we must convert the generic
"neighbor" who is to be loved into the plural "neighbors."
The plural is already implicit, but practical conscience has
to make it explicit—in order to avoid the oversimplifying,
Tolstoyan notion that love wears blinders, never calculates,
sees only the one-to-one *immediate* neighbor who is to be
loved, one at a time.[13]

However, the main thing to emphasize is that only a
misdirected and confused conscience has to wrestle with
such pseudo issues as justice *versus* love, or justice *or* love,
or even justice *and* love. Like the Roman moralists, both

Brunner and Niebuhr separate them into two independent categories—relating them either by opposition ("against"), by option ("or"), or by alteration ("and"). But this conception has only managed to muddy the waters of ethical relativism. Christianly speaking, we know that justice *is* love! Justice is *agape* working out its problems. Justice is Christian love using its head—calculating its duties. The Christian love ethic, searching seriously for a social policy, forms a coalition with the utilitarian principle of the "greatest good of the greatest number." Of course it reshapes it into the "most love for the most neighbors." Faith provides the value principle of love and rejects utilitarianism's hedonistic value, using only its *procedural* principle, its method. In any such coalition there is obviously a risk that love may be thinned out by calculation, but this is the "calculated risk" which all-inclusive love is bound to take.

A resident physician on emergency service, deciding whether to give the hospital's last unit of plasma to a young mother of three or to an old skid-row drunk, may suppose that he is being forced to make a tragic choice between love "or" justice—he may think that choosing the good of the mother and her children means ignoring love's impartial and "nonpreferential" concern for every neighbor. But love must make estimates; it *is* preferential. To prefer the mother *in that situation* is the most loving decision, and therefore just. If love does not calculate the immediate and remote consequences, it turns irresponsible and subverts its own high office. Roman moral theology, agreeing with Niebuhr that love and justice can come into conflict, has settled for the maxim that we may sometimes deny love but never justice![14] This is perhaps the best they can do—this demotion of love—given their initial mistake. Actually, the choice is only between either sentimental or discerning love, not between love and something else. *Love and justice are the same, for justice is love distributed.*

PROPOSITION IV

Love wills the neighbor's good whether we like him or not.

To love Christianly is a matter of attitude, not of feeling.
Love is discerning and critical; it is not sentimental. Whatever we may think about his thesis as a whole, Anders
Nygren's analysis in *Agape and Eros* (1932) has at least
provided us with a valid distinction—and Christian love
is definitely "agapeic," not erotic. As Canon Quick puts it,
"whereas in *eros* desire is the cause of love, in *agape* love is
the cause of desire."[15] *Agape's* desire is to satisfy the neighbor's need, not one's own, but the main thing about it is
that *agape*-love precedes all desire, of any kind. The ethic
of *agape* is a *Gesinnungsethik*, an attitudinal ethic. It is not
at all an emotional ethic. It is volitional, conative.

As Richardson's *Theological Word Book* shows, New
Testament love "has neither the warmth of *phileo* nor the
intensity of *erao*" and refers to "the will rather than to emotion."[16] Bishop Stephen Neill calls it "the steady directing
of the human will towards the eternal well-being of another."[17] According to Kierkegaard, to say that love is a
feeling or anything of that kind is an unchristian conception of love.[18] Therefore C. H. Dodd says that "it is not
primarily an emotion or an affection; it is primarily an active determination of the will. That is why it can be commanded, as feelings cannot."[19] *Loving and liking are not
the same.*

Pinned down to its precise meaning, Christian love is
"benevolence," literally. *Good will.* It is, of course, true
that the word "benevolence" and the term "good will" have
by usage acquired a tepid, almost merely *polite* sense.
Nevertheless, this is what Christian love is. It does not
seek the deserving, is not judgmental when it makes its
judgments; it does not reserve itself to the congenial or the
responsive. We can say properly that Christian love is a
matter of loving the unlovable, the unlikable. Indeed, it

is even more radical than that in its nonreciprocity and
noncongeniality—Matt. 5:43–48 puts it with the bluntest
extremism: "Love your *enemies*. . . . For if you love those
who love you, what reward have you?"

To require or to claim that we *like* everybody is a hypocrisy and an impossibility. Kant observed that love cannot
be commanded, yet in his own way he understood that
while *eros* (and for that matter, *philia*) cannot be ordered
at will, *agape* can. Referring to Jesus' Summary of the
Law, in the second part, he explained that "it is only
practical love that is meant in that pith of all laws."[20]
There is nothing sentimental about Christian love.

Admittedly there can be no command, no obligation,
no duty to love if love is affection—as it assuredly is in
both romantic love (*eros*) and in friendship love (*philia*).
Genuine affection—what psychologists call "affect" to
mark it off from conation or will—cannot be turned off
and on like water from a faucet, simply by an act of will.
But kindness, generosity, mercy, patience, concern, "righteous indignation"—these things are dispositions of the
will, *attitudes,* and therefore psychologically speaking they
are perfectly possible requirements of duty and commandment, of covenant.

The radical obligation of the Christian ethic to love even
the enemy implies unmistakably that every neighbor is not
a friend and that some are just the opposite. But Christian
love, which is not a matter of reciprocity at all, is agapeic
—not erotic or philic. *Love wills the neighbor's good
whether we like him or not!*

PROPOSITION V

Only the end justifies the means: nothing else.

Given our present perspective, it is amazing that Christian ethics down through the centuries could have accepted almost unanimously the sententious doctrine that

"the end does not justify the means." We have to ask now,
"If the end does not justify the means, what does?" The
answer is, obviously, "Nothing!" Indeed, unless justified
by some end in view, any action is literally meaningless—
i.e., means-less, merely random, pointless. It is in fact
only the end that justifies any means. Trying to absolutize
Paul's remark in Rom. 3:8 ("We may not do evil that
good shall come")—a remark clearly implied, although
not positively stated—classical Christian ethics has lent
itself to a vast amount of equivocal and downright con-
tradictory opinion. The endless debates and talmudic
"pilpul" ground out to rationalize war's ruthless methods,
capital and corporal punishment, diplomatic subterfuge,
surgical mutilation, and a host of other "lesser evil" practices—all derive from the inconsistency of paying lip
service to a maxim that the practices in question obviously
contradict!

We have already seen, in connection with our Proposition I, that the "intrinsic" theory of value traps its holders
into either absolute prohibitions of certain actions regardless of circumstances—for example, forbidding a lie which
could lead to a great good—or into stigmatizing as a "lesser
evil" such loving actions as stealing a neighbor's gun to
keep him from shooting somebody in anger. As Paul said
twice in his first letter to Corinth (chs. 6:12; 10:23),
this approach fails to perceive that it is not its being "lawful" that makes a thing good but whether it is expedient,
edifying, constructive—whether it builds up. What *else*
could make a thing "lawful" (i.e., loving) except agapeic
expediency? Theodore Roosevelt was either not quite candid or not very thoughtful when he said, "No man is justified in doing evil on the ground of expediency."[21] He was
much too mired down in "intrinsic" moralism.

Once we realize that only love is intrinsically good, and
that no action apart from its foreseeable consequences has
any ethical meaning at all—only then will we see that the

proper question is, "Does an evil means always nullify a good end?" And the answer, on a basis of "due proportion" or situational estimate, must be "No." All depends upon the situation, i.e., the relative weight of the ends and means and motives and consequences all taken together, as weighed by love. Bishop Kirk came close to this standpoint when, speaking of the old rule about means and ends, he said: "The correct form of the maxim, in fact, is 'circumstances alter cases.' And this is obviously true. An act which is right in some circumstances may be wrong in others."[22] However, be it noted, he did not say that an act which is wrong in some cases can be right in others. His bid for freedom was too fainthearted.

Only the end justifies the means. It cannot justify itself! What was once charged as an accusation against the Jesuits is here frankly embraced: *finis sanctificat media*. This is what our doctrine of extrinsic or contingent value entails. And therefore, in the relativities of this world where conscience works, we may do what *would* be evil in some contexts if, *in this one,* love gains the balance. On this ground we must flatly oppose the classical rule in moral theology which allows us to omit a preponderantly good action just because the necessary means happens to entail some evil. If the emotional and spiritual welfare of both parents and children in a *particular* family can be served best by a divorce, wrong and cheap-jack as divorce commonly is, then love requires it. Love's method is particularity. Getting a divorce is like eating the altar bread in this particular case. *Only the end justifies the means: nothing else.*

Proposition VI

Decisions ought to be made situationally, not prescriptively.

It seems almost a self-evident finding of culture analysis that our age is one of relativistic thought forms—not only in scientific "fact" opinions but also in "idea" and "value" opinions. Lynn White in a recent symposium on anthropology describes four major shifts in the canons of culture —all in the direction of relativity: (1) from an occidental to a global outlook, (2) from language and logic to symbols and image communication (think only of television, for example), (3) from rationality to the unconscious as the foundation of human behavior, and (4) from a hierarchy to a spectrum of values—i.e., from the idea that some things are better or worse than others to the view that they are only different, that they shade back and forth into each other according to the situation and culture context.[23] With some of our contemporaries this takes the radical form of *de gustibus non est disputandum* and "what's one man's meat is another man's poison"—a kind of "absolute relativism" or true antinomianism.

Ethical relativism has invaded Christian ethics steadily ever since the simultaneous appearance in 1932 of Brunner's *Divine Imperative* and Reinhold Niebuhr's *Moral Man and Immoral Society*. This was a quarter century ago, the year of the New Deal! They built on the principle that the divine command is always the same in the *Why*, but always different in the *What*.[24] Ever since then the shift has been away from code ethics, from stern and ironbound do's and don'ts, from prescribed conduct and legalistic morality. Torah law is in this era suffering a second eclipse, even more radical than when Jesus and Paul first attacked it—because the culture context, the milieu controls, are more appropriate today to such an eclipse than in the apostolic and patristic period.

Contemporary Christians should not make the blunder of underestimating this relativism—either as to its general trend or its Christian form in particular. Christian ethics is already drawn into it and fully "implicated" by its doctrine of man as a finite and therefore, sinful creature, and by the Biblical warning, phrased by Isaiah (ch. 55:8),

"For my thoughts are not your thoughts, neither are your ways my ways, saith the Lord." This primary concept of creatureliness cries "relativity" on every human score.

There is a comic desk sign which reads: "My Mind Is Made Up—Don't Confuse Me With The Facts!" This joke is no joke for ethics. It points to a spiritual insecurity which makes people long for an ethical "system" of pre-fabricated morality, of rules to lean on. Contextual, situational, clinical, circumstantial case method or casuistry is too full of variables for them—they want only constants. As life and culture become increasingly complicated and wide-scoped, our ethical problems and decisions grow complex. Then it is that "prefab" code ethics reveals itself as a neurotic "security measure" to simplify personal decisions. Many people prefer to fit reality to rules rather than vice versa. Legalism always emphasizes order and conformity, while "situation ethics" puts its premium on freedom and responsibility. Situation ethics always suspects prescriptive law of falsifying whether it is the *Scripture* legalism of Biblicist Protestantism or the *nature* legalism ("natural law") of Roman Catholic philosophy. One writer recently complained that most people do not want "paradoxical ambiguities"—they prefer something definite[25] This is no doubt true. But they are going to have to learn love's tactics, and put away their childish rules.

If actions are right only *because* they are loving, then they are only right *when* they are loving. The righteousness (rightness) of an action does not reside in the act itself but "holistically" in *the loving configuration* of the factors in the situation—in the "elements of a human act" —i.e., its totality of end, means, motive, and foreseeable consequences. The rightness is in the *Gestalt* or shape of the action as a whole, and not in any single phase or dimension of it.

When love's decisions are made, they are relative—if love reigns and not law. Love plots the course according to the circumstances. Only the obligation is absolute—the obligation to stand by our decisions—but the decisions themselves are *relative* to the situation. The metaphysical moralist with his intrinsic values and laws says, "Do what is right and let the chips fall where they may." The situational moralist says, "Whether what you do is right or not depends precisely upon where the chips fall!" John Kasper, a racist agitator, was convicted in Tennessee in November, 1958, of inciting to riot in a school desegregation situation. Judge Homer Weimer told the jury that we all have a right to make public speeches but we must answer for the consequences. A Christian situationist would say to Kasper: "You may claim a 'natural' or 'God-given' right to speak, but whether you have *a right to exercise your right* —i.e., whether you actually have any right at all—depends on the situation."

This contemporary shape of Christian ethics was accurately described and labeled as "existential" or "situational" by Pope Pius XII in an allocution on April 18, 1952.[26] He denounced it, of course, pointing out that such a nonprescriptive ethic might be used to justify a Catholic leaving the Roman Church if it seemed to bring him closer to God, or to defend the practice of birth control just because personality could be enhanced thereby! Four years later, February 2, 1956, the Supreme Sacred Congregation of the Holy Office called it "the new morality" and banned it from all academies and seminaries, trying to counteract its influence among Roman Catholic moralists. The "situations-ethik" is more and more openly invading nonfundamentalist Protestant ethics—cultivating a kind of neocasuistry among the neo-orthodox! Not only Roman Catholics but conservative and even liberal Protestants still fear it, charging that a justified antilegalism is ending up in an unjustified antinomianism, and even using epithets such as "moral nihilism" when referring to situation ethics. To this, in one way or another, the new moralists such as H. R. Niebuhr, Alexander Miller, James Gustafson, Paul Lehmann, D. D. Williams, Kenneth Underwood, and Albert Rasmussen—to mention only a few—continue to reply that *decisions ought to be made situationally, not prescriptively*.

POSTSCRIPT

Situationism, then, is the crystal precipitated in Christian ethics by our era's widespread reaction against legalism. In plain fact men have always been situationists, more or less, but the difference now is that they are situationists as a matter of rational and professed method. Gone is the former sense of guilt and of cheated ideals when we tailor our ethical cloth to fit the back of each occasion. We are, for this reason, closing the gap between our overt and covert cultures!

In the closing paragraph of his *Moral Man and Immoral Society,* Reinhold Niebuhr, summarizing his thesis that man's hope for "perfect justice" is an illusion, ended by saying, "One can only hope that reason will not destroy it [i.e., the illusion] before its work is done."[27] What a pious and wishful note, to first discredit abstract ideals with such a devastating analysis as his was—and then still want to keep their dynamic force! We cannot eat our cake and have it too. The actual trend, of course, has been that reason progressively banishes all perfectionism from Christian ethics, more and more by an open declaration and repudiation.

This is a neocasuistry—this situationism. It is, like classical casuistry, case-focused and concrete, concerned to bring Christian imperatives into practical operation. But unlike classical casuistry, this neocasuistry repudiates the attempt to anticipate or prescribe real-life decisions in their existential particularity. There is, after all, no discredit to the old-fashioned casuists, nor to the Talmudists, in the old saying that they continually made rules for the breaking of rules. They were turning and twisting in their own trap to serve love as well as law, but unfortunately the only result is a never ending tangle of legalism in any ethics which attempts to correct code law with loving-kindness. The reverse of these roles is vitally necessary. It is love which is the constitutive principle—and law, at most, is only the regulative one if it is even that.

The neocasuists do not always render justice to the classical casuistry. In his "Approach to Protestant Casuistry," Edward LeRoy Long has confused casuistry with *compromise!*[28] Doubt and perplexity about obligation are not necessarily compromise, and even the old casuistry was not motivated merely by a desire to cut corners or water the milk. Dietrich Bonhoeffer was not entirely correct when he identified ethical "formalism" with casuistry. As a matter of fact, Bonhoeffer's own neocasuist *Ethics* makes it plain that Christian conscience can be free of formal fetters and still be both "entirely concrete" and case-focused, yet obedient to love.

Moralists like Long and Bonhoeffer are, in any case, clear about the heart of the matter—the absoluteness of the Word and the relativity of the deed. For the Christian conscience the total context of decision, the whole situation, is always "circumstances under the law of love."[29] Situational Christian ethics has a tactical formula for the strategy of love: *the indicative plus the imperative equals the normative.* What is, in the light of what love demands, shows what ought to be.

Said Paul to the saints at Philippi: "And this I pray, that your love may abound more and more in knowledge and in all judgment." (Phil. 1:9.) Here are the four pillars of the method of Christian ethics: (1) a prayerful reliance upon God's grace, (2) the law of love as the norm, (3) knowledge of the facts, of the empirical situation in all its variety and relativity, and (4) judgment—i.e., decision—which is responsibility in humility.

II

Love Is the Only Measure

THE NEW MORALITY, so called, is taking a long, hard second look at some of our assumptions. It does not oversimplify the issues at stake, even though some of its professed advocates do, yet it most certainly poses the essential questions. It might be said to be a revolt against what Henry Miller, the paper tiger of the sex rebels, calls "the immorality of morality" (in *Stand Still like the Hummingbird*).

Any serious discussion of the new morality should begin with philosophical candor. Let it be understood, then, that the new morality is a form of ethical relativism. A *locus classicus* might be Paul Tillich's blunt statement: "The truth of ethical relativism lies in the moral law's inability to give commandments which are unambiguous both in their general form and in their concrete applications. Every moral law is abstract in relation to the unique and totally concrete situation. This is true of what has been called natural law and of what has been called revealed law."

An old joke can serve to pose the problem. When a rich old man asked a lovely young woman if she would sleep the night with him she said, indignantly, "No." He then

A statement in a "dialogue" with Father Herbert McCabe, O.P., editor of the London *Blackfriars*, published in *Commonweal*, the Catholic lay-edited weekly, January 14, 1966, with rejoinders afterward by both writers.

asked if she would do it for $100,000. She said, "Yes!" She even agreed to $10,000, but when he came down to $500 she exclaimed, "What do you think I am?" He replied: "We have already established that. Now we are haggling over the price." Is any girl who has "relations" (a debased way to use the word) outside marriage *ipso facto* a prostitute or loose woman, guilty of sin or wrong? Or, as the new moralist would say, does it all depend upon the situation?

There are at bottom just three lines of approach to moral decision making. One of them, perhaps the least followed but having at least some following, is the antinomian or lawless (nonprincipled) method. It operates with spontaneous decisions. Christian antinomians or extemporists, such as those Paul opposed in Corinth, often claim to be above any moral law (since they are "saved" or guided directly by the Holy Spirit). In any case they repudiate not only all rules of morality but even general principles. Non-Christian antinomians, such as Jean-Paul Sartre, make their moral decisions with "autonomy" and "instantaneity," i.e., without help from general maxims, unpredictably, wholly within the situation, in the belief that one "moment" of existence is entirely discontinuous from others—so that we cannot generalize about our decision making.

For example, even if you described in the most complete detail all the facts involved and all the considerations pro and con joining a labor union where the antinomian works, or whether he should respond to a plea for a loan from a good family man or from a hopeless wastrel, he could not possibly say how he might decide until he was there, then, led by God's spirit or his own. Spontaneity is the key to his method.

At the opposite end of the spectrum of approaches is legalism. In this ethical strategy the "situational variables" are taken into consideration, but the circumstances are always subordinated to predetermined general "laws" of morality. Legalistic ethics treats many of its rules idolatrously by making them into absolutes. Classical Christian ethics and moral theology ("seminary" or "manualistic" ethics and casuistry), like the conventional wisdom, has been mainly of this kind. Not all legalism is cruelly rigid or callous about sticking to the letter even if the spirit is ignored, but too much of it is guilty on that score. The Scriptural law of Protestant morality and the natural law of Catholic morality, each in its own way, have treated principles as rules rather than maxims. In this kind of morality, properly labeled as legalism or law ethics, obedience to prefabricated "rules of conduct" is more important than freedom to make responsible decisions.

For example, if you were a Roman Catholic husband and found that, for whatever reason, the only method of family limitation which worked was contraception, you would either have to go on begetting unwanted children beyond a responsible number or cease the unitive lovemaking which is a vital part of a good marriage. This would be because contraception is declared (at least as of this writing) by your church to be always "against nature." If you were a Jehovah's Witness, you would refuse a blood transfusion to save your life, or even your child's, because "the Bible says we must abstain from blood" (which it does, however differently you might exegete the "texts" cited).

The third method of approach is that of the "new" morality. This is situation ethics. In this moral strategy the governing consideration is the situation, with all of its contingencies and exigencies. The situationist enters into every decision-making situation armed with principles, just as the legalist does. But the all-important difference is that his moral principles are *maxims* of general or frequent validity; their validity always depends upon the situation. The situationist is prepared in any concrete case to suspend, ignore, or violate any principle if by doing so he can effect more good than by following it. As Dietrich Bonhoeffer said in his prison-written *Ethics,* after conspiring to assassinate Hitler, "Principles are only tools in the hand of God, soon to be thrown away as unserviceable."

Adultery, for instance, is ordinarily wrong, not in itself but because the emotional, legal, and spiritual entailments are such that the overall effects are evil and hurtful rather than helpful—at least in our present-day Western society. But there is always the outside case, the unusual situation, what Karl Barth calls the *ultima ratio,* in which adultery could be the right and good thing. This writer knows of such a case, in which committing adultery foreseeably brought about the release of a whole family from a very unjust but entirely legal exploitation of their labor on a small farm which was both their pride and their prison. Still another situation could be cited in which a German mother gained her release from a Soviet prison farm and reunion with her family by means of an adulterous pregnancy. These actions would have the situationist's solemn but ready approval.

How Is One to Judge?

With these three ethical perspectives in mind, how are we to "judge" the Puerto Rican woman in Bruce Kenrick's story about the East Harlem Protestant Parish, *Come Out the Wilderness.* She was proud of her son and told the minister how she had "made friends" with a married man, praying God she'd have a son, and eventually she bore one. The minister, dear silly man that he is, told her it was okay if she was repentant, and she replied, "Repent? I ain't repentin'. I asked the Lord for my boy. He's a gift from God." She is *right* (which, by the way, does *not* mean a situationist approves in the abstract of the absence of any husband in so many disadvantaged Negro and Puerto Rican families).

It is necessary and important to note this: that situation ethics or the "new morality" is *not* the existentialists' or antinomians' method. Unfortunately the waters of debate have been badly muddied since the Second World War, because some observers, both Catholic and Protestant, have got the two all mixed up and confused. Future historians of modern ethics may fix the start of this confusion in the advice of Roman Catholic moral theologians which led to an allocution by Pope Pius XII on April 8, 1952. He used the terms "existential" and "situational" as synonymous. On February 2, 1956, situation ethics in another papal utterance was called "the new morality," and ever since then the debate has been at sixes and sevens. The *situationism* of the "new" morality is definitely *not* existential, in the sense that secular and atheist exponents of it use the term.

There are three, not just two, alternatives open to honest people who want to choose their moral course, whether they happen to be Christians or not. We don't have to be either legalists who absolutize ethical principles, or extemporists who make decisions without any principles at all. We can choose (and I would urge it) to be situationists, acknowledging our heritage of canonical and civil principles of right and wrong but remaining free to decide for ourselves responsibly in all situations which principles are to be followed, or in some cases to decide that the "relevant" principles are to be rejected because they would result in more evil than good.

What, then, is good? Asking this question drives home the basic fact that the "new" morality, situationism, is a moral strategy or procedural doctrine that has to be seen in tandem or partnership with a substantive companion doctrine—personalism. And "personalism" here means the ethical view that the highest good, the *summum bonum* or first-order value, is human welfare and happiness (but not, necessarily, pleasure). Good is, first and foremost, the good of *people*. Christians call it "love," meaning neighbor-concern or *agape*. This love means, of course, a social attitude, not the romantic emotion that the word has come to connote in popular literature. The great commandment orders Christians to love, i.e., to seek the well-being of people— not to love principles. Non-Christians may call it something else, for example, "justice" or "altruism" or "humanism" or the like, but whatever label they use, it is a personalist devotion to people, not to things or abstractions such as "laws" or general principles. Personal interests come first, before the natural or Scriptural or theoretical or general or logical or anything else.

SEXUAL ETHICS

When we think about the conflict between the old or classical morality, the law ethic, and the new morality, the love ethic, we can see that the nub of it is the choice between the notion that a thing is right or wrong inherently and intrinsically, given in the nature of the thing (maybe because God created it "to be what it is"), as legalists or absolutizers would say, or only contingently and extrinsically right or wrong, depending on the circumstances, as situationists or relativists would say. It goes back, in intellectual history, to such controversies as the realist-nominalist debate. The intrinsic idea of moral quality is Thomist, the extrinsic idea is Occamist. The situation ethic is extrinsicalist; it claims that moral quality is nominal, not real. Practical men may not recognize that this kind of philosophical issue is at stake, but it is.

It all depends on the situation, say the extrinsicalists. In some situations unmarried love could be infinitely more moral than married unlove. Lying could be more Christian than telling the truth. Stealing could be better than respecting private property. No action is good or right in itself. It depends on whether it hurts or helps people, whether or not it serves love's purpose—understanding love to be personal concern—*in the situation*.

The situational-personal ethic, in short, subordinates principles to circumstances and the general to the particular, as well as making the "natural" and the Biblical and the theoretical give way to the personal and the actual.

For the sake of a clear and striking illustration we might turn to sex relations and the ethics of reproduction. And, furthermore, let us address the subject in terms of the *Christian* version of situation ethics. (We could use truth telling, or buying and selling, or diplomacy and national defense, or something else. The same considerations would come into play whatever the area or "field" of decision making might be.)

Alas, the very word "morals" in popular use means sex conduct, as we can see in newspaper headlines about a "morals charge." (This ridiculous reduction of morality to sexuality probably got its start in English translations of references in the Bible to fornication, as when I Thess. 4:3 is rendered "abstain from immorality." The Greek and Latin texts without pruriency or evasion say "fornication.") Actually, the "new morality" is a wide-ranging ethical theory of far more varied bearing than sex, but that is what it is focused upon in the street debates. So be it. Suppose we look at sex, to give our discussion a specific set of operational terms.

Sexual intercourse may or may not be an act of love. Love, as understood in the Christian situation ethic, is an attitude of concern and not an emotion of desire. A *Playboy* cartoon went to the heart of the matter by showing a rumpled young male saying to a rumpled young female in his arms, "Why speak of love at a time like this?" The point is that, Christianly speaking, sex which does not have love as its partner, its *senior* partner, is wrong. If there is no responsible concern for the *other* one, for the partner as a subject rather than a mere object, as a person and not a *thing*, the act is immoral.

The new morality, therefore, requires its practitioners to be who-askers (who will be helped or hurt?)—not, as with legalistic morality, what-askers (what does the law prescribe?). Immanuel Kant, even though he was a legalist himself, was nevertheless right about his maxim: treat persons as ends, never as means. This is essentially the personalism of the Summary of the Law in the Gospels: love God and neighbor, with nothing about following a code of law or a set of abstract, before-the-fact rules.

It comes down to this: people are to be loved and things are to be used. "Things" include material objects and general principles. Immorality occurs when things are loved and people are used. When anybody "sticks to the rules," even though people suffer as a consequence, that is immoral. Even if we grant, for example, that generally or commonly it is wrong or bad or undesirable to interrupt a pregnancy, it would nevertheless be right to do so to a conceptus following rape or incest, at least if the victim wanted an abortion. (Legalism of the Protestant, "Scriptural law" variety has no Biblical prohibition of abortion, and like Jewish opinion, approves of therapeutic abortions and is divided over the morality of nontherapeutic reasons for it.)

The Christian situationist says to all men, to all who care about others, whether they are Christians or not: "Your love is like mine, like everybody's. It is the Holy Spirit. Love is not the work of the Holy Spirit, it *is* the Holy Spirit—working in us. God *is* love, he doesn't merely 'have' it or 'give' it; he gives himself, to all men of all sorts and conditions: to believers and nonbelievers, high degree and low, dark and pale, learned and ignorant, Marxists and Christians and Hottentots."

Long ago, Chrysostom said the essence of sin is in the substitution of means for ends. Modern social analysts are saying the same thing when they speak of "the error of substituting instrumental for terminal values!" Chrysostom meant that sin treats means as if they were ends in themselves. But in the Christian ethic (at least in its situational version) things are means, and only persons are ends. We could restate it by the assertion that sin is the exploitation or use of persons. This is precisely what prostitution is. Therefore in a familiar phrase, the prostitute is far more sinned against than sinning. She is infinitely closer to righteousness than are her customers. In the same way, on the same logical base, we can say that the classical capitalist commodity theory of labor, largely a dead letter now due to trade unionism's struggles, is or was a sinful, evil principle.

In teen-age social life if a boy seduces a girl in order to appear in his own eyes or his friends' as a Big Man, he is using her; he is guilty of sin or "moral evil." If a girl seduces a boy out of curiosity or some such motive, she is committing the same wrong; if she seduces him in order to lure him into marriage she is committing a far greater sin than simple fornication ever could possibly be, even if they are married to make it legal. Such married sex is legal prostitution and a case of sinning not only formally and materially but also with malice! Even if she lured him into marriage *without* fornication the guilt lies just the same. What is more despicable than a technical virgin, male or female? The new morality weighs motive heavily in its scales, along with means and ends. The new morality is not *soft* morality.

As we have noted, Karl Barth, the Swiss theologian, who speaks of "law" a great deal, nevertheless allows for what he calls the *ultima ratio,* the outside chance that in a particular situation what the law forbids can be excused. In this way Barth, like many Catholic moral theologians, is prepared out of mercy and compassion to excuse an act of fornication or a loveless marriage *in the situation,* in the rare case. But it would be a matter of excusing an evil (because unlawful) act. For Barth and Catholic metaphysics, the evil is "real"—objectively given *de rerum natura* in such categories as fornication, adultery, homosexual acts, contraception, abortion, sterilization, and the like.

IS ANYTHING INHERENTLY GOOD OR EVIL?

This is not the situationist's view. For him nothing is inherently good or evil, except love (personal concern) and its opposite, indifference or actual malice. Anything else, no matter what it is, may be good or evil, right or wrong, according to the situation. Goodness is what *happens* to a human act, it is not *in* the act itself. This is, in a way, a "nominalistic" doctrine. Like the situationists, Emil Brunner, another Swiss theologian, is more plainly in the camp of such a morality. To use language not his own but in keeping with his thought, he sees that *goodness* or *rightness is a predicate of actions, not a property of them!*

A clarion statement of this position is William Temple's: "The rightness of an act, then, nearly always and perhaps always, depends on the way in which the act is related to circumstances; this is what is meant by calling it relatively right; but this does not in the least imply that it is only doubtfully right. It may be, in the circumstances, certainly and absolutely right." That is, the action even if unlawful, even if it violates a moral maxim or rule, will be positively right; not merely an excusable wrong!

Bishop Pike of California, following the situational method in large part, has turned in his ethical treatise (*Doing the Truth*) to the story of how Judith used her sex to save Israel from Holofernes' army. The Bible obviously approves and applauds her action, her deliberate sexual seduction. (They wrote the story in such a way as to leave her technically chaste by getting away before Holofernes got her into bed with him, thus illustrating the ethical dishonesty of legalism, as well as its willingness to accept the lesser of evils. But this is what the notion of intrinsic evil always degenerates into!) A situationist would also applaud Judith's action, but wouldn't be driven by the theory to extricate her from the logic of her seduction. In any case, the Biblical Judith is a model for governments that use a woman's sex to entrap enemy espionage agents in blackmail, to inactivate them. Is the girl who gives her chastity for her country's sake any less approvable than the boy who gives his leg or his life? No!

True chastity is a matter of personal integrity, of sincerity and purity of heart. It is not sexual. Righteousness or virtue is willing the good of the neighbor. Von Hügel said that "caring is the greatest thing, caring matters most." Not all legalists and not all relativists are agreed about sexual promiscuity, of course, but the chances are that the Christians among them look upon promiscuity as irresponsible, careless, insincere, even as indifference. They (we) believe that promiscuity ignores and flouts the value and integrity of persons, turning casual sexual partners from true subjects into what some psychologists significantly call "love *objects*." It turns them into things. In the same way that sex is right or wrong according to its treatment of persons, so with the so-called "obscene." Frankness about sex is not wrong. As somebody said recently, obscenity is the word "nigger" on the lips of a Bull Connor type cop.

Even a transient sex liaison, if it has the elements of caring, of tenderness and selfless concern, of mutual offering, is better than a mechanical, egocentric exercise of conjugal "rights" between two uncaring or possibly antagonistic marriage partners. Sexual intercourse is not right or good just because it is legal (by civil or canonical law), nor is it wrong just because it is outside the law. So-called "common-law marriage" recognizes this.

The personal commitment, not the county clerk, sanctifies sex. A man or wife who hates the partner is living in sin. A couple who cannot marry legally or permanently but live together faithfully and honorably and responsibly, are living in virtue—in Christian love. In this kind of Christian sex ethic the essential ingredients are caring and commitment. Given these factors, the only reason for disapproving sexual relations would be situational, not legal or principled. It would be because the circumstances, realistically and imaginatively weighed, with a responsible eye on remote as well as immediate consequences, balance out against the liasion rather than for it. There is nothing against extramarital sex as such, in this ethic, and in *some* cases it is good.

As an example of the fact-weighing problem (situationism is *very* data conscious) we can cite a recent proposal by a Unitarian-Universalist minister in Michigan. He recommends that teen-agers be prepared for sexual maturity in temporary trial marriages of limited duration and with parental consent. From a Christian perspective, most situationists (if not all) would hold that the teen-agers would simply be practicing on each other, and the mere fact that their using each other would be *mutual* would only compound the evil, not justify it. The scheme seems unbelievably naïve on the score of emotional and cultural risks.

Advocates of Hugh Hefner's *Playboy* doctrine of promiscuity, arguing that sex is just "fun," are backing a naturalistic hedonism which is poles apart from the Christian ethic. Their argument is that anything sexual is all right if it does not hurt anybody. A lot hangs on that big word "hurt." But Christians say that nothing is right unless it *helps* somebody. Here lies the true issue of sex ethics—not moral maxims nor sentimentality nor romanticism nor antisexual fears. We do not praise a technical virgin whose petting practices are sexually unrestrained, nor do we condemn a loving transgressor of the law who is emotionally honest although technically unchaste.

If a defensive maneuver can be forgiven here, suppose we hear Msgr. Pietro Palazzini, a Catholic moralist and Secretary of the Sacred Congregation of the Council, in his article about situation ethics in the *Dictionary of Moral Theology*. He says that situation ethics "must not be understood as an escape from the heavy burden of moral integrity. For, though its advocates truly deny the absolute value of universal norms, some are motivated by the belief that in this manner they are better safeguarding the eminent sovereignty of God."

One last word. The *Christian* criteria for sex relations are positive: sex is a matter of certain ideals of relationship. These ideals are based upon a certain faith: about God, Christ, the church, who man is, and his destiny. Therefore, if people do not embrace that faith (and most don't), there is no reason why they should live by it. And most do not! It is time we faced up to this. Nowadays in the "secular city" it is easier and easier to see who are committed Christians and who are not. On any serious view of the matter, sex is not the decisive thing. Character shapes sex, sex does not shape character. Virtue never goes out of style but styles change. If true chastity means a marital monopoly, then let those who believe in it recommend it by reason and example. Nothing is gained by condemning the unbeliever. Indeed, to condemn him is more unjust (immoral) than a sexual escapade!

The fact is that all along churchmen have relied on *prudential* arguments against sexual freedom—the triple terrors of conception, infection, and detection—not upon Christian sanctions. But modern medicine and urban anonymity have made sex relatively safe. The danger argument is almost old hat. It is true, of course, that coital adventures may bring on delayed emotional reactions, but the same is true of petting. And in any case, these feelings are largely guilt feelings which changing cultural norms are making archaic or even antediluvian. The guilt is going. If Christians honestly and seriously believe that there are matters of *principle* at stake, as distinct from situational factors, they had better make them clear. And whatever they come up with, they aren't going to make a good case for absolute, universal, and unexceptionable ethical negatives. Or positives. The new morality is a better morality than that—than the old morality.

III

Love and Justice Are the Same Thing

The Question

The theme here—a perennial one in theological ethics —is the relation between love and justice. The thesis is that they are actually one and the same thing.

If I am right about this, a great deal of time and thought has been wasted or imprisoned in a kind of conceptual revolving door, going around and around a "point of tension" which itself never gets anywhere. It is the purpose of this chapter to show how the love-justice relation has been treated in representative modern moralists' work, and to explain why so much of it has been only "arrested development."

A few years ago Sammy Davis, Jr., a popular American entertainer, repudiated his Christian identity and became a Jew. "As I see it," he said, "the difference is that the Christian religion preaches love thy neighbor and the Jewish religion preaches justice, and I think justice is the big thing we need."[1] As a Negro who has suffered the injustice of discrimination he has our quick sympathy, but what about the inferred conception of love and justice in

A chapter in *Lux in Lumine,* edited by Richard A. Norris, Jr., in honor of Prof. Norman Pittenger (The Seabury Press, Inc., 1966). "Love" and "justice" might be rendered as "concern."

his words? The problem of conscience his revolt points at is obvious enough, bitterly obvious; but what of the *ethical understanding,* or misunderstanding, behind it?

The relation or tension between love and justice has been a central focus of Christian ethics and moral theology in all ages, but thus far without any result except confusion and foolishness. It does not arise in the same way in philosophical ethics and the cultural mores, nor do they get bogged down in conceptual worries and constant re-examination. This is because of two peculiarities in Christian ethics. (1) "Love" in the theological lexicon carries a nonromantic and nonaffectionate meaning. (2) The primary or pivotal imperative of the Christian ethos (possibly the only one) is the commandment to "love" one's neighbor. How then is this prime imperative of "love" to be related to the universal search for justice? Justice tends to be the core category in nontheological morality, love in theological morals. What is their true relation? And what *are* they?

THE PROBLEM

We might draw a parallel between the love-justice and the faith-works problems. Some theologies treat the latter as faith *versus* works, some as faith *or* works, some as faith *and* works, some as faith *is* works (i.e., simply put, "faith works"). In the same pattern we could find four different ways of relating love and justice: love *versus* justice, love *or* justice, love *and* justice, or love *is* justice. Are love and justice to be opposed to each other, served separately or alternatively, linked in coalition, or coalesced?

Bishop Anders Nygren's motif research came close to making them an antithesis, by embedding justice in *eros* (enlightened self-interest) and opposing *eros* to *agape* (disinterested love).[2] Denis de Rougemont has done the same thing.[3] But Father Martin D'Arcy has challenged them, arguing that the two "loves" (*agape* and *eros*) are not mutually exclusive, and hence, justice is "on the side" of love.[4] Reinhold Niebuhr has in effect made them alternatives, regarding Christian love as impossible and only relative justice as within the range of possibility.[5] (Note, however, that Niebuhr's constructive ethics are somewhat equivocal through his use of "mutual love," meaning a relative, contingent, historically possible love.) In another way both Emil Brunner and William Temple have given love and justice separate and different relevances, holding that "love" is an imperative in interpersonal relations and "justice" in intergroup relations—Brunner speaking of "systems" and Temple of "organizations."[6] Brunner says that they are "radically different" although "akin." On the other hand, this separation of love and justice is challenged by Bishop Gustav Aulén in his *Church, Law and Society*.[7] G. Ernest Wright holds the same view, based on Biblical studies: "These two conceptions simply cannot be separated because they are united in God."[8] And like Aulén and Wright, Canon Quick says that justice is "but one aspect or consequence of his [God's] all-creating and all-redeeming love," thus including the one in the other, yet not equating the two.[9]

Again love and justice are linked in coalition and mutual reinforcement by some—for example, by Paul Tillich who says that love "is the ground, the power, and the aim of justice" and, therefore, "Love without justice is a body without a backbone."[10] Indeed Tillich's treatment of love and justice, in relation to the factor of power, comes very close to the fourth approach to our problem, i.e., of coalescing or combining them into one. He actually says that love is "the ultimate principle of justice."[11] But this is not close enough. The fourth way of relating them has not actually been put forward in such straightforward terms as yet. This chapter will do so. That is the only reason for writing it.

How, then, shall we set up the problem for careful scrutiny and analysis? There are, I suggest, three conceptual questions at stake here, and the way we answer them will determine how we relate love and justice. Put in their plainest fashion they are: (1) Are we to understand that "love" is emotional, a matter of feelings, while "justice" is volitional, a matter of "will" or determination? (2) Are we to regard "love" as personal and interpersonal, and "justice" as impersonal and "objective" (even putting a blindfold on it)? (3) Are we to think of "love" as particular and specific, and of "justice" as general and dispersed?

It seems evident that each of these three questions is inherent in the others, and therefore I propose a fourth coordinate question: Do not our answers to the second and third depend upon how we answer the first? This way of putting the question hints at the answer that I believe to be the right one: "Yes, all depends upon whether 'love' as such is an emotion or a volition. Let us firmly declare that it is a *volitional* category, not an emotional one. And therefore it is like 'justice'—in fact, the same thing."

However, if we are to attempt a fresh and independent construction of the question of the meaning of Christian "love" (*agape*) in relation to justice, we must go about it carefully, that is, with some care for the way others treat it. This can be done in a limited way which nevertheless reveals the variety of opinion available and the elements of equivocation which infect the whole discussion. Some of these equivocal elements may seem merely semantic, but we have learned not to say "merely" when we depart from the use of univocal terms in any serious discussion.

THE DISCUSSION

In a single, short book review recently, I found the following typical conceptual confusions: "Love cannot be indifferent to justice"; "Justice is not complete without love"; "Love is a constituent element of justice"; and "We must act both justly and lovingly." Yet the reviewer's problem is not his alone. Let us look briefly at what representative moralists have said about the three questions we have framed.

1. *Are we to understand that "love" is emotional, a matter of feelings, while "justice" is volitional, a matter of "will" or determination?* A great majority answer in the affirmative, but it is a consensus only, not a universal agreement. For example, Nicolas Berdyaev treats Christian love as feeling.[12] Albert Schweitzer despaired of keeping any agapeic meaning in "love" and, faced with such interpretations as Berdyaev's, began using "reverence for life" instead, turning "love" over to friendship and romance as categories of mild or intense emotion.[13] Karl Barth, perhaps annoyed by Nygren's oversimple dichotomy of *eros* and *agape,* simply mixes the two.[14] Roman Catholic moral and ascetical theology has traditionally treated "charity" as an appetite, along with justice and kindness and reverence, but their insistence on the supremacy of reason has tended to put "will" in charge as charity's primary quality. Thus Jacques Maritain and Bernhard Häring have followed St. Thomas in regarding Christian love as *"friendship* with God and man"—making *agape* into *philia* in the manner of the Fourth Gospel.[15]

Most writers are more unambiguously insistent on the volitional nature of Christian love. According to Ethelbert Stauffer in the article on *agape* in Kittel's *Wörterbuch,* the Bible's use and distinction of three terms we translate as "love" was not consistently maintained, but generally its usage indicates: (1) *eran* as passionate desire, (2) *philein* as friendship feeling, and (3) *agapan* as more disinterested, without the intensity of *eran* or the warmth of *philein.* (*Agapan's* disinterestedness is none too clear in pre-Biblical Greek, but its pre-Biblical use is also infrequent.) Nevertheless, perhaps because of the suggestiveness of the Bible's different terms, constructive theologians are overwhelmingly in favor of assigning the "love" of the commandment (*agape*) a primarily nonemotional meaning. (They often say "primarily" because of their recognition that with the end of the old faculty psychology went any idea that the cognitive and conative or volitional functions of the human psyche can ever be entirely free of some admixture with affective or emotional dynamics.)

For example, C. H. Dodd says that *agape* "is not primarily an emotion or an affection; it is primarily an active determination of the will. That is why it can be commanded, as feelings cannot."[16] To illustrate, how could the promise to "love" in the marriage service be possible if "love" meant feeling? We cannot promise how we will *feel*. Hence Kant's conclusion about the great commandment, "it is only practical love [that is, benevolence or goodwill] that is meant in that pith of all laws."[17] Canon Herbert Waddams says even more forcefully in his *New Introduction to Moral Theology*: "It is extremely important to understand that love in the Christian sense is not primarily a matter of the emotions, although the emotions may be engaged. It is a matter of choice, choosing to submit to the will of God and to follow his path, and as a matter of choice its essential nature consists of an act of the will."[18] Almost all writers in the Anglican tradition have said the same, starting with Jeremy Taylor's assertion in his *Holy Living* (ch. 4) that love is purpose rather than passion, that it is *not* liking. Another, more modern moral theologian, Bishop Kirk, reiterates the same point.[19] Still another, R. C. Mortimer, puts it this way: "The theological virtue of love is not primarily an emotion, its seat is in the will" and therefore "man is enabled to love God in the sense that by an act of the will he prefers God above everything else."[20]

Rudolf Bultmann is insistent. It is, he says, "now clear that *love does not mean an emotion* [his italics] . . . but a definite attitude of the will." And again, "Only if love is thought of as an emotion is it meaningless to command love: the *command* of love shows that love is understood as an attitude of the will."[21] C. E. B. Cranfield in the *Theological Word Book of the Bible* says "*agape* refers to will rather than emotion, and often conveys the idea of showing love by action."[22] Millar Burrows, the Biblical archaeologist at Yale University, in his *Outline of Biblical Theology* explains: "What Jesus demands is not an emotion but an attitude of the will. . . . To love one's neighbor is not to feel affection for him but to wish and seek his good."[23] H. Richard Niebuhr and Waldo Beach put it very baldly: "To say love is a feeling or anything of that kind is really an unChristian conception of love."[24] And Reinhold Niebuhr agrees: "The ideal of love is first of all a commandment which appeals to the will."[25]

Martin Buber, a Jewish theologian Biblically oriented, in his distinctive way says "the act of relation is not an emotion or a feeling. . . . Feelings accompany love, but they do not constitute it. . . . Hence love is not the enjoyment of a wonderful emotion, not even the ecstasy of a Tristan and Isolde, but the responsibility of an *I* for a *Thou.*"[26] And further, he says that "love thy neighbor" certainly "does not mean loving feeling but loving action. One cannot command that one *feel* love for a person but only that one deal lovingly with him."[27]

Perhaps the most unpretentious way to understand *agape* is T. E. Jessop's, as a "certain bias or set" of the will! He held that "love as an emotion is more or less momentary or spasmodic; it is only love as an attitude that is continuous or lasting. The former is an effect of the latter, and only one of its effects."[28] As Tillich has pointed out, "One of the reasons for this misunderstanding of love is the identification of love with emotion. Love, like every human experience, of course includes an emotional element," but its essential nature is volition, choice, commitment, purpose.[29] It is discerning and critical, not sentimental. Its purpose is to satisfy the neighbor's need, not one's own, but the main thing about it is that *agape*-love precedes all desire of any kind. Its ethic is *Gesinnungsethik,* an attitudinal ethic, not emotional.

The point should now be clear. *Agape,* as distinguished from *philia* and *eros,* is the "love" of the commandment. And it is an attitude, a will-disposition, a matter of the conative—not the emotive. Only a perverse and stubborn sentimentalism will persist in treating it as feeling, although "feeling" is not to be deprecated or minimized as such, nor is it to be denied when it plays a part *in* the "bias" of *agape.* Yet the result is that we are to love the unlikable. Only in this way can we make sure we grasp the meaning of "Love your enemies."

In the same way, "justice" is conative, volitional, decision-oriented, purposive, dispositive—as *agape* is. As in the case of *agape,* we might, of course, "feel strongly" about justice too, but in their primary meaning both "love" and "justice" are volitional rather than emotional in the Christian interpretation. *They are not different*—love being a matter of "feeling" and "justice" a matter of "willing." They are not even merely alike. They are the same.

What of the second question?

2. *Are we to regard "love" as personal and interpersonal, and "justice" as impersonal and "objective" (even putting a blindfold on it)?* As we have seen, both Temple and Brunner found it possible to separate love and justice because they held the former to be relevant to persons only, reserving the latter as a norm or imperative for relations between "impersonal" or *group* entities. This is, of course, also the way that Martin Buber looks at the question in his influential *I and Thou,* and in *Between Man and Man.*[30] Yet we should take careful note that Buber has

not put groups of related or even organized *I*'s and *Thou*'s
into the world of *it*'s. Fraternities, associations, and even
collectives (e.g., Buber's cherished *kibbutzim* in Israel)
are still human and still personal.

Temple reasoned in *Christianity and Social Order* that
there cannot be "love" between a labor union and a corporation or between one nation and another.[31] Yet, like Buber,
Temple never actually characterized groups of persons as
"impersonal." On the contrary, he defined a "person" as
an individual who has been socialized by interaction with
others, even using Buber's dialogic I-thou-it conception,
although in complete ignorance, at the time, of the Continental Jewish philosopher.[32] Brunner, in maintaining
that love belongs to the world of persons and justice to the
world of "systems," meant that love is interpersonal while
justice is social. Thus he claimed that in society the Christian has to "change his love into the current coin of
justice."[33]

Brunner would, unlike Temple and Buber, finally and
fundamentally divorce love and justice as entities. In *The
Divine Imperative,* his *magnum opus* on Christian ethics,
he flatly asserted that "love is never given to a collective
body, even if this body were to consist of two people
only; real community (*Gemeinschaft*) only exists between
the 'I' and the single 'Thou.'" He added that once a third
person enters the scene we are "no longer in the 'personal'
sphere"——we are in "the realm of the 'orders' of human
life." At the same time he acknowledges that such a "purely
personal relation of love" to the neighbor is nonexistent,
and that in fact we "*have* to deal with him as a member
of the historical community."[34] To suppose, as Brunner
does, that the Sermon on the Mount is addressed only to
Robinson Crusoe and Friday is to make it more irrelevant
and inviable than the most legalistic and pietistic exposi-
tions. And the human "person" he describes as a "single
Thou" (he had no reference to God) is a sheer abstrac-

tion, a fiction of his theological imagination. Such a "person" is as fictitious as the "fictitious person" of the corporation in civil law; one is as unreal as the other.

On any calm, untendentious view, it is clear that we cannot separate the social from the personal. Each dimension of human existence is presupposed in the other. Therefore, to speak of love as the "personal" and justice as the "social" is to unite the two terms.[35] But a more realistic view of things rejects both categories as separate entities. Personal and social are phases of being human, distinguishable but not separable, and the words "justice" and "love" are simply verbal signals that thinkers such as Brunner apply when they relate the norm of the "will of God" to the two phases. Justice is as "personal" as love, and "love" is as "social" as justice. We are commanded to love all our neighbors whom we do not know interpersonally, even as we are to be just to the neighbor who is "nigh" or *here* in person. All men are *thou*'s, not *it*'s; they do not become *things* because they are too numerous or too distant. Therefore *agape* and justice require imagination and the ability to "care" for more people than we "know."

This leads us, by a logical entailment, into the third question.

3. *Are we to think of "love" as particular and specific, and of "justice" as general and dispersed?* If these three questions are as logically inherent in each other, coinherent, as I have suggested they are, then this one too must be answered "No"—as the first two were.

The one and the many, the particular and the general; these are age-old problems in the history of metaphysics: Parmenides' and Plato's universals over against the "empirics" of theirs and all times. The realists versus the nominalists. This is the archaic antinomy of archaic philosophy. But none of it has ever helped to settle any real issues, whether they are directly at stake in the debate or only remotely involved. Certainly it brings no light to the question under scrutiny here, probably because the attempt to distinguish *and to separate* the particular from the general or the one from the many is as artificial—as much a falsification of reality—as the attempt to separate the personal from the social, as the attempt to separate love and justice themselves.

Since God's love is the source and "type" or prototype of *agape,* it is of interest here to observe that even though there are many references in the Old Testament to will-love or "goodwill" (*aheb* or *chesed*), the love of God for human beings is ordinarily, indeed consistently for collective subjects rather than particular individuals. God's "love affair" is with the covenanted nation or people or community, or even (as in the universal covenants) with mankind, in "Adam" and Noah. For that matter, the "particular" covenants beginning with Abraham's in Gen., ch. 22, are not with individuals either, but with them and their seed forever.

We all know the pitfalls of word study: how *chronos* can do duty for *kairos, didachē* for *pistis,* and so forth. Biblical theology must take whole statements for the Bible's meaning, not words alone. Yet even so, in the New Testament "love" is, like justice, mainly understood as will or attitude and commitment. The way they are practically equated in Luke 11:42 ("the justice and love of God") is revealing. In another episode the centurion is said to "love our nation," and the term is *agape,* as with God's love. There is no notion here like Kierkegaard's that love is only for the "single one" and that a collectivity is a falsity. Only in the Fourth Gospel is love often rendered by *philia* instead of *agape,* or mixed up practically interchangeably, as in the famous instance of John 21:15–18. This being so it comes as no surprise that the "love" of the Fourth Gospel is interpersonal, a friendship relationship ("greater love than this has no man") along the lines of Brunner's thesis, or that the term "justice" is not present in that Gospel anywhere. This nonsocial or selective-exclusive meaning of "love" in the Fourth Gospel (for the "brother" or fellow believer but not for the "neighbor") is in contrast to the wider or more general reference of *agape* in the Synoptics and Paul.

There is a certain reasonableness back of the fear that the woods can blind us to the trees. William Blake's warning reminds us of it: "He who would do good to another must do it in minute particulars; general good is the plea of the scoundrel, the hypocrite, and flatterer."[36] Yet we are still faced with the hard fact that the tree is a part of the wood. In a forest fire we do not have to give each tree its own "name" in order to love it and do it justice by beating back the flames. It is too much and too simple to say, as Barth does, that "the State, the most impersonal because the most comprehensive of institutions, knows nothing of love."[37]

The problem of the relations of the particular to the general is like the problem of the personal and the social. The relationship is one of coinherence. To think or speak of the one is to think or speak of the other.

Justice is not alone in recognizing that there is more than one tree in the woods, more than one pebble on the beach. Love does too. This is why Augustine said that love calls for "more than good will, and can be done only by a high degree of thoughtfulness and prudence."[38] He meant that love in the same way as justice has to figure how to *distribute* its favors among many beneficiaries. The question of how to love justice is how to be just about love. *Love must be justice.* Granting the Aristotelian-Thomist-Brunnerian view that justice is giving to each man what is his due, how are we to calculate and "balance" love's benefits among so many claimants? This is precisely the problem of justice; the problem of love is no whit different. For love, *agape*, plays no favorites, exactly as "God is no respecter of persons" or "shows no partiality" (Acts 10:34; Rom. 2:11; Eph. 6:9; Col. 3:25; etc.).

Because we exist in community, love-justice is compelled to be calculating and distributive. The "neighbor" whom we are commanded to love is a generic *pleision*— neighbors in the plural. "Thou shalt love thy neighbors, all of them, as thyself." Only in this way can we avoid the oversimplifying, Tolstoyan notion that love wears blinders, never calculates, sees only the one-to-one *immediate* neighbor who is to be loved, one at a time.[39] To embrace such a notion, as so many have, is to fail to see that love is justice, justice love. For justice is no respecter of persons, shows no partiality, loves all alike, exactly as "God is no respecter of persons," and chooses no friends. Behind such a phrase as "love is the soul of justice," getting close to the simple truth, is a recognition that love is the effective principle of justice; and justice is love balancing interests and claims, calculating, "sorting its mix" (in the language of the game-theory analysts). The upshot of all this is that "love" and "justice" are to be related not as one plus one, which equals two, but as one times one—which equals only *one*.

The Solution

There are at least three summary things to be said now, which are supported by the thesis we have been developing.

The first thing is that "love" and "justice" equally are volitional, when Christianly understood—even though susceptible often of an emotional admixture. Both are, at the same time, at once personal and impersonal. They are also, both of them, particular and general. What may be said properly of either of them applies to the other.

The second thing is that "love" and "justice," as classical terms with a long and noble history in Christian moral theology, mean exactly what is meant in philosophical ethics by "goodness" or "the good." As with goodness, so with love and justice, we must never forget that such terms or epithets are predicates, not properties. "Love" and "justice" are something that *happens*, not something that is. Each is extrinsic and contingent in any action or relationship, not intrinsic or given. The theological observation is that only the love of God, who *is* love, is a property. It follows, therefore, that the love-justice which God commands and requires of men may only be *predicated*, if and when they are obedient—but only if and when. *Agape* or neighbor-love is not something we have or give. It is something we do or do not do. And so with justice.

All serious English ethical analysis since G. E. Moore's *Principia Ethica* at the turn of the century has seen for what it is (a phantasm) any reification or objectification of "good" or of value concepts. Moore's "naturalistic fallacy" has always undermined and misdirected those who attempt to "thing-ify" love and justice. I would go farther. I would have to agree with Stephen Toulmin's brilliant demonstration that such notions, whether taken as "values" or "imperatives," are not even "nonnatural" or "unanalysable" properties.[40] They just are not properties at all, only predicates, except for God himself—since as Jesus pointed out, "With men this is impossible, but with God all things are possible" (Matt. 19:26). This is why H. Richard Niebuhr could insist that "Jesus never commanded love for its own sake."[41] Love that pretends to *be* something in and of itself is a self-contradiction. It is on this elemental level of ethical theory that we have to oppose Tillich's attempt in *Love, Power and Justice* to give love and justice an ontological status, even though he pleases us by refusing to separate them or to give one a higher "value" than the other.

The third thing is that all of this means, in the simplest and most direct language, that love and justice are one and the same thing. Hence the persistence in the past of such maxims as "justice is the soul of love" and "love is the soul of justice." What we call love is justice, as justice is love. Neither is a phase nor a partner nor a prerequisite nor a consequence of the other. They are coeval, coterminous.

Their complete identity may be recognized in this way
—by seeing how they both "go out" to their many neighbors on all hands, responsibly ignoring Tolstoy's notion
(his anarchist notion) that love cannot count and knows
no future, and trying instead to balance its favors among
them all with a realistic eye to consequences. Then it can
be recognized. Love is justice, love is just. Justice is loving
—using its head, calculating its duties, sharing its obligations, seeking the good of as many neighbors as possible.

The idea of Reinhold Niebuhr's, that love and justice
are different, love being "higher" and justice more "possible," has its counterpart in Roman Catholic moral theology. There it has actually been held that love and justice
can come into conflict—in which case love may be denied
in order to do justice.[42] Actually, when the love-ethic removes the blinders which narrow its field of vision to one
neighbor at a time, it forms a coalition with the utilitarian
principle of "the greatest good of the greatest number."
In this partnership or "front" the *procedural* principle of
utilitarianism ("the greatest number") and the normative
principle of the commandment ("love your neighbor") result in "the greatest amount of *agape* for the greatest number of neighbors possible." That is justice. And even if we
define justice as "paying what is due" (a rather static notion), the *Christian* understanding of "what is due" to our
neighbor is "all the love possible." Love and justice are the
same.

THE CONCLUSION

All of this is a serious thesis about a serious question in
theological ethics. Paul Tillich has called upon the Christian church to "demonstrate in teaching, preaching, and
liturgy the unconditional demand of justice in the very
nature of *agape*."[43] Justice is the very nature of Christian
love, and love of justice.

A practical difficulty is the semantic confusion. In a
worldwide usage the word "love" has a romantic connota-

tion. Qualifying "love" with "Christian" does not eliminate the sentimental suggestion. (Even in Japan, when *agapē* is translated as *ai* the same confusion and red herring ensues as in English with "love.") Tillich says, "I believe it would be salutary if the word 'love' in the sense of *agape* could be avoided for a long time, and the word *agape* introduced into modern language."[44] *Agape* at least comes to people as a new word, so that they ask, "What's that?" and thus hear better what is meant than if, by misconstruing, they respond with, "Oh!"

But I have another recommendation. *The best practice is never to use the word "love"* in Christian ethical discourse. Every time we think "love" we should *say* "justice." For justice has not been hopelessly sentimentalized, or romanticized, or individualized. Not only *is* it Christian love but, as communication, it *says* it. It says what the Biblical *agape* means. If we are to have one ethical *logion,* as Paul put it in Gal. 5:14, then let it be *justice.* (And it is possible, at least, that Paul was leaning in the same direction by his frequent use of *dikaiosunē*—that justice or righteousness which is the mark of the man in Christ, who is the Man for *all* others.)

Jeremy Taylor, that Anglican bishop and casuist who spoke as much for the Puritans as for the high churchmen of the Caroline seventeenth century, said flatly in *Ductor Dubitantium:* "God cannot do an unjust thing, because whatever he wills or does is therefore just, because he wills and does it, his will being the measure of justice."[45] Exactly so. Love is *his* being, justice is what he wills for *our* doing. Our Christian business is not to try to be God, but to do God's will—that is, justice.

Perhaps because I coalesce love and justice in this direct way I shall be accused of being too Old Testamentish. If so, I don't mind. I am no crypto-Marcionite. If we take seriously the prophetic genius of the Bible, we should have no trouble seeing the *henōsis* of love and justice or using "justice" as its name.

IV

The Ethics of Natural Law

THE NATURAL-LAW theory's storied and continuous role in the development of classical Christian ethics and moral theology has nonetheless always failed to win it immunity from attack and outright repudiation. Yet never has it suffered as much skeptical criticism, from within as well as from without the camp of those who live by the *depositum fidei,* as right now in the twentieth century. Indeed, it seems most unlikely that it can survive conceptually in any recognizable guise.

In the fifty years since the First World War the most creative and compelling work in both "theological" and "special" Christian ethics has taken shape out of ecumenical dialogue and interconfessional confrontation, especially in the study commissions of the World Council of Churches —*yet the natural-law doctrine has been given practically no attention in any of this work.* Has this been because Protestantism has been so indifferent or antagonistic to-

A chapter originally entitled "Anglican Theology and the Ethics of Natural Law" in *Christian Social Ethics in a Changing World,* edited by John C. Bennett (Association Press, 1966), the first of four volumes of preparation studies for the World Council of Churches' Conference on Church and Society in Geneva (Switzerland), July 12–26, 1966.

ward it and perhaps in need of the stimulus of recent encounter with the Roman Catholic theologians to give this discussion the urgency and sophistication it requires? Possibly. But this view does not do justice to the question, for there have always been some exponents of natural law in the non-Roman churches from the very beginnings of "Life and Work" and of "Faith and Order." Among these, Anglicans have been both numerous and influential. Their views, therefore, call for a closer scrutiny, if we are to analyze the "natural-law issue" in Christian ethics today, especially in relation to church and society.

ANGLICANISM AND NATURAL LAW

In ecumenical circles there is a widespread but erroneous impression that the natural law doctrine is a fixed feature of Anglican theology. Every student of the history of ideas is familiar with the role of the concept in the English common law tradition and jurisprudence, and how it began to lose its force and tenability as early as the seventeenth century. It managed to keep its hold upon English theology for a somewhat longer time and, after the "Catholic revival" under Pusey and Newman, even regained its vigor and acceptability for a while, particularly in the "Christian sociology" circles of the Anglo-Catholic wing of the Church of England. Soon after the Reformation, Anglicanism's tie to the natural law was plainly put by Richard Hooker in his *Ecclesiastical Polity,* where he declared with bland confidence that its (natural law's) "general principles are such that it is not easy to find a man ignorant of them."[1] English Christianity has always kept a place for "natural theology" (the religious perception of natural reason apart from special revelation), and like Hooker two hundred and fifty years earlier, Archdeacon Paley stated its view bluntly: "Now, there are two methods of coming at the will of God on any point. I. by his express declarations, when they are to be had, and which must be sought for in Scripture. II. by what we can discover of his designs and disposition from his works; or, as we usually call it, the light of Nature."[2] Bishop Butler, Paley's contemporary, was of the opinion that "almost any fair man in almost any circumstance" would know the right course to follow, but rationalist though he was, he made his own system stand on other grounds than natural law precepts.[3]

However, there has always been a measure of ambiguity in the Anglican treatment of natural law. The Caroline divines—Puritans, such as Richard Baxter, William Ames, and William Perkins, and churchmen such as Robert Sanderson, Joseph Hall, John Sharp, Jeremy Taylor, and Thomas Barlow (all bishops)—were more or less in the "following" of the classical doctrine. But it is wise to use such qualifiers as "more or less" since these men were inclined to trace with (the then uncanonized) Thomas Aquinas the sequence from eternal law to natural law to "right reason"; yet as Reformation theologians they took sin and its blinders seriously and constantly "hedged" the classical doctrine of natural law in such a way that it was never the clear-cut theory the schoolmen (and later neo-Thomists) made it. Jeremy Taylor twisted and squirmed in an effort to follow the line, yet he confessed that though "all men talk of the law of nature," they differ as to its precepts and how they are discovered, "whereas if the law of nature were such a thing as is supposed generally, these differences would be as strange and impossible as that men should disagree about what is black, or what is yellow."[4] Taylor could foresee that natural law would be "used" comfortably by Nazis and anti-Nazis, Thomists and humanists, naturalists and theists.

From the start, English Protestants, taking their more independent and indigenous line of approach to theological doctrine and ethics, have had more trouble with the "discernment" of natural law than with belief in its objective reality. They had no difficulty in believing that God wills what is right and good, whether he wills it because it is good (the realists) or it is good because he wills it (the nominalists). Their belief that his will infuses his creation was like the *anima mundi* of the Stoics from whom early Christians took the natural law idea and baptized it. But they were uneasy about the *epistemology* of the classical doctrine, for reasons we shall shortly discuss. On the one hand, they sympathized with Aquinas' theory of analogy whereby they could assume that there is enough in common between the minds of God and man so that the latter may discern something of God's will (eternal law) naturally and without revelation. Yet they were troubled by the Reformation conviction that human sin and finitude set too great a distance between the divine mind and the mental capacities of fallen humans, to say nothing of their moral or volitional powers! They never quite shrugged off Isaiah's warning, "For my thoughts are not your thoughts, neither are your ways my ways, saith the Lord."[5]

At the same time, the English tradition in *social* ethics has fairly consistently adopted the heuristic notion that certain of what Luther, with the schoolmen, regarded as created "orders" (*die Ordnungen*)—Bonhoeffer's term "mandates" denotes the same thing—are God-given or "natural" institutions. Anglican thought focused especially upon the family and the state; work or vocation was less readily recognized as such. Yet quite as many Anglican theological treatises, perhaps most of them, "derived" their defense of and demands upon these orders of life and society from the Bible and revelation as from any alleged "natural" or "self-evident" principles.

A brief inspection of Archbishop William Temple's treatment of the natural-law concept will show the ambivalence, the ambiguity, and the subordination which it has encountered in Anglican theology all along. The plain truth is that Temple never developed an explicit *method* of social-ethical analysis. Most of what he wrote about moral values and social policies was constructed by dogmatic derivation (drawn by logic out of Christian doctrine, in the manner described by Barth as "analogy"[6]). Temple tended to use "natural law" and "natural order" interchangeably, although he preferred the latter phrase. Significantly, he never once used the term or the concept in his Gifford lectures, *Nature, Man and God* (1934). By "natural order" he meant nothing more than a logical relation between appropriate means and "true" ends—for example, subordinating private profit to social need. The natural law ethics of Aquinas, in Temple's view, tried to fix Christian norms in the feudal and medieval culture-pattern.[7] At the same time, he was influenced by the heuristic idea of Aristotle's "final cause"—a *phusikon dikaion* in which "true ends" are simply given or ordained in the nature of things.

Furthermore, Temple was inclined to assume in traditional fashion that "natural order" can be discerned through (1) "universals" or what men generally hold to be good, and (2) the use of reason to figure out the "true" purposes of life. His principles of "natural order" were, abstractly expressed in terms of obedience to God, respect for human dignity, freedom, fellowship, and service. Except for the first of these, the motivational principle, they are all ideals that any humanist could adopt or any cynic reject. Indeed, as already noted, he founded them not on natural law, but rather on the "implications" as he saw them of such doctrines as creation, the trinity, the incarnation, resurrection and atonement, the church, and the Sacraments.[8] Temple's peripheral and opaque use of natural law analysis confirms him as a representative of modern Anglicanism.

But certain serious efforts have been made to revive or rehabilitate the concept. A dramatic attempt was made at the wartime conference at Malvern on "The Life of the Church and the Order of Society" (in 1941), which Temple called together to discuss a coherent Christian scheme of war and peace aims.[9] One of the groups participating was "the Christendom group"—a company of rather Anglo-Catholic clergy and lay people devoted to the intellectual tasks of "Christian sociology." Because he obviously hoped to get from them a set of working formularies, based on their deductions from the natural law, Temple had several of them read papers (W. G. Peck, Maurice Reckitt, Dorothy Sayers, V. A. Demant, and T. S. Eliot). Little or nothing crystallized. Donald MacKinnon, now a philosopher at Cambridge, took issue with natural law, declaring that "to specify the content of the natural law, as it affects men, is a task of appalling difficulty." He opted instead for a dogmatic analogical approach combined with pragmatic reasoning. Temple himself spoke of "derivative maxims worked out by theologians," but they were to come from *doctrine,* not nature. Demant wanted churchmen "to *develop* a theology of the natural Law" for social criteria, but he himself produced none.

In *Prospect for Christendom,* a symposium by the Christendom group published in 1945, Canon Demant again pleaded for a natural-law ethic, joining "natural law" and "natural order" in a way which would have been familiar to Temple (who had died in 1944). And in his *Theology of Society* he argued again that "only a theological conception of a natural order can identify the permanent central data"—without indicating what those data were or might be.[10] Theologically regarded, this is an interesting inconsistency; it demands that natural law be theologically supported and presumably made a part of *theological* ethics, thus abandoning the classical doctrine that natural law ethics are a part of God's providence known by human reason, rather than a part of God's redemption known by divine revelation! Anglicans have always been blandly evasive of the problem of knowledge in natural law and have never made the frank admission of the First Vatican Council (1870), that the church's *magisterium* is in the end needed to decide what "nature" requires—thus, in effect, abandoning the natural law's epistemological assumption, and leaving only its ontological assumption (an objective divine will or intention)![11]

Demant's conclusion that natural-law precepts and rules are needed is like the yearning conclusion of a group of English Protestant and Roman Catholic churchmen, which met periodically for several years in the hope of finding "a guiding principle for social life equivalent to the traditional conception of 'the law of nature' (while realizing) the impossibility of simply recalling to life any ancient or medieval form of the conception."[12] Needless to say, after their years of labor they concluded only that good is to be done and evil avoided. Beyond that they could only leave every problem of justice to "theonomic thinking," since "there is no ready-made or text-book method of settling what is good or evil in every situation." Their conclusion, which is entirely sound but for reasons altogether different from that offered below, stands in sharp contrast to the explicit and integrated *system* of social ethics, for example, in a Roman Catholic treatise like that of the Viennese theologian, J. Messner, *Social Ethics: Natural Law in the Modern World* (1949).[13] Almost all the English natural-law works are, and always have been, of the indeterminate and prospective kind—this and that "will be" or "could be" or "should be" or "needs to be" worked out! They have wrestled helplessly with the dozen different meanings of the term "nature" and the equivocations it introduces into all discourse in which it is used. This confusion is found, of course, in all the historic versions of the natural law—Stoic, Roman, Augustinian, Scholastic, Calvinist, Rationalist (as in the French and American "rights of man" declarations).

Growing Disaffection

In 1921, Kenneth Escott Kirk, who became, some twelve years later, Regius Professor of Moral and Pastoral Theology at Oxford and who was subsequently bishop of the diocese, wrote a very complete, systematic, and learned Anglican treatise on moral theology, and in it he gives only one and a half pages out of 413 to natural law! He says rather blandly that it is "the accepted Christian belief" even though moral standards among cultures "vary almost indefinitely." As to its content, he says merely that its precepts may be *deduced* from the "cardinal" virtues.[14] In *The Threshold of Ethics* (1933), Kirk developed a phenomenology of moral experience without a single reference to the natural law! In 1947, his successor in the Oxford chair, R. C. Mortimer (who is now Bishop of Exeter and who was succeeded in the Oxford chair by Demant), also wrote a treatise on moral theology in which we find the most positive affirmations of natural law in formal Anglican treatises, but it ends in the usual style by admitting that it "may seem there is little of value" in natural law. He then identifies it with the *jus gentium*, while allowing that the latter could just as well be accounted for by positive law theory!

Another *inter bellum* leader in the Christendom group, W. G. Peck, made vigorous claims for the natural law, but in actual practice, like most Anglican ethicists, he followed the method of Karl Barth ("analogy" or logical inference from dogma) and Temple ("inference" drawn from doctrine), rather than the neo-Thomist method of "analogy" by logical deduction from the "natural law." Striking examples of Peck's work are *The Divine Society* (1925) and *The Social Implications of the Oxford Movement* (1933), the latter being lectures given in America. In the same way but more recently, an Anglican layman and economist, D. L. Munby, has, in *Christianity and Eco-*

nomic Problems,[15] called upon natural law while ignoring it in practice. Munby confesses that the concept is so murky that he risks the *odium theologicum* in referring to it (he calls his own version "descriptive" rather than legal or moral), but claims to find in it "proximate norms" such as that material things are good but subordinate, men are to work, they may own privately but should avoid pride in wealth, they are to live in social groups, and there must be government. Obviously these maxims do not need either Scripture or natural law to suggest them; and, in fact, Munby proceeds thereafter in a quite rational and pragmatic way to deal with economic questions. He *refers* to Christian ideas and church writers, but has no constructive need of them to validate what he says!

Anglican philosophical theologians in the last quarter of a century have exemplified this sketchy and peripheral treatment of natural law. It was true of Lionel Thornton's work and of Eric Mascall's, as of Norman Pittenger's in America, to mention only three. This should not be surprising to anybody who is familiar with official or semi-official formularies in the Church of England. There is no mention of natural law in the Thirty-nine Articles of Religion in the prayer book.[16] In *Doctrine in the Church of England* (1933) the phrase occurs only a single time, properly enough under "providence"—but even here it carries the scientific, *nonethical* meaning, and is never mentioned once in connection with creation, revelation, love-justice, sin, or conscience![17]

For the past decade and a half there has been little or no talk of natural law, until quite recently. In 1964 there were three English Anglican treatises, but with none of the grandeur and scholarship of Kirk, which revive the notion. They are generally conservative on most of the issues of the times. The first of these is Canon Herbert Waddams' *New Introduction to Moral Theology*, with a section on natural law containing more skepticism than affirmation. In effect, he bows to the views of Professor

J. A. Boorman, of McGill University, Canada, that the classical Christian (Roman Catholic) doctrine is a two-story ethic with Aristotle on the first level and the Bible on the second—a "prudential ethic" bearing little resemblance to that of the New Testament.[18] The second is Lindsay Dewar's *Moral Theology in the Modern World.* Canon Dewar's defense of the idea is equivocal: even though "there be no doubt as to what *are* the agreed principles of the natural law—and the doubt has been magnified by some recent writers—there is, to say the least, no less doubt as to the exact interpretation of the Sermon on the Mount."[19] As we shall see, his remarks upon the problematic character of the Protestant Scriptural law ethic are well enough founded, but they do not strengthen the natural law position (and there is an alternative still open to Christian ethics). The third work, *The Right and Wrong,* by J. H. Jacques, is a brief and very traditional affirmation of natural law, lacking any concrete "precepts." Jacques wants politics formed "according to the precepts of the natural law" (p. 112), but these never emerge—only "searching" questions. Nevertheless, he actually calls natural law (p. 117) "a bridge from reason to belief."

Anglican moralists are not alone, of course, in this stubborn but equivocal "loyalty" to the tradition of belief. We should recall that even Ferdinand Toennies in his *Gemeinschaft und Gesellschaft* (1887) tried to find a "sociological basis of natural law," even though it had little ethical connotation. Nathaniel Micklem, a distinguished Congregational theologian, principal of Mansfield College, Oxford, 1932–1953, took the same loyal stance.[20] Americans and Englishmen looking toward the Continent are intrigued by the spectacle of Jacques Ellul, in France, vaguely and ambiguously defending the natural law in a Christian legal treatise,[21] while Paul Tournier, of Switzerland, prefers a personalistic ethic for medicine.[22]

In America, there are persistent champions of natural-law philosophy, of whom Robert M. Hutchins, of the Fund for the Republic, is a leading example. Many of those who lean upon it appear to use it politically, as Origen did long ago, to justify civil disobedience, especially in relation to dictatorships and on behalf of civil rights.[23] John C. Bennett, the editor of the volume *Christian Social Ethics in a Changing World*, is a leading American ethicist in social questions who refuses to "break with" the natural-law concept, even though his obvious attraction to it is formally disclaimed by such statements as this one in *Christians and the State:* "Whether or not it is wise for Protestants to avoid the use of the phrase 'natural law' (I am not sure about it)," they ought to make clear "that Christians and non-Christians do have much in common in their moral awareness and moral convictions."[24] There is something strange in the persistent notion that natural law still provides common ground with nontheological social thought, when in fact it has just the opposite effect. Walter Marshall Horton once asserted the doctrine for this reason, in the American ecumenical journal, *Christendom* (Winter, 1944, IX. 1), and traces of the same *penchant* are to be found in the work of a Methodist theologian, Walter G. Muelder.[25]

But in Anglicanism generally for the past twenty years, as well as in English and American Protestantism, natural law has suffered the same scant treatment it was given in 1950 by the group appointed by the Central Committee of the World Council of Churches to reexamine it in relation to international order: they quickly by-passed the natural law ideal altogether. After much hesitation most non-Roman theologians, Anglicans included, are inclined to agree with Canon Ronald Preston (of Manchester) on traditional moral theology:

> There is too much law in it, too many hair-splitting legal distinctions, too little attention to empirical evidence (for instance in psychology and sociology), too simple a notion of the term "natural," and too little concern for perfection as against minimum obligations.[26]

THE ISSUE: ETHICAL KNOWLEDGE

In America the "conservatives" among Christian moralists cling halfheartedly to the natural law, or at least to the term, while "liberals" reject it. It is rarely mentioned, and even more rarely treated constructively. In the World Council, most of the ethics have been based on what a Roman Catholic analyst—making use of a distinction first suggested by J. H. Oldham[27]—has called "inspiration" rather than ends. By "inspiration" he meant the motivation of neighbor-love, *agape,* and by "ends" the teleology of the Aristotelian-Thomist natural-law doctrine. As Father Duff makes clear, the former is Protestant, the latter Catholic, and hence inevitably "the ethic of inspiration" has prevailed. Natural law received no serious attention in the social ethics of the Oxford Conference on Church, Community, and State in 1937, nor at Amsterdam in 1948, Evanston in 1954, New Delhi in 1961. It was to be expected that evangelical ethicists would ignore it, but what is significant is the absence of any vigorous or committed support even from Anglicans.

Even Emil Brunner's influence among Continental thinkers has not advanced its cause—perhaps because his support is only halfhearted.[28] (We may take note, as an example of *Natur-Recht* analysis, that Brunner rests the case for private ownership on it, whereas Melanchthon in his *Loci* of 1521 took it to favor common ownership!) Brunner's predicament is the one in which any Christian finds himself when he tries to build social ethics on the natural law. He analyzes the problem more thoroughly than any Anglican has ever done. In *Justice and the Social Order* (p. 88), he says that Paul embraced the Stoic notion, and that the Reformers likewise "unanimously and unhesitatingly applied the concept of the natural law presented by the church fathers and the schoolmen, as an integral part of their social ethics." But a critical examination of his treatment shows that he accepts only half the concept—namely, that right and wrong are objectively real as God's will; *he does not accept the claim that by natural reason men can know what "nature" teaches.* In brief, he accepts its ontology but not its epistemology—its substantive but not its cognitive claims. Its first part fits the Christian faith, but its second part clashes with the fact of finitude. Yet surely the natural-law doctrine includes both.

The year 1932 was important as the emergence point of three most influential works: Brunner's *Das Gebot und die Ordnungen,* Reinhold Niebuhr's *Moral Man and Immoral Society,* and William Temple's *Nature, Man and God.* Temple and Niebuhr completely ignored natural law, but in Niebuhr's case this was more definitely due to a fundamental insistence on human limitations and the relativities of knowledge and of history. It is this relativism which is our era's birthmark. All three approaches, however, were relativistic or "contextual" or "situational." Brunner spoke of "the occasionalism of love" and his method-principle was: "The basis of the Divine Command is always the same, but its content varies with varying circumstances." Niebuhr's very similar approach is well known. Temple put it: "There are no moral laws that are absolute except the law to love one's neighbor as oneself."[29]

Although C. H. Dodd showed in a scholarly way that the natural-law idea, in the ontological or substantive sense of the term, had been implicit in the Bible, English or American writers betrayed no interest.[30] In Europe, Werner Elert has been undecided about its utility and validity and therefore has made no use of it.[31] Helmut Thielecke (*Theologische Ethik,* 1955) introduces still another variation on the theme by separating the "order of nature" from the "order of creation," the former being "fallen" enough to come into ethical conflict with the latter![32] This challenges Luther's "orders" and Bonhoeffer's "mandates" and doubles the difficulty of discerning what it is that is "ordained."

A neat and succinct repudiation of natural law, which voices the opinion of most of us, is that by James Pike, the Episcopal Bishop of California.[33] He calls it a "holy noise" and "color words." He gives four main grounds for rejecting it: (1) its "universal precepts," such as "avoid the evil, do the good" and "to each according to his due," are platitudinous; (2) it has been used in history to defend anything and everything—feudalism, capitalism, socialism, fascism, both the "divine right" of kings and democracy, denial of political and religious liberty ("error has no rights"), and affirmation of the same ("conscience is always to be followed"); (3) cultural anthropology has made it plain that there is disagreement "on every subject" in morals—there is no *consensus gentium;* (4) its—the natural law's—conclusions are always built into its premises, and the premises are based on faith assertions, entirely legitimate but not a matter of reason at all!

Now that the ecumenical dialogue is widening to include Roman Catholic moralists and social-ethics thinkers, the discussion of natural law will almost certainly be given a depth, coherence, and competence which it has not had from Anglican and Protestant theologians. Yet even in Roman Catholic circles the battle is being waged or rewaged. In 1963, in a Roman Catholic–Protestant colloquium at Harvard (attended by Cardinal Bea), Roman Catholic theologians indicated that there are those among them who minimize natural-law theory and the "manualistic treatment of conscience," preferring instead such lines of approach as (1) charity and eschatological concern, (2) the particularity of decision—"every concrete situation is unique," and (3) "the demands of love."[34] Their openness to the relativity of ethical insight was expressed as a rejection of St. Bernard's view that one who in good faith follows an erroneous conscience commits sin, a view based on the "mystical" theory that conscience is the voice of God, and therefore any error or departure from the natural law (which is God speaking to man's reason) is due to man's *bad will!*

In the lively Roman Catholic debate about birth control centering on a schema of the Second Vatican Council, some theologians may still allow the phrase "natural law," but they depart radically from its conventional use—so radically that the phrase loses definition. The Dutch Dominican, Edward Schillebeeckx, has proposed a personal instead of a biological interpretation, so that the "nature" to be respected becomes not the reproductive processes but "what is worthy of a human being"—freedom, planning, control of physical nature to serve human nature![35] The American Jesuit, R. O. Johann, undergirds Schillebeeckx, with a personal philosophy directly challenging natural law.[36] F. E. Flynn has agreed that man's vocation is actually to frustrate nature as do medicine and technology, if rational needs and purposes require it.[37] In a different genre, the Australian Father Eric D'Arcy, in his antilegalist *Conscience and Its Right to Freedom* (1961), asserts not one but four reasons against the classical natural-law doctrine of man's ability to know and do the right thing by an innate knowledge of the principles of ethics (*synderesis*).[38]

This is the heart of the problem—in the natural-law theory of ethical knowledge we can postulate the presence of right and wrong objectively in the nature of things, *de rerum natura,* if we appreciate that kind of metaphysics. But this does not entitle us to claim that we *possess* such "values" cognitively. Such epistemological complacency has become impossible since the establishment of cultural relativism by Edward Westermarck in his *Origin and Development of the Moral Ideas* in 1912. On the basis of the "radical monotheism" in Christian theology, we may believe (heuristically postulate) "natural laws," but we cannot pretend to *know* them as universals or as universally obligatory. The natural law may persist as an ontological affirmation, but it is dead as an epistemological doctrine. This is an age of relativism in Christian terms of humility: the old "canon" of rationality has been shaken by depth psychology; the old "canon" of the occidental perspective has been superseded by a global or even interspatial perspective; the old "canon" of logic and language has been replaced by nondiscursive and symbolic reason. In the same way, the old "canon" of a hierarchy of values has been converted into a *spectrum*—a sliding scale of ethical relativities and a pragmatic temper.[39] With some this becomes *de gustibus non est disputandum* or an "absolute" relativism, but it cannot become so for Christians because of Jesus Christ, the man who is the measure of all things. As Brunner put it, the *Why* is always the same, no matter how much the *What* may vary. The point is that the *What* does vary.[40]

SITUATIONAL OR CONTEXTUAL ETHICS

What, then, becomes of Christian ethics, social and personal? Is it now simply a matter of "intuition" or "guidance" or "spontaneity"? Certainly not.

There are three lines of approach to right-wrong, good-evil judgments. The first is legalism. Generally in the past Roman Catholicism has relied upon the "law" of nature, and Protestantism upon the "law" of Scripture. The legalist enters into every decision-making situation with an array or apparatus of prefabricated principles, precepts, and rules, and forces the life situation to fit procrusteanly the "relevant" rule. The second approach, at the opposite extreme, is antinomianism—the spontaneity or impulse of the moment, experienced as "intuition" from within or "guidance" from without. The antinomian enters the decision-making moment unencumbered but unarmed by any prevenient principles whatsoever. We see this in some Protestant groups, and the secular existentialists such as

Simone de Beauvoir (see, for example, her *Ethics of Ambiguity*, 1948). One American Lutheran has spoken of "conscience" as "the swoop of a gull."[41] But there is a third approach, the "contextual" or "situational" method. And it is toward this ethical strategy that Anglican and "Atlantic" Protestant theologians lean sharply.

Whereas the legalist prefabricates his ethical choices, and the antinomian or spontaneist acts on "the spur of the moment," the situationist or contextualist enters into his decision making *well armed with "principles generally valid" but prepared to modify, suspend or even violate any principle or "general rule" if in the situation the command to love the neighbor is better served.* The situationist always remembers that he is commanded to love persons— not precepts nor even principles! This is Bonhoeffer's idea of "formation"—"no abstract ethics." All things may be lawful but they may not be constructive, upbuilding, edifying (I Cor. 6 : 12; 10 : 23). There is nothing fixed or absolute or "natural" about any guideline in this strategy. When the only law is the "law of love" (understood according to the commandment in the Summary and in Rom. 13 : 9–10) *anything* may be right or good, depending on the circumstances. Otherwise, as Bultmann has argued, principles are idolatrous. This brings an end to all legalisms—natural, Scriptural, or doctrinal! When love is the norm, we work with *maxims* but not with rules.

There is a widespread and erroneous idea that the situational or contextual ethic is existentialist and utterly *undisciplined*. But only the antinomian strategy is truly existential. When Pope Pius XII proscribed the nonprescriptive ethic as both "existential" and "situational," he confused the two.[42] This confusion is seen in the writings of Karl Rahner, S.J., who mistakenly believes that situationalists have adopted the existentialists' ontological theory of *radical discontinuity*.[43] On the basis of this theory, the fabric of experience is denied; there is no connective tissue in events, all is unique. There is no web of life to relate one moment of decision to another, and hence no basis for generalizing. According to the theory of radical discontinuity every situation has only its particularity. It would force us to the "absolute particularism" of *tout comprendre, tout pardonner*. On such an ontology the existentialists rightly reject all principles or "generally valid" ethical propositions—as well as those legalistic rules of Torah which absolutize or idolize maxims and fix them into rules.

On the contrary, situational or contextual ethics, the "new morality," as Bishop Robinson has called it in his *Honest to God* (1963), is *not* existential, at least in the philosophical sense that a Kierkegaard or a Sartre would suppose. It simply refuses to accept *any* principle, other than neighbor concern, as always binding. It is, therefore, an ethic of tremendous personal responsibility and initiative—and an ethic for a social policy which is nondoctrinaire and elastic. This is seen in the thought of another English writer, Canon Douglas Rhymes, as well as that of the "Cambridge Question Askers"—almost all of them Anglicans.[44] Even Karl Barth allows for the *ultima ratio,* the outside chance that love will cancel out a principle. Indeed, while situationalism is willing to operate with principles or maxims, kept in their proper place, it nevertheless rejects precepts or rules as inevitably rigid and legalistic.

In America this alternative to legalism (natural or otherwise) and antinomianism has its exponents: this writer; another Anglican, Professor George Easter of Philadelphia; Bishop Pike, already quoted. There are non-Anglicans, too—Paul Lehmann of Union Seminary; James Gustafson of Yale; A. T. Rasmussen of California; and others.[45] Alexander Miller in his *Renewal of Man* (1955) held that "the absolute is an absolute loyalty, not an absolute principle," nearly the same language as that of Archbishop Temple's ethical theory: "What acts are right may depend on circumstances. . . . But there is an absolute obligation to will whatever may on each occasion be right."[46] In his *Ethics,* Bonhoeffer put it thus: "The question of good is posed and is decided in the midst of each definite, yet unconcluded, unique and transient situation of our lives, in the midst of our living relationships with men, things, institutions, and powers, in other words, in the midst of our historical existence."

The basic issue at stake between this situational ethic and the natural-law theory is the locus of value. Wherein does the goodness or badness of an act lie? Is adultery wrong always and in itself because it breaks a law, or is it wrong only *if and when* it hurts and betrays the persons involved? The same may be asked of fornication. Is a theft wrong any time and any place, regardless of circumstances—even if by stealing we are doing *the most loving thing in the situation?* (See Matt. 12:3–4.) Can abortion be right if it saves the mother's life? What of her health, her family's welfare, her freedom? What "makes" a personal act or a social policy right or wrong, good or evil? As the old realist-nominalist debate recognized long ago, the question is: Is the moral quality or "value" of a thing or action intrinsic or extrinsic, inherent or contingent? Is it "in" a right act or policy, or does it happen *to* it?

The Anglican tradition includes an elastic, nonlegalistic ethical method which calculates the greater good or the lesser evil—a system called compensationism.[47] But this sought only to establish that for love's sake we may sometimes do what is evil. The situational method, on the contrary, holds that whatever is most loving in the situation *is* right and good—not merely something to be excused as a lesser evil! *Agape* is its only law. The principles of the Christian *sophia* are at most maxims, never rules or precepts, and they illuminate situations but do not dictate decisions. Temple and Oldham, back in 1937, called them "middle" axioms. But in the *kairos* of decision the facts and technical data require careful calculation, *ex factis orbitur jus*—a Christian *sophrosunei*. Then, finally, as personal and responsible, *decision* must be made. This is not an ethic of "inspiration" or of "ends," but of *decision*. It is a Christian ethic, radically different from the preponderant legalism of the Christian past, as well as from its sporadic antinomianism. It is theonomic, or more carefully put, Christonomic.

Tillich has shown that to have personal status means to have in some sense the power of self-determination, of *being free of one's given nature, as well as of subpersonal nature.* So say situationists. Tillich holds that true theology arises where a question in the situation asks for an answer from the *message*—a "situational theology." Just so, true ethics arise where a situation poses questions to principles! What Tillich calls the method of "correlation" applies to moral theology as fully as to systematic or philosophical theology. Therefore, the situational ethic is *ex casu* and thus far, at least, closer to existential decision than to natural-law ethics which tries in a desperate way to decide according to precepts *per naturam.* Situational ethics declares that all qualifiers such as "always" and "never" and "perfect" and "complete" and "certain" must be thrown aside.

ISSUES FOR ECUMENICAL STUDY

The situational ethic poses many theoretical, practical, and prudential questions. We may close this chapter by pointing to three of these issues of basic theory or rationale:

1. Are "good," "evil," "right," "wrong," and so forth predicates or properties of personal and social actions? Do they *happen* or are they *given*? What of the situationist

view that the Christian good, that is, responsive love to God through concern for our neighbors, is a formal principle, not substantive; and that only with God is love a property? "Why do you ask me about *what* is good? One there is *who* is good" (Matt. 19:17). With men and life and history, all is relative.

2. Can we divorce right from good? Is it true, as men sometimes say, that there are tragic situations in which the best we can do is evil? Is it possible to say that the *best* we can do (that is, the most loving thing possible for the most neighbors) is wrong? For example, is suicide always wrong? What about espionage? Simple affirmatives come from those who innocently and uncritically accept the intrinsicalist-realist metaphysics.

3. Since we are commanded to love the neighbor (Christian social ethics points out that *pleision* is generic, meaning the plural neighbors), and since the word "love" in most languages is romanticized and sentimentalized and personalized out of all relation to *agape,* should we not use the term "justice" instead? Justice is love calculating complex, pluralistic situations, using its head, distributing its services and concern. Justice is love facing the social and circumstantial dimensions of life and history. Does it not actually better express the meaning of the Summary of the Law?

PART TWO

SITUATIONS
FOR
ETHICAL DECISION

V

A Moral Philosophy of Sex

THE TWO elemental, rock-bottom problems of the natural man are production and reproduction, or wealth and love, property and sex. Indeed, productive relations influence sex relations; according to the Kinsey report one's class position often determines his sexual mores. It was found, for example, that people in the low-income bracket show a rate of premarital intercourse which is seven times higher than the college population's, and that college students show a much higher rate of petting, subsexual, and semisexual activities than the low-income, noncollege group. The more broadly "sex" is conceived (beyond directly genital procedures) the more influential and numerous are the things that affect it. Like economic role and class position, there have always been certain specially important influences (religion and scientific knowledge among them), and it is the business of philosophy to place them in a meaningful reference to each other.

Dynamic psychology and anthropology, with their idea of the "libidinous component" in emotion and behavior, have taught us to think of sex as the whole sphere of action

Contributed to a symposium, *Sex and Religion Today,* edited by Simon Doniger, editor of *Pastoral Psychology* (Association Press, 1953). This book included a fine historical paper by Roland Bainton, "Christianity and Sex," subsequently published independently.

and feeling dominated by the relations between men and women: a pervasive force in all aspects of human personality. It encompasses much more of life than merely the physiology of sex functions and differentiation. In this broad and generic sense the term "sex" is a modern one; it is not to be found in Greek or Latin literature, nor in the Bible, nor do they have any equivalent concept.

Our word comes from the Latin *sexus*, meaning "gender" (maleness or femaleness), probably from *secare*, "to cut," meaning thereby a division or segment of mankind. I believe that this is at least a possible explanation of the word; it is only necessary to point to the ancient myths telling how male and female were originally one, as in Aristophanes' tale of love being a reunion of separated halves (in Plato's *Symposium*), and by implication in one of the Creation stories in Gen. 2:18–25 where a prototype woman is made out of a prototype man and thus man and wife (again) "shall be one flesh" being "bone of his bone and flesh of his flesh." But sex as we modern people see it, particularly psychologists and counselors, is nowhere to be found in ancient literature such as the Bible's.

(The New Testament is strikingly fragmentary in its treatment of sex problems and ethics. Jesus, for example, had nothing whatever to say about courtship, perversions, masturbation, sex manners, codes of reproduction and parenthood, multiple marriage, incest, birth control, artificial insemination, feticide, and the like. Apart from his divorce teaching Jesus spoke only of the subjective side of sex. Like the Stoics, he was primarily concerned with the inwardness of merit, that is, with the motives rather than the means or the consequences of an action, as we see in Matt. 5:28, "everyone who looks at a woman lustfully has already committed adultery with her in his heart." Modern depth psychology reveals so much about the unconscious and involuntary causes of our thoughts that some feel Jesus' ethical subjectivity was unjust. The only other sex *logion*—in John 8:3–11, KJV—is a bit of "fringe" tradition, early but not part of the original Gospel, and had to do with mercy and the evil of self-righteousness and hypocrisy, not with extramarital sexuality.)

I remember saying several years ago at the Harvard Law School, in a debate with Margaret Mead and Gregory Zilboorg, that the ideals of sex are no lower (ethically) in the present time than in the past but that the sanctions enforcing them are weaker and fewer, and that technology (especially medical technics) is the fundamental factor of change. It is precisely with regard to these three things (ideals, sanctions, and technics) and their relations to each other that we can work out a relevant, realistic, and constructive philosophy of sex.

First of all it needs saying that the Christian churches must shoulder much of the blame for the confusion, ignorance, and unhealthy guilt associations which surround sex in Western culture. In the Old Testament and in Judaism generally, sexuality has been honored as a part of the divinely ordered nature of human beings, although the law and the prophets and rabbis steadily held to the view that sex is a purposive or *instrumental* value, a means to procreation rather than an end in itself; sex for its own sake was always scorned. But there have been, beginning in the primitive church, many puritanical Christians, both Catholic and Protestant, who have treated sexuality as something inherently evil. I am of the opinion that their reasons for doing so, when we examine them carefully, are rather more of a "psychogenic" kind than rationally theological.

Although Paul (I Cor., ch. 7) advised against marriage and parenthood except in cases of urgent sexual appetite (a kind of race-suicide doctrine), Augustine reversed the apostle by advising against sexual intercourse except in cases of marriage and parenthood! Methodius ranked virginity high above marriage, and Jerome could only praise marriage (the only permissible sexual partnership) because it produced virgins! Augustine went so far as to argue that coitus is sinful even within wedlock unless the specific purpose is always conception. We may be grateful that a wiser view prevailed in the classical tradition of moral theology, where it was allowed that "married love" is a proper part of marriage (even though secondary to procreation in terms of *relative* importance).

This marked antisexual bias may be attributed to a phenomenon which is almost universal, a psychosexual tendency to find a conflict between "holiness" and sexuality, due in its turn to incest taboos or other "depth charges" in the human psyche. It comes, I think, perilously close (philosophically) to the Manichean dualism which was formally denounced as a heresy because it cut across the symbiotic meaning of the incarnation ("the Word was made flesh"). This central Christian doctrine was at loggerheads inevitably with any naïve ontology which looked upon the body as "bad" and the spirit as "good." This dualistic (Persian) brand of "antimaterialism" or bogus "spirituality" has persisted through the Reformation to modern times in many forms of popular piety based upon false asceticism and prurience.

The general assumption has been that only by suppressing instinctual demands can "goodness" be achieved. Leaving aside certain romantic movements of the Middle Ages, it is actually only since the turn of the twentieth century that we have seen a sound rebellion against this repressive pattern and its false dualism. On the whole, furthermore, it has been psychological insights (not monistic theologies or philosophies) that have turned the trick. We have better insights now into what makes people "tick," not only the sinners and their undisciplined conscious sexuality, but also the saints and their undisciplined *un*conscious sexuality!

People commonly have been inclined to make sex Evil Number One, ignoring or minimizing equally or even more important ethical issues. They have identified (I would say *confused*) morality with sex questions, and virtue with obedience to the sexual taboos. The more decisive problems of our social attitudes and spiritual destiny have been ignored. Such evils as lack of love, ego aggrandizement, emotional isolation, envy, lust for power—these were treated as less important than failing to respect the sexual conventions. The ethical "pharisees" (of whom there are too many) fail to see that the most evil and destructive traits are not those of the sexual appetite, which is biologically given and morally neutral in itself, but the irrational emotional passions such as hate, fear, greed, ulcerous struggles for discrete status—all of our self-regarding ("sinful") and antisocial impulses. And none of this, in any case, actually reduced our interest in sex; it activated it at a sly and prurient level of secrecy, behind-the-scenes humor and debate, and such "mental maneuvers" as erotic advertising. The result was that more time and attention was given to "ignoring" sex than to anything else!

Our twentieth-century revolt against hole-in-corner sex was, therefore, a healthy and wholesome thing, taken for what it was. But alas! it soon went in its reaction to the opposite extreme. It fell into the equally absurd and subversive idea that sexual behavior lies outside any kind of ethical code or philosophical meaning whatever. It became a sort of Kantian *Ding an sich,* a thing in itself without relation to or qualification by anything else, whether it might be God, society, beauty, family, partnership, or self-discipline. Yet it is obvious, on second thought, that if our attitude toward others (relationship) is the concern of ethics and philosophy and theology, then sexual behavior—one of the most vital and powerful expressions of our relationship with others—*is decisively important* in morals and faith and world view.

Sigmund Freud, who precipitated so much of this change, began his analysis of people with a quite self-contained and psychogenic view of the individual person.

He tended (with his biological frame of reference) to abstract people from their environment and social matrix, conceiving them as isolated personalities somehow self-determined (by id, ego, and superego) without any "structuring" from the surrounding culture and conditions of life. Now we know more fully how "conditioned" people are; all are agreed including Freud's followers such as Karen Horney and Abraham Kardiner. We understand that personality is a complex of interpersonal relations, an interaction and not something that grows by itself. Our "character" is formed through social experience. The values and standards which shape our behavior have been "structured" into our personalities. *It is not sexual behavior that determines character; it is character that determines sexual behavior.* Contrary to a lot of pseudo psychology based on Freud's earliest formulations, sex ("libido") does not determine what kind of persons we will be; but rather the kind of person we are determines our pattern of sexual behavior. This is important to get straight, for it puts first things first.

A "character" who is dominating and likes to manipulate others will very likely treat others as a mere means to satisfy his sexual needs. Meeting his sexual partners in a pattern "I" to "it" rather than to "Thee," he will enter readily but fitfully into relations with prostitutes and casual "pickups" along the way. (See Paul's two interesting objections to promiscuity, based on relationship theology, I Cor. 6:15–20.) If he is highly aggressive (a "consumer personality"), hungry for power and success, he will disregard his sexual partner's needs and pleasures, perhaps even engaging in sadistic practices of inflicting pain. If he is emotionally mature, capable of both giving and accepting love, he will behave accordingly. *The point here is that character, the system of values and philosophy by which we live, is what determines the particular ways in which we handle and satisfy the sexual drive.*

Any person worth his salt is humble before the truth, and for this reason we are all in debt to psychology and anthropology. But we ought also to realize that the scientific collection of sex facts (as in the much-publicized research of Kinsey and his colleagues) misses the most important side of the matter. Our ethical interest is in the ends people seek, the goods they want, the values they live by and for. In this perspective, sex is a means to an end or ends, not an end in itself. Psychiatry says that anybody who treats sex as an end in itself is sick, whether you call him a victim of "satyriasis" or something else. He has ceased to live a life in productive and creative relationship. This means, of course, that in all but pathological personalities it is the *motives* of sex behavior that are the most important facts, and statistics cannot measure them or discover them.

For example, a factual study describing premarital intercourse in three couples could record the class position, income, age, education, religion, vocation, and the like of all six persons, but the *meaning* of their behavior would be undisclosed. The first couple might be planning to marry (a committed relationship), the second merely seeking "release" from sexual tension (a mutually utilitarian view of each other), and the third couple might be "using" each other with no concern or respect at all (an exploitative relationship: what Erich Fromm calls the "nonproductive, exploitative orientation").

We often hear it claimed by "oldsters" that sex standards are lower today than they used to be, whether the younger generation that is "going to the dogs" has its growth security smashed by the oldsters' wars or not! I do not believe it, not for a second. What is true, I am sure, is that sexual promiscuity (especially before marriage) is more common than it used to be; and also it is much more widespread among the fair sex (as the decline of organized prostitution would suggest). Now this is the kind of statement for which (in the nature of the case) it is hard to find proof. But I believe I can show that it is *probably* true by explaining why I do not think that sex ideals are any lower. (If this sounds like a paradox, just have patience for a few minutes, and it will clear itself up.)

There is no convincing evidence that young people today are any less conscientious than their parents, or less successful at maturing emotionally. That is to say, they are no less capable of avoiding sexual promiscuity since they are just as able as their forebears to relinquish short-term satisfactions for the sake of long-term satisfactions. (This is a criterion of maturity, of being grown-up or adult, or of "ego sovereignty over the id.") There is, in short, no reason to think that today's youth have less moral stamina or weaker fibers than their elders. *But* our patterns of moral action involve more than ideals; the *inducements or motivations or incentives* of morality include "sanctions" as well as ideals. We walk in the paths of virtue because there is an expectation of rewards and punishments in the background; this is true of some people all of the time, and of all people some of the time. (Just look at the prizes and penalties held out in the Sermon on the Mount, Matt., chs. 5 to 7!) Our *ideals* of love and of sexual expression are as high as ever but *the sanctions behind our loyalty to the ideals have changed.*

In the past people stayed "in line" as far as sex goes because they feared the consequences if they got out of line. A sharp-sighted modern limerick puts it this way:

> There was a young lady named Wilde
> Who kept herself quite undefiled
>   By thinking of Jesus
>   And social diseases
> And the fear of having a child.

It is true that there is a place for religious sanctions, as well as for practical prudence in such matters as health and social disgrace. But the *prudential* sanction is the one that has changed. The *technology of sex,* prophylaxis and contraception, have removed the triple terrors of conception, infection, and detection. This is true for married love as well as for premarital sex; hence, the modern Mother Goose:

> There was an old woman who lived in a shoe;
> She had so many children because she didn't
>   know what to do.

But that is the old situation, not the new one. Sex is becoming safe! There is also added protection in the anonymous-stranger patterns created by the automobile and the apartment house.

Indeed, even the religious sanctions of obedience and loyalty to God are weakening in this "secular" age, sometimes described as a post-Christian culture. The old religious threat of hell is gone, as a negative sanction. And now what? With the loss or weakening of religious sanctions, and the disappearance of prudential sanctions under the new technology of sex, the only motivating force to turn to, to buttress our sexual ideals, is the positive one of love rather than the negative one of fear. It means that our sex standards will have to find a foundation in loyalty and devotion to some loved one—based, that is to say, in a high-commitment relationship—whether that person be human or divine. For the humanist it will be only the former; for the theist it will or can be both. *But the fundamental truth to get straight is that our sex standards in an era of medical technology and urban anonymity depend for their sanction upon devotion rather than dread.*

To use the language of formal ethics, a "prudential" sex standard will no longer work, if the ideal is premarital continence and marital monopoly. And when people have stuck to ideals out of the fear of what will happen when they cheat, they are helpless when that crutch is gone. Fear as a motive *is* a crutch, a sign of weakness and not of strength.

I do not mean to make out that there is a quick or easy way to build up positive sanctions, with which to replace the old outmoded negative sanctions. On the contrary, the task of finding substitutes is enormous, subtle, and (so I believe) a matter of "grace" beyond nature. It is so difficult that many students of sex ethics are convinced that the old ideals of premarital continence and marital monopoly of sex are dead and gone, unworkable in a civilization of sex hygiene, postponed marriage (the prolonged bachelorhood of education and war), and small families. Unfortunately there is a lot of truth in the old saw that "the spirit is willing but the flesh is weak." Paul says there is a law in his members that wars against the law of his mind (Rom. 7:22–25), and for this reason alone, without any empirical evidence, we can suppose that with old sanctions gone there is more sexual promiscuity. Old ideals or standards tend to die with old sanctions, if no remedy or tonic is provided.

If fear is a discarded crutch, what help have we, what other motivation? Humanists will say it must be loyalty to personal integrity and the common good, social conscience. That is part of the answer, no doubt; but I do not believe it can succeed by itself. In the first place it is a fact that even in the past prudential considerations (of self-realization and human well-being) did not always support marital sex monopoly as their ideal. Many societies and cultures have had other and "looser" sex standards. Moreover, human selfishness is such that I do not think most people can "identify" with their neighbors completely enough for altruistic ends. By our very constitution we are too self-centered. Psychology calls it egocentricity, theology calls it sin; in either purview it makes for only limited communality of interest.

The loyalty needed to keep modern people hewing to the line of the old ideal must, therefore, be born out of grace, out of the spiritual power of religious conviction. Religious faith is not needed to tell us *what* is good, but it *is* needed to make us *want* it enough to do it. (Of course, this whole discussion assumes without question that the true and best sex ideal is, as it was in the prescientific Christian era, a marital monopoly. Yet most of what is said here is valid if the old code is rejected in whole or in part.) In any case, as things are now we have to act out of love, not out of fear. It requires very grown-up people. To use a misused word, we have a *crisis* in sex ethics involving profound levels of religious experience.

Sex is dynamite. Unchanneled by high character it leads to chaos and destruction. It can be the fiercest cement of relationship, but it can also be the lever that breaks people apart. Conceived broadly as "libido" it is the most "dynamic" of assets as a means to good ends, including love as well as procreation. Our danger is that while technology (medical and industrial) makes intercourse easier, our moral *ability* to serve our ideals has not kept pace. The ideal no longer finds support in the "facts of life." This is what is called the moral lag, a religious and moral (not scientific) problem. It is much like the new atomic energy: science gives us the new power, but to what end will we use it? For better living, or for self-destruction?

Sex Offenses: An Ethical View

INTRODUCTION

"ST. PAUL'S advice is as sound today as it was two thousand years ago," says Morris Ploscowe. "It would be a great deal better if men and women remained continent sexually or got married and then adhered to their marriage vows. Much emotional disturbance, human misery, crime, disorder, and illegitimacy would be averted if humanity could abide by St. Paul's teachings. It never has."[1]

Because the "flesh is weak" in most people some of the time and in some people most of the time, with resulting offenses either to the persons or the opinions of others in the community, the law has erected fences of prohibition and of penalty. How effective these fences are is, at the very least, questionable. One distinguished writer on jurisprudence, Edmond Cahn, has observed that "the criminal laws relating to sex have very little systematic enforcement anywhere. Most of them ought to have been repealed long ago."[2] There is some evidence, based on one serious, although debatable, attempt at research into sexual behavior,

Reprinted, with permission, from a symposium, *Sex Offenses*, appearing in *Law and Contemporary Problems* (Vol. 25, No. 2, Spring, 1960), published by the Duke University School of Law, Durham, N.C. Copyright 1960, by Duke University.

that if existing laws were actually enforced, about 95 percent of the male population in America would go to jail.[3] If this finding even remotely reflects the realities, it is plain that there is room to wonder whether our criminal sex laws are legally viable, and possibly also to question their ethical validity.

Why are these unenforced laws still on the statute books? Morris Ploscowc, in another place, has explained their presence as "dead letter legislation" kept there "because of the fear that a vote for repeal would be branded as a vote for immorality."[4] Writing more than a quarter century ago, Walter Lippmann offered a second explanation, saying that "what everybody must know is that sexual conduct, whatever it may be, is regulated personally and not publicly in modern society. If there is restraint, it is voluntary; if there is promiscuity, it can be quite secret."[5] Here, in these two comments, we have a large part of the reason for our continued lip service to unenforced sex laws: *fear of appearing indifferent to morality* if we advocate cutting out the dead wood, in the eyes of those who think by what recently has been called the conventional wisdom;[6] and the plain fact that *most sexual activity is clandestine* and, therefore, not easily subjected to control by public policy and judiciary. The rules of evidence in our law are such that the secretive nature of sexuality removes a great deal of it from ordinary criminal procedures.

However, "evidence" is a technical legal question and outside the scope of this article. The present discussion will be restricted to the ethical side of the problem. Lord Russell has asserted what he called "the well known fact that the professional moralist in our day is a man of less than average intelligence."[7] In spite of the grim possibility that his harsh judgment may be well grounded, it is necessary, just the same, to place the whole question of criminal law and sex offenses within the ethical perspective and frame of reference. It is even possible that a "professional moralist" might share Glanville Williams' dissatisfaction over the present state of affairs in which "proposals to extend the law of crime and sharpen its penalties receive ready consideration, while proposals to restrict it are almost impossible to realize."[8] If it is true that "law is the rule of reason applied to existing conditions,"[9] then moral values and ethical analysis are an important part of that reasoning. Morality is as much at stake in our laws themselves as it is in the behavior which our laws ostensibly seek to regulate. Justice Holmes once remarked that "law is a statement of the circumstances in which public force will be brought to bear upon men through the courts."[10] Since morality is meaningless apart from freedom, moralists naturally seek to reduce "legalism" to a minimum, keeping the range of choice and personal decision or responsibility as wide as possible. In the language of classical Biblical theology in the West, grace reinforces law and sometimes even bypasses it, but it does not abolish it nor can it replace it until sin itself is no more.

There are some who seem to imagine that law and ethics can be divorced, as if law were not a matter of translating morals (value judgments) into formal social disciplines. Every law is the fruit of a decision about good and evil, right and wrong. "It is a pretty safe rule," as Felix S. Cohen once put it, "that whenever a judge says, 'This is a court of law,' and then goes on to say that he cannot be guided by moral or theological considerations, he is actually being guided by moral or theological considerations without knowing it."[11] There certainly are differing ethical doctrines; we do not all derive our values from the same source or, to alter the figure, base our norms on the same foundations and premises. A lawmaker's ethic, and a court's, may be utilitarian or hedonistic, based on a striving for happiness or pleasure as the highest good; or it may be a sheer duty-ethic, based on commandments from God or from some other authority such as the state or a leader. But whether pragmatic or formal, there *is* an ethic at work, no matter how covert or obscure it may be.

Some forms of sexual activity are historically and conventionally related to criminal law, such as fornication, adultery, abortion, bigamy, indecent exposure, rape (both forcible and statutory), homosexuality, prostitution, psychopathic sexuality, incest, and crimes against children. The problem of obscenity might be included, along with pornography—which D. H. Lawrence called "the attempt to insult sex."[12] Roman Catholic theologians would add artificial insemination from a third-party donor ("adultery"), divorce ("legal adultery"), and contraceptive birth control ("unnatural," as with sodomy, bestiality, etc.). For general purposes of discussion, however, the laws affecting marriage, divorce, and annulment only *indirectly* regulate sexual acts, and we should focus here upon the acts which are directly regulated by law.

THINGS AS THEY ARE

The relativity and variety of sex laws, even within the common framework of "Christian civilization" in the West, may be seen when we compare the network of statutes in the United States and England to the French *Code pénal,* for the latter ignores entirely all sexual acts which are adult, private, and consensual.[13] It should be carefully noted that the whole objective of recent studies and reviews of sex laws, such as the Model Penal Code proposals of the American Law Institute,[14] is to encourage the adoption of legislative principles and statutory codes which approximate the laissez-faire code of France.

The Anglo-American policy has been a very confused and inconsistent one, tending to "dead letter" laws and hypocrisy. In England, law reformers find it something of a puzzle that adultery, fornication, and prostitution are not criminal offenses; nor is homosexuality between females an offense, although between males it is; nor was it until a scant fifty years ago that incest was made a crime.[15] In the United States, with its fifty separate lawmaking states, there has been a veritable mare's nest of statutory laws. Since Elizabethan and Jacobean times, for example, courts and legislatures have tended to follow Lord Coke's line that homosexuality is "a detestable and abominable sin among Christians not to be named,"[16] with the result that the statutes outlawing it are commonly so broadly and evasively worded as to make it difficult, if not impossible, to draw an indictment that allows the defense any bill of particulars. A quick reading of Ploscowe's survey of the obscurities, contradictions, and loopholes of American law shows why he ended his work declaring that the criminal law needs "a complete reorientation in the field of sex crimes."[17]

The logical difficulties are compounded by the moral evasions accompanying them. It has been seriously estimated that in the United States, there are about 40,000 sex crimes reported annually and perhaps ten to twenty times as many actually committed.[18] Most state legislatures obviously do not regard their "sex crimes" as real crimes at all. For example, in Virginia[19] and West Virginia,[20] only twenty dollars is the maximum penalty for fornication; in Rhode Island, it is only ten dollars.[21] In Arizona, the penalty might be imprisonment for three years;[22] but in North Dakota, it is only thirty days.[23] Police departments, except for Boston's, simply do not make arrests for adultery.[24] "Men and women copulate in sovereign disregard for penal statutes," and there is little that police, courts, or prosecutors can do about it unless we throw away the constitutional principle that safeguards privacy and frowns upon its invasion.[25]

The hypocrisy of these laws is nothing new or "modern." It has revealed itself not only in the broad secular patterns of behavior, but also among such special and exemplary circles in the social order as the clergy. In medieval days, concubinage was common among the supposedly celibate priests, and the church authorities did not try to enforce the canons against it, even though they had the canons.[26] The Bishop of Winchester licensed prostitutes, or "stews," and collected the taxes on them; yet he forbade them the rites of the church and Christian burial on the ground that brothels were forbidden by "the law of God."[27] It is a comfort, as we shall see, to find that many distinguished churchmen are much less hypocritical in our own times.

There were, of course, other reasons than hypocrisy and venality for the failure of the eccleciastical courts to deal effectively with forbidden sexuality, either heterosexual or homosexual. Their statutes, like many of the modern ones, were poorly drawn and defined, procedures were faulty as to evidence and judgment, and penalties were commonly meretricious. The penances imposed were so often commuted to money fines for the sake of the income that church courts lost status even where there was, as in England, a religious establishment with civil authority.

When the civil courts in England in 1533 took jurisdiction over sex sins and changed some formally into crimes,[28] they were far more punitive than the church courts had ever thought of being. For example, death was made the penalty for male homosexual acts (ignoring "lesbian" behavior altogether); and it was not until 1828 that this was reduced to life imprisonment, to be reduced again, with typical gyration, in 1885 to a maximum of two years![29] Penalties in the United States range from one day in New York[30] to life imprisonment in Nevada;[31] some states have a five-year maximum,[32] others a five-year minimum.[33] It seems fairly evident that the common-law courts have never managed to work out a comprehensive or coherent code of forbidden sexual acts. Following a precedent of harshness by the early Puritans, some states have gone very far; for example, an Indiana statute actually made self-masturbation an offense punishable on the same terms provided for sodomy.[34]

Prostitution might serve as another example, although not as much of confusion as of evasion. The "call girl" phenomenon in America today is simply a sophistication of the older practice. Christian culture has always been two-sided about prostitution—unfairly condemning prostitutes, while winking at or even justifying toleration of prostitution as a necessary evil.[35] Thomas Aquinas reasoned that God allows it "lest certain goods be lost or certain greater evils be incurred."[36] In the United States, it is a criminal offense in all states, defined as the indiscriminate offer of sexual intercourse for hire; but in England, it is not in itself an offense, although certainly the law there prohibits certain features that commonly attend it, such as street and public solicitation.

And so with other statutory offenses. Similar varieties, duplications, contradictions, inequalities, and lacunae are to be found on other scores of sexual behavior. To correct the trouble, we have a swelling stream of suggestions. Glanville Williams urges, for example, that bigamy should not be an offense, since it is actionable already as a fraudulent obtaining of intercourse and a deliberate registering of a void marriage.[37] In the same way, it has been argued that bestiality can be left to the general provisions covering cruelty to animals, and that incest be dropped as a statutory offense and reliance made upon existing laws on family relations, mistreatment, and assaults on children—as in Belgium.[38] The range and complexity of sex laws at present "on the books" is a monument to tongue-in-cheek legislation and to the "prohibitionist fallacy."

The Moral Question Posed

The conclusion that "the American sex revolution" has trapped us in a "listless drift towards sex anarchy"[39] is no doubt overdrawn. Still, there has been a change in sex attitudes and practices of a truly revolutionary caliber; this is a patent truth accepted generally among present-day culture analysts. Perhaps a typical symptom can be seen in the recent furor within British Medical Association circles over a booklet, *Getting Married,* by Eustace Chesser, M.D., and Winifred de Kok, M.D. It was written and published by the BMA, but had to be withdrawn after some members resigned in protest shortly before the first printing was exhausted. As an American commentator at the University of Oklahoma expresses it, the protestants disavowed the booklet's claim that chastity is "outmoded and should no longer be taught young people."[40] Nevertheless, the fact that it could reach the advanced stage of publication and discussion it did is significant.

Parallels and cross-cultural traits as between England and America are a commonplace. Transatlantic attitudes and customs have always maintained a marked degree of similarity, in spite of typically chauvinist disclaimers in the journalism of both countries. Therefore, it is important, even vital, to keep abreast of British developments as we carry on our American discussion of sex ethics and sex law. We have a significant development of this kind in the proposals of a recent parliamentary committee chaired by Sir John Wolfenden,[41] and in the testimony formally submitted to it by the Church of England Moral Welfare Council.[42] These studies are as appropriate to our own American legal and ethical problems as to Great Britain's. Proposals in the American Law Institute lean heavily in the direction of the English ones, but by comparison, they seem to lack the sharp edge and clarity we need to reach and explore the issues at stake. Perhaps the most succinct statement of the core issue as between ethics and sex laws is one in the testimony of the Anglican Council. It declared that[43]

> it is not the function of the State and the law to constitute themselves guardians of *private* morality, and thus to deal with *sin as such* belongs to

the province of the church. On the other hand, it
is the duty of the State to punish crimes, and it
may properly take cognizance of, and define as
criminal, those sins which also constitute offenses
against *public* morality.

The heart of the ethical question, for lawmakers and en-
forcers, is precisely this distinction between public and
private interests, between illegality and immorality, between crime and sin. The Anglican Council, which is not
an official agency, even though it carries great weight,
"unreservedly" condemned as "sinful" all violations of
Christian teaching on chastity. Yet, it insisted that "there
should be no departure in specific instances from the
generally accepted principle that the British law does not
concern itself with the private irregular or immoral sexual
relationships of consenting men and women," and that
"the action of the State should be therefore limited to the
protection of the citizen from annoyance or obstruction."[44]
We have here two legally relevant distinctions. One is
the distinction between immoral and illegal offenses; the
other is the distinction between private and public acts.
The laissez-faire nature of this approach is self-evident.
Thus, Eustace Chesser has called these distinctions the
moral of the Wolfenden Report, which followed the line
proposed by the Anglican Council.[45] The Anglican Council
and the Royal Committee, on this common basis, called
for a radical minimization of statutory laws controlling
and penalizing both heterosexual and homosexual activities, whether in prostitution or in noncommercial relationships.

The fact is that recent tentative drafts of the Model
Penal Code for the American Law Institute are very simi-
larly inclined. Published private opinions, too, are increasingly of the same kind. To give one example, Albert Ellis,
a psychiatrist, has published views that have much popular

support (outside of legislative halls) and a wide reading, even though the almost truculent hedonism he espouses would generally be repudiated.[46] In his basic ethical norms, he is poles apart from the Anglican Council, since he gives his approval to any and every kind of sexuality, but his viewpoint parallels the Council's as far as the law is concerned. He insists that[47]

> society should not legislate or invoke social sanctions against sex acts performed by individuals who are reasonably competent and well-educated adults; who use no force or duress in the course of their sexual relations; who do not, without the consent of their partners, specifically injure these partners; and who participate in their sex activities privately, out of sight and sound of unwilling observers. If this and only this kind of limitation were applied in modern communities, only a few distinct sex acts would be considered illegal and illegitimate. Included would be seduction of a minor by an adult; rape, sexual assault and murder; and exhibitionism or forms of public display.

In connection with its proposal to remove homosexuality from the list of proscribed acts in the criminal law, the Royal Committee, like the Anglican Council, held:[48]

> Unless a deliberate attempt is made by society, acting through the agency of the law, to equate the sphere of crime with that of sin, there must remain a realm of private morality and immorality which is, in brief and crude terms, not the law's business. To say this is not to condone or encourage private immorality.

The core consideration here is the separation of public and private morality. There is no suggestion that what is private or nonpublic is not subject to moral judgment, or that what is done in secret is *ipso facto* righteous.

In developing its appeal for clarification of the circumstances that might make prostitution illegal, the Wolfenden Report simply said:[49]

> It should not be the duty of the law to concern itself with immorality as such . . . it should confine itself to those activities which offend against public order and decency or expose the ordinary citizens to what is offensive or injurious.

In our common-law tradition, a premium has always been put on privacy; the law has frowned upon its invasion. Police and citizens alike are forbidden to trespass. No general right of search is provided. The principle is that "an Englishman's home is his castle," and consequently wiretapping, interference with mail, or any other such maneuver is subject to close scrutiny by the courts. The public-private distinction has some legal history. And besides, there has always been a real respect for ethical pluralism and for private convictions in our liberal inheritance, as well as for private *actions*. As an American Law Institute report expresses it, "to use the criminal law against a substantial body of decent opinion, even if it be minority opinion, is contrary to our basic traditions."[50]

These two distinctions, then, between morality and legality (sin and crime), and between public and private interests, set the major terms of the problem of sex laws in relation to social ethics.

An Ethical Analysis

Morality and Legality

The old crackerbarrel phrase is, "You cannot legislate morals." Experience with our sex laws, as with the "noble experiment" of prohibition in the '20s, seems to show that the ethical standards after which we aspire cannot be imposed by force of law. It has occasionally been argued that law encourages and inculcates higher standards of behavior and that the proper role of positive law is not merely to reflect the consensus of the society enacting it, but to anticipate and pioneer it. But this doctrine has little prospect of being adopted in democracies. A more cautious view might hold that law can inhibit as well as prohibit behavior, operating as "a conditioner of conduct," but even this is questionable.[51] And the opposite can be true; Westermarck refers to a homosexual who said "he would be sorry to see the English law changed, as the practice would then lose its charm."[52]

Law certainly does not seem to be edifying in its moral influence, even if it is thought to be a restraint on one or more levels. Ethical analysis of law reveals that its real function is to *limit* obligation. Law says, "This specifically (i.e., *only* this) you are to do, or to refrain from doing." Law's definition of obligation is inherently a limitation of obligation. It does not—it cannot—prescribe ideals or even an optimum discipline. This is precisely the reason for Paul's revolt from code law (Torah) and the rise of the term "pharisaism" to describe the practice of hiding behind the law to evade the unbounded demands of grace (an evasion as common in Christian as in Jewish conduct). The radical Christian love-ethic is so grace-focused that its own built-in danger is a tendency to ignore our need of law to make sure that justice is served in a world of still-selfish rather than neighbor-concerned citizens.

The Wolfenden Report and Anglican Council testimony favored the elimination of most of our existing sex statutes for these two reasons: first, law does not build character; and second, it tends to stunt the sense of moral obligation and provide defenses for the complacent. In the same spirit, the American Law Institute has allowed that the criminal law on sex offenses "cannot undertake or pretend to draw the line where religion and morals would draw it."[53]

There is a third reason for separating sin, or moral fault,

from crime, and that is that compelled (law-enforced) behavior is not righteous behavior anyway. No merit, or moral credit, accrues to obedience under the *imperium* of positive law. Only voluntary obedience, under the *auctoritas* of the moral law, represents ethical achievement. Sir George Frazer once suggested that it is better for men to do the right thing for a wrong reason than the wrong thing for a right reason.[54] He was speaking of the role of superstition; but whether the reason is superstitious or legalistic, it is a dubious principle to follow. The only possible ground for *compelling* people to do "the right thing" is concern for justice. We cannot permit innocent third parties to be victimized by the exercise of such high principles as personal freedom and responsibility, desirable as they are, if in some situations, freedom from law means that those who enjoy that freedom exercise it to the injury of others. It was for this reason that the Anglican Council, when recommending freedom (*legal* freedom) for sexual promiscuity, added the condition that it must be adult, consensual, and not a public nuisance.

There is still another related consideration. Most of our sex statutes do not take adequate account of the element of psychological compulsion. Modern depth psychology has revealed the wide extent to which many sexual acts, hetero- and homosexual, are compulsive. Both civil law and ethical analysis make it a principle (*mens rea*) that an act must be *internally* free to be blameworthy, as well as *externally* free to be praiseworthy. The compulsive are not culpable, and this rule applies to many sex crimes. Hence the maxim: *Actus non facit malum nisi mens sit rea*—an act is not criminal unless the mind is guilty. The courts have said, "Our collective conscience does not allow punishment where it cannot impose blame."[55] We have passed beyond the appeal of the Gilbert and Sullivan song, "Let the punishment fit the crime," to the insight that the punishment should fit the criminal as well. In the effort to establish a new rule that some sins are not crimes, we must remember the reverse proposition too: some crimes are not sins.

In pleading for the separation of sins and crimes, this chapter asserts quite simply that it is not the business of law to punish sin at all. It is the business of law to prevent or punish wilful injuries to individuals or to the common order. There is no idea here that ethics, whether religious or not, is to be separated from society and social practice; on the contrary, ethics always limits individual or private freedom by subordinating it to the social or public interest —to neighbor-concern. Nor is the separation of sin and crime a matter of any one orientation or philosophy. Both religious and nonreligious moralists could oppose criminal actions against sexual wrongdoing, holding such actions to be the wrong remedy. Thus, the one-time Archbishop of Canterbury, Geoffrey Fisher, said of nonprostitutional homosexuality, "Some of us think that this particular evil could be more effectively dealt with pastorally if it were not regarded as criminal."[56] At the same time, he favored putting both adultery and prostitution on the statute list as, in his view, inherently injurious to other individuals and/or the collective good. (Even more controversially, he held that artificial insemination from a donor is adultery and should be proscribed. This is the papal position, too.)

In brief, it seems axiomatic that the law cannot rely upon a doctrine that its citizens are legally entitled to disbelieve. There are some ethical doctrines that do not render an adverse judgment (*moral* judgment) upon many sexual acts commonly held to be crimes or sins or both. For example, ethical standards based on natural-law theories, as in Roman Catholicism, or on Scriptural-law rules, as in Protestant literalism and fundamentalism, are *not* the standards of humanists, naturalists, and others. They have not, in fact, been acceptable even in the law for a long time—especially in the American positive-law tradition. Sin is already divorced from crime in our pluralistic culture, and the only real sanction for criminal law is *the common interest,* public order, or the collective good. On this basis only may an ideologically free and pluralistic society frame its moral principles or judgments as to right and wrong and enforce its standards by legal weapons. Society has a right to *protect* itself from dangers within and without, but not to enforce a monistic and monopoly standard of personal (in the sense of private) conduct. The question is: What, if anything, is discretely private? This leads us on to the second crucial distinction.

Privacy and Community

Ethically regarded, the distinctions between private and public moral standards and conduct would be irrelevant and even meaningless in societies in which cultural monism obtained—i.e., in societies that had a single, monopolistic faith or philosophy. Such was the case in the era of church establishment, for example, when the state was the secular arm of the church. But that kind of uniformity (as distinguished from unity) has suffered Queen Anne's fate; it is dead, and its resurrection seems, at least, a highly eschatalogical hope. For some of us, it seems far better, anyway, that there should be a diversity of religions and philosophies and political doctrines. For out of their rubbing together, their competition in the free market of ideas, truths and insights are revealed that would not have emerged in a monochrome culture. Many colors are needed in the democratic coat.

This belief that variety provides creativity, uniformity yields only conformity, is not held by all. At the political level, communists and many anticommunists strive for a one-party state. At the religious level, many Christians and Jews long for a one-faith, one-morality order. For example, Roman Catholic moralists often claim that "truth has rights which error may not enjoy."[57] They have defended their wish to outlaw contraceptive birth control on the ground that it is a practice that violates the natural law (what Thomas Aquinas called a *vitium contra naturam*) and further claim that the natural law is binding on *all* people, Roman Catholics and others alike.[58] The obvious difficulty with this doctrine is that it relies upon the *magisterium* of the church hierarchy to decide which moral judgments are correctly adduced from nature and which ones are not. It is clearly not a matter of *consensus communis* and, therefore, incommensurate with democratic principles. Although careful democrats will not claim that "the voice of the people is the voice of God," they are not likely, for the same reasons, to acknowledge that any ecclesiastical party is either. This is clearly, and persuasively, the reason why legal positivism has triumphed in American law and jurisprudence, rather than natural-law doctrines. As Lon Fuller has pointed out in his discussion of these "two competing directions of legal thought," positive law is skeptical about any attempt to bridge "Hume's gap" between what is and what ought to be, whereas natural-law theory does so confidently.[59]

Our American tradition is, therefore, pragmatic and utilitarian, not metaphysical and dogmatic. We cannot be otherwise in the face of different and conflicting schools of natural-law morality and law, deriving their norms and criteria from such various sources as the nature of God, or the nature of man, or the nature of things. The same position would hold in relation to Kant's categorical imperatives of practical reason—as, for example, his conclusion deduced from the principle of requital (*jus talionis*) that those who engage in an act of bestiality should be expelled from society and deprived of human rights.[60]

Again, then, there is no just and realistic way in law to take account of the pluralistic situation, except by distinguishing between private and public standards. There

is no ambiguity here, but there is an ambivalence. Wiley
Rutledge once said: "I believe in law. At the same time I
believe in freedom. And I know that each of these things
may destroy the other. But I know too that, without both,
neither can long endure."[61] He referred to the neat balance
we must maintain between the *areas* of private choice and
public policy. Only by means of distinguishing private
and public (preserving privacy and responsibility, and
protecting the public order for the sake of justice) can we
give life to the truth that freedom and order presuppose
each other. On the one hand are the moralists who covet
the widest possible range of freedom according to conscience; on the other is the equally imperative obligation
of the lawmakers and courts to fulfill what Holmes called
their "duty of weighing considerations of social advantage,"
which is the "very ground and foundation of [legal] judgments."[62] Freedom without control by law—i.e., without
concern for the collective interest and protection of the
innocent—invites disaster either in the form of anarchy or
dictatorship.[63]

This pragmatic distinction is already partially recognized in the law and the courts. It is sufficiently illustrated
in a Missouri case where the appellate court reversed a
conviction for adultery on the ground that the appellants
had not been guilty, according to the act, of *open and
notorious* cohabitation. "It is not," said the court, "the object of the statute to establish a censorship over the morals
of the people, nor to forbid the violation of the seventh
commandment. Its prohibitions do not extend to stolen
waters nor to bread eaten in secret."[64] Here is the operation
of the principle embedded in the Wolfenden Report and
the Anglican Council's recommendation. In the same way,
the American Law Institute's latest draft proposal extends
the legal grounds for abortion from the present restriction
to therapeutic reasons only, to include the mental and
physical health of the mother, to prevent physical or

mental defects in the child, and to end pregnancies after rape and incest. Soon, we may be sure, statutory rape will be added. The Institute's discussion has also referred to further possible grounds such as pregnancy in a deserted wife, a working mother having to support a dependent husband and children, a prison inmate or other institutionalized person, or an unmarried woman who could not rear her child. Says the draft commentary, "the weight of critical and public opinion probably favors much more restricted applications of criminal sanctions than present laws contemplate."[65]

But *can* sex conduct be a private matter? In terms of ultimate meaning, the probable answer is "No." As Edmond Cahn has expressed it, although each of us has our own unique being and integrity, yet "each human being is also a cell in the social organism and in the complex tissue of its members, operating always as a socius with others, never through himself alone."[66] In the same vein, Archbishop Temple said, "Personality is inherently social. We can only become fully personal through the interaction of our own and other selves in the fellowship of society"— there are no "hard, atomic cores of individuality."[67] Nevertheless, in opposing a merely monadic view of people, we must avoid a false solidarism or collectivist view. There is *some* boundary between personal existence and the social membership. There is some range for private choice and personal taste.

Sylvanus Duvall, whose ethical analysis of sex conduct is far from puritanical or doctrinaire, has concluded that the greatest danger in our day is a kind of antinomian selfishness about sex. "Nobody," he says, "frankly repudiates the whole idea of morality and defends his position in a logically organized statement."[68] But he thinks a-moralism lurks behind much of the discussion, like a weasel in the henhouse. "The non-moral are those who . . . recognize no obligation beyond their own wishes and desires except those dictated by prudence."[69] All such autonomies, whether they be sex for sex's sake, or business, or art, or science, or even "America First," are the sworn enemies of law with its concern for the common good.

The English jurist Sir Patrick Devlin said in opposition to the Wolfenden Report that "it is wrong to talk of private morality" and "the suppression of vice is as much the law's business as the suppression of subversive activities."[70] But this appears to be a position based on a radically solidaristic view of community and personality, and perhaps it predicates the natural-law theory of universals. It is entirely tenable, however, to hold that any sexual act that seems directly or indirectly to affect the public interest adversely, either through its overt consequences, such as illegitimacy, or its remote consequences, such as the influence of its example, may be statutorily forbidden. Since it would hurt the public interest, it is a matter for the law. This would not be taking the line that we cannot distinguish between private and public affairs. It would be up to the consensus, expressed through democratic lawmaking channels, to determine the issue in each form of sexuality.

Conclusion

Ethics and moral philosophy are concerned with character on the practical side, as well as with a critical analysis on the theoretical side. It is doubtful whether sex laws can build character (raise sights), and it is even probable that unenforced and/or unenforceable laws, through the attendant hyprocrisy or outwit-the-cops spirit, actually weaken character and standards. Modern medicine and its technology have brought about a revolution. Lippmann has caught it in a phrase: contraception and other means of control have provided a sexual freedom that is a "transvaluation of values" in sex ethics.[71] This revolution has removed from sex conduct the triple terrors of conception, detection, and infection. Sex is safe. From now on, it will be personal conviction, not fear, that will hold people to chaste standards if they are to be preserved.[72]

Looking at the relation of ethics to law in general, we may assert four propositions:

1. Value (i.e., moral) considerations enter into law-making.
2. Law should be the means of making social morality effective.
3. The prelegal, value-finding process lies in the consensus of the community as to the common welfare.
4. What is held to be private, in the consensus, is not the law's business.

As to sex laws in particular, offenses should be restricted to (1) acts with persons under the legal age of consent; (2) acts in situations judged to be a public nuisance or infringement of public decency; and (3) acts involving assault, violence, duress, or fraud.

VII

On Fertility Control

THE SITUATION

THE TERM "birth control" now ordinarily means family planning. The term "fertility control" on the other hand is broad enough to cover *population* control as well as family limitation. These are the two urgent nonmedical or nontherapeutic sides of a problem which have almost taken first place in serious social ethics. The problem is: Should we use rational controls for humanly chosen purposes in fertility? Its two sides are concern with family welfare and concern with social welfare.

Staggering rates of criminal abortion, the tax costs of public assistance for welfare clients, the living-space problem of urban civilization, the rising costs of adequate education for children facing employment in modern times, and a rising demand of mothers and fathers for the right and the know-how to separate lovemaking from babymaking—such factors as these are strong motives behind the family planning ideal. These concerns are now aggravated by a threatening "population explosion" long predicted by demographers. Various startling, sometimes overdrawn, but always sobering statistics have been published

Written as a debate document or position paper for the Episcopal Church bishops of Latin America, meeting in Puerto Rico in May, 1965, as a part of their agenda.

as to birth, fecundity, and mortality rates. In all of this the main thing for a broad social analysis is the *population* rate, i.e., the rate of population increase according to a combination of birth and death rates. Due to good medicine and sanitation, death is ceasing to be an ally of population control.

Latin America, which cannot feed its 220,000,000 people now, will have three times as many mouths to feed (nearly a billion) within only 35 years. Population is like compound interest, it increases geometrically—not arithmetically. A sensible capsule statement of our present position globally would be something like this: the earth's population will likely double in 40 years, to total nine billions within a century. It took 50 centuries to reach a billion in 1830, yet in only one more century (by 1930) it was doubled to two billions. In the following 25 years (one *quarter* of a century) another half billion was added. The *decade* ending in 1965 has seen still another half billion added. Another whole billion will have been added by 1980 (i.e., in only 15 years' time). The rate of increase is greatest in Latin America.

This is not due to increased fecundity but to good medicine, sanitation, and public health policy. Here is at least one *ominous* result of medical care, immunization, insecticides, and antibiotics—ominous, that is, if human fertility remains uncontrolled. In the mature, developed economy of the U.S. market our analysts and businessmen are delighted to see four million new babies a year, for their consumer-potential's sake. "More babies are more customers." The same idea is expressed in Western Europe. But is this the wisest and most prudent way of looking at it, even in terms of enlightened self-interest? Here we may have one of the few remaining phases of the old and classic "people vs. profits" antinomy. In areas such as Latin America, India, and Africa all attempts to achieve capital formation and a higher standard of living are literally "eaten up" by what the Lambeth Conference in 1958 called "an ungoverned spate of unwanted births."

The U.S. Agency for International Development (AID) is now offering technical advice and assistance on fertility control throughout the world, both on population planning and family planning. AID personnel are often "population officers" in Central and South American countries. The rate of illegal abortions in Latin America is higher than anywhere else in the world, because contraception is widely and generally forbidden. Brazil is one of the large nations where AID's services are being fully engaged, and some Roman Catholic clergy there speak out favorably for control—by means of "the pill." Puerto Rico, a Catholic land, is one of the world's pioneering nations in both kinds of control ("public" and "private") at all levels—medical, legal, and personal-ethical. The birth control doctors there meet the question whether they are opposed by Catholic doctors with a grin: "We are all Catholics." And so with their patients—all Catholics. In 1960 a church party, opposed to the Government's birth control program, received only 51,000 votes out of nearly 789,000! Indeed, 20 percent of Puerto Rican women ages fifteen to forty-five are sterilized.

There is a worldwide revolt against rhythm, with its 40 percent rate of failure. In Britain it is estimated by maternal health experts that 100,000 Catholic women practice contraceptive birth control. Much the same estimate obtains on the Continent. In the U.S., Gallup polls show that 81 percent of the whole population favor birth control freedom, and as high as six out of ten Roman Catholic women do! Archbishop Thomas D. Roberts, S.J., former primate of Bombay, in the introduction to the symposium *Contraception and Holiness,* says, "Thus far I have not been persuaded by any of the natural-law arguments against contraception." The ten contributors, theologians and experts, declare a need of some form of contraception. So with Michael Novak's *The Experience of Marriage,* in which thirteen anonymous couples take the same position—the "pill" and Dr. John Rock's plea for it holding the center of attention. William Birmingham in his *What Modern Catholics Think About Birth Control* argues that Roman Catholics must free themselves from a narrow and discredited *biological* interpretation of "natural law." Novels like Margaret Culkin Banning's *The Vine and the Olive* give literary backing to the new theological and medical reasoning of various Roman thinkers—who usually try to follow a personalist rather than a legalist ethic.

Rome is not alone in its embattled opposition on "artificial" birth control. The bishops of the Eastern Orthodox churches have held more or less steadily to the same policy. The Anglican bishops did not fully agree on an endorsement until 1958. Protestant Christianity seems to have reached a consensus (caught up with historical reality?) soonest. But now theory and practice are moving swiftly. Pope John XXIII in his *Pacem in Terris* dealt with overpopulation by calling for free migration, with not a single word about fertility control, but his successor, Paul VI, not only called upon a commission to reexamine the problem and report to the Vatican Council in 1965 but subsequently he warned them not to drag their feet![1] Nor is this solely a Christian or Jewish development. It is also to be seen at work in the utterances of Hindu, Muslim, and Buddhist religious and civil leaders. The power of the movement lies in the combination of population explosion with "the revolution of rising expectations"—the excitement of the prospect of a good life constantly imaged on TV and radio and in the movies and magazines.

METHODS

Not only have Christians to satisfy themselves as to the principle of fertility control itself, but also they must make a conscientious judgment as to the methods to be used.

There are five kinds of birth control and nearly thirty different means—mechanical, chemical, and biological. The five *kinds* are: (1) total abstinence, (2) rhythm or periodic abstinence, (3) contraception, (4) voluntary sterilization—the "surest" kind of preventive control, and (5) abortion. Most Christian moralists have insisted, citing I Cor., ch. 7, that abstinence must be by mutual agreement of the spouses. Rhythm (called by some rebellious Catholics "Vatican roulette") is being rejected because of its unreliability, although out of compassion for those who are ordered to rely upon it the U.S. Public Health services and institutes are doing what they can to research and improve it. (An attempt was being made—indeed still is —by some moral theologians to "prove" that the steroid pills are not contraceptives or temporary sterilizers but *aids* to "nature's purpose" of regular menstrual periodicity, and hence fall within the definition of control by rhythmic calculation. This is the theory of "ovarian repose" as distinguished from temporary sterilization, suggested by the work of Drs. John Rock and Nino Passeto.)

Contraception is by far the most widely favored kind of birth control, by a variety of mechanical and chemical devices. Voluntary sterilization, because of its certainty, has been a growing practice, especially where large families are already procreated. The best estimate puts the U.S. number at 1,500,000, at a rate of 100,000 per year. This has no doubt been influenced by medicine's success in restoring fertility in one third of cases, when wanted. A University of Michigan study found that at least one partner in one out of ten couples has been sterilized. Its use in India has strong governmental support, as in Japan. Abortion, the artificial termination of a pregnancy, by whatever means, is nowadays the least favored kind of fertility control, except in Japan. Abortion is, in point of fact, the only kind of fertility control which is actually "birth" prevention—all the other kinds being forms of *conception* prevention!

The two latest innovations are the "pill" and the "ring" or "coil." The pill is at the center of Roman Catholic attention just now. Its ordinary use is in an astrogen-progestin compound which properly taken suspends ovulation in a controllable fashion. These steroids may someday, however, also be used to inhibit the production of male sperm. As anovulents they are, on any objective view, temporary sterilizers.

The "coil" (or equivalent intrauterine devices of plastic or steel such as spirals or loops) is the latest breakthrough in control methods. *Its mere presence* in the uterus causes the fertilized ovum to fail to implant and develop. Because the intrauterine device is cheap (a few cents), easy to use (can be inserted in a few seconds and remain for as much as two years), and reliable, it is the most promising method yet found for fertility control. Contraceptives have a failure rate of 10%, rhythm of 40%, but the IUD's of only 1%! Some 144 doctors in 51 different countries have reported on their use. In Hong Kong, Taiwan, and Korea (more slowly in Japan and India) there are now 100,000 patient-hours of use as a statistical basis. From one to two out of ten patients do not "retain" them; those who do report or show unprecedented success and no pathological side effects.

CULTURE CONTEXT

The problem of every culture, as of every person, is growth and change. What was once viable and functional may become quite maladaptive when circumstances change. This is especially true of the primary events of life—birth, reproduction, and death—which easily acquire moral regulations of taboo strength, not easily altered or raised to a higher level of insight and practicability. With respect to big populations as a matter of national interest, and to big families as a matter of social status or pride, modern realities are against them but they re-

treat reluctantly. Modern military technology has no need
of vast land armies, modern industrial technology has no
need of large labor forces, modern urban families have no
need of many willing hands, as they did in an agrarian
society. But Marxian and Roman Catholic ideology still
treat population and birth control as a cover-up for an
unjust economic system—an "imperialist" attempt to
downgrade colonial peoples. Thus a serious program of
control in Red China was cut off by an "orthodox" reaction. (Peking's latest twist again favors control and family
limitation.)

There is also the "demographic miracle" notion, that
with rising economic levels population mysteriously de-
clines. An interesting version of this form of cultural-
ideological resistance is Josue de Castro's theory in *The
Geography of Hunger,* where he argues that high fertility
(or fecundity) is due to protein deficiency; therefore raise
the diet from poverty levels to protein adequacy and the
birth rate drops. This "ploy" has the double effect of being
simple and avoiding the problem!

Upper-class or elite theories explain the problem by
claiming that the poor or "the masses" either actually want
large families or do not care. There is no research to support this. Cross-cultural studies show that three children
is an ideal number, and usually with four no more are
wanted. In "mature" cultures many couples are content
with two. Investigation in South America has shown that
mothers want to keep the children they have, understand-
ably, but if asked more abstractly what they think is the
"right" number to have, their replies favor fewer than they
have.

Cross-cultural study indicates that in areas like Latin
America there are certain common but correctable obstacles
to fertility control. (See, for example, J. Mayone Stycos,
in *Marriage and Family Living,* 25 [1963], 5–13.) Ignorance of the physiology of sex and reproduction is far
more basic and general than people in advanced countries

realize, and old taboos on discussion have reinforced it.
It is due to their ignorance that they are indifferent, i.e.,
they just don't think of control as possible. Another obstacle is a certain amount of cultural ambivalence, since
a vestigial pride in big families hangs on. Late motivation is
yet another obstacle; women do not "feel" the need to plan
until they are swamped with multiparity, and sexual behavior by that time is apt to be routinized. The *religious*
blockage is of course obvious, and while investigation
shows that direct religious teaching has remarkably little
influence, it nevertheless carries a cumulative effect. Our
beliefs and attitudes change more easily and often than
our biological constitutions can, but unfortunately we
know much less about the dynamics of attitude than we do
about human biology!

Culture analysis throws light also on strategy and tactics. Experience shows that the male is too much ignored
and uncultivated by family planning propagandists. He
is often more open to new insights than his wife because
his social role favors wider understanding and imagination.
More resources and teaching should go into nonclinical
channels—to key shopkeepers, midwives, druggists,
healers, barbers. The mass media should be given more
emphasis, even in nations of relatively high illiteracy.
What gets read gets repeated. The economic and social
disadvantages of excessive childbearing should be stressed,
especially with young couples. And we need to appreciate
that trends start in cities and spread to the country, that
fertility in cities is lower, and that cities will grow and
increase for a long time to come.

ETHICAL ISSUES

None of us believes that we are obliged to bring as many
children into the world as we are biologically and physio-
logically capable of procreating. The only issue as to the
morality of birth control arises around the means em-

ployed, not about the end sought. The ethical dividing line has to do with the relation between means and ends. We may, on the one side, hold that (as Kant put it) to will the end is to will the means—subject, of course, to the principle of proportionate good. In this case, the means we employ to realize a proper end or purpose will be chosen in an empirical and pragmatic temper, choosing means according to their efficiency. On the other side, we may take the position that our actions are inherently either good or evil, so that some means are immoral no matter how good the end they might serve. In this case, we will choose the means we employ in purposive acts according to their metaphysical or "intrinsic" morality, regardless of their contributory efficiency.

The second, or "intrinsicalist," approach is the one followed in Roman Catholic moral theology. Their position has been that anything which prevents "an end intended by nature," i.e., any fertility control practice other than total or periodic abstinence, is inherently evil and therefore immoral.

It is not too clear how we should regard the position taken by the Lambeth Conference in 1958. The bishops said, "The means of family planning are in large measure matters of clinical and aesthetic choice, subject to the requirement that they be admissible to the Christian conscience." What is meant by "in large measure" and "admissible"? The Conference report, issued by a committee chaired by Bishop Stephen F. Bayne, Jr., excluded as unjustifiable such practices as unilateral abstinence, *coitus interruptus,* nontherapeutic abortion, and artificial insemination from a donor (allowing it only homologously from the husband). Sterilization was not outlawed. The bishops' last prohibition rejects a *pro*-fertility procedure, not an anti-fertility one! Are these control methods not "admissible" because they are intrinsically evil, or because on the principle of due proportion they ordinarily do more harm than good, so that a good end cannot outweigh it? Here is a question which calls for clearing up, since if the second basis is the one that applies, all such pragmatic judgments are subject to challenge and possible revision. If the first reason applies ("intrinsic evil"), then the Anglican bishops are in the curious position of agreeing with the Romans that moral quality is a property, not a predicate, yet evidently having an undisclosed theory of evil different from the Romans', since they do not agree that contraception or sterilization are evil but *do* agree that *coitus interruptus,* nontherapeutic abortion, and AID are!

The National Council of the Churches of Christ in the U.S.A., too, has declared that "motives rather than methods form the primary moral issue," yet its statement goes on to question—while not condemning—the morality of sterilization and abortion. Here, however, as compared to the Lambeth statement, the basis for questioning noncontraceptive fertility control is clearly pragmatic and extrinsic, not metaphysical and intrinsic.

In between these two positions, the NCC's and Lambeth's, is that of the Bangkok meeting of the East Asian Christian Conference in 1964. Like them it favored contraceptive controls, yet unlike the NCC it favored sterilization and like Lambeth opposed abortion! The churches suffer from a typical incoherence and ethical superficiality.

For those theologians whose approach is by intrinsicality, such as the Catholic natural-law doctrine that some evils are given in the nature of things, *de rerum natura,* perhaps the most puzzling problem is the one raised by the intrauterine devices. What exactly are they?

They are not contraceptives, since they do not intervene between or prevent the meeting of sperm and ova. They are not, like the "pill," temporary sterilizers, since they do not suspend or impede ovulation. Are they, then, a form of abortion? By definition an abortifacient directly attacks a pregnancy, but the "ring" functions by indirect, side effect. The definition of abortion has never before included an unimplanted, preuterine fertilized ovum, except for pathological cases of ectopic or tubal pregnancy. The intrinsicalists will need to think carefully through this question *when* is abortion and *what* is it, and *is* an IUD an abortifacient? Science and medicine pose nonpragmatic ethics with problems far faster than they can be handled by principles based on either Scriptural law or natural law.

PROSPECTS

A "position paper" or "debate document" of this sort should take a quick peek at the future. Just around the corner are once-a-year anovulents for both men and women, sperm banks by deepfreeze processes, artificial insemination with donated ova (instead of sperm) for sterile wives—many things which only the naïve wave away as mere magazine sensationalism.

One thing we can confidently foretell. There will be an increase in man's power of rational control over subhuman natural phenomena, and more urgent need all the time to exercise it, posing the question whether there is *any* natural process to which he must submit regardless of humanly, freely chosen goals, and—if so—what processes are they, and what—*if any*—are the humanly devised or discovered methods of control he ought not to employ.

The ecumenical dialogue with our Roman Catholic brethren will sooner or later drive itself down from the relatively superficial level of dogmatic theology to the far greater depth and dynamism of moral theology—of Christian ethics. At that point the ecumenical boys will be separated from the ecumenical men! Moral issues—such as the ethics of reproduction—deal with the vital, feeling-freighted primary questions of human existence.

Surely our task here is to see the issues *as others see them*. Our Christian duty is to explore these questions in such a way as to make the task of aggiornamento workable, for *all* Christians, not just the Catholics, and to avoid driving anybody into an ethical corner. In the meantime we can rejoice in the general support given to legal changes which allow fuller responsibility and freedom of choice, such as we see in Cardinal Cushing's support of a proposal in Massachusetts and Connecticut to end the outlawry of contraceptives, and support to that same end by the Catholic Council of Civil Liberties.

Let us who are non-Roman Christians be as clear and articulate about our own principles and application of them, and about our own ethical method, as they are.

SOME CONCLUSIONS

By way of some capsule or summary conclusions, let me seriously suggest these five propositions:

1. *Making babies is a good thing but making love is, too,* and we can *and should* make love even if no baby is intended. There ought to be no unintended or unwanted babies.

2. The best way to make love without making babies is to prevent their conception; the next best way is to prevent fertility itself; and the least desirable way is to end a pregnancy already begun. *But any of these methods is good if the good to be gained is great enough to justify the means.*

3. Some methods of birth control may be morally better than others, but if so it will be because they are the most loving and creative and constructive means available; it will not be because they are "artificial" or "against nature," because *all* medicine and art and science is an "interference" with brute nature, using it *or* outwitting it, for the sake of *humanly chosen ends.* To be artificial or against nature is often the highest good, in terms of moral values. In short, the natural-law ethic is self-contradictory, problematical, and dead as Queen Anne.

4. Only one thing is *intrinsically* good, that is, in-

herently and always good and right, regardless of circumstances; and that one thing is love, namely, concern for others. All else is, at best, only *extrinsically* good and desirable, because of the situation. Nothing else, only love, is unconditionally good. And therefore nothing but malice or ill will is unconditionally evil. Everything is good or bad according to the circumstances, including abortion and sterilization and contraception. This is *theological* relativism, based on the proposition that *God is love* and *only* God is *un*conditional and absolute.

5. Finally: if there are people who believe that any of these things is wrong or sinful, let them conduct themselves accordingly. But let them not try to deprive their neighbors, who see it differently, of *their* freedom and responsibility. That is, let them not try to hold down the moral stature of others, which is measured by how much control we have over our natural processes—so that we can choose like people, not submit like sheep! There is in a culturally pluralistic society like America's a vital need never to forget the difference between a "sin" and a "crime," between what is morally wrong and what is *legally* wrong. Without a *consensus,* a democratic agreement about what is immoral, there can be no true civil law: only tyranny, hypocrisy, culture lag, and bigotry. This is the lesson we are all learning anew these days.

VIII

Ethics and Unmarried Sex

EVER SINCE BIRTH CONTROL separated lovemaking and baby-making the resistance movement, principally in our Christian churches, has warned us that sooner or later "they" would be recommending it for "everybody"—even the unmarried. The time has come—*der Tag* is here.

Before the Second World War, Lewis Terman predicted that premarital sex would be accepted in the near future.[1] Now, in 1966, the press is picking up and publishing news that several universities and coeducational colleges are being faced with a policy question by their health services: Should unmarried students be informed, supplied, and guided in the use of fertility control devices upon request? Last year a report of the Group for the Advancement of Psychiatry, entitled "Sex and the College Student," gave its support to the principle of privacy and accordingly challenged the theory that an institution of higher learning should try to be *in loco parentis*. The psychiatrists concluded that "sexual activity privately practiced with appropriate regard to the sensitivities of other people should not be the direct concern of the administration."[2]

A paper delivered in May, 1966, at the University of North Carolina. Copyright © 1966 by the Carolina Population Center. This paper, together with those of other authors, will be published in a book, prepared by the Carolina Population Center, on population policy in the United States.

However, in this matter as in most, the usual distance between the conventional wisdom and critical reflection separates town and gown. Going to bed unwed is not regarded favorably in the sidewalk debate or at the coffee klatches after church. A Gallup poll in October, 1965, showed that 74 percent of American adults disapproved of allowing college or university women to have oral contraceptives, or at least of *giving* them to them. This means, logically, an equal disapproval of making mechanical means such as diaphragms or intrauterine devices available to undergraduates, as well as other nonsteroid pharmaceutical methods. Elements of psychodynamics and cultural taboo are strong in the general public's opposition; it is far from being simply an informed and critical opposition to a proposed ethical innovation. The "ancient good" is stubbornly grasped no matter how "uncouth" it may be alleged to have become. Shakespeare put the grass-roots temper very neatly in *The Tempest,* where he had Prospero warn Ferdinand:

> If thou dost break her virgin-knot before
> All sanctimonious ceremonies may
> With full and holy rite be minist'red,
> No sweet aspersion shall the heavens let fall
> To make this contract grow; but barren Hate,
> Sour-eyed Disdain and Discord, shall bestrew
> The union of your bed with weeds so loathly
> That you shall hate it both.

But Shakespeare did his thinking in a very different milieu. Approximately forty percent (40%) of the sexually mature population are unmarried. Just in terms of statistical weight this shows, therefore, how many people are affected by our question, and we can also make a good guess as to the extent of the hypocrisy which surrounds it. Social competition penalizes early marriage, and the postponement required by a lengthening period of training for career roles and functions pushes marriage farther and farther away from the biological pressure following puberty. Physical maturity far outstrips our mental, cultural, and emotional development. It is said that menstruation in girls starts in this epoch on the average at the age of thirteen and a half years (13½), compared to seventeen (17) a century ago.[3] No human culture in past history ever levied as much tension and strain on the human psychophysical structure as ours does. And since the Kinsey reports, it is an open secret that male virility is greatest in the late teens—when young men used to marry and rear families. But now they go to high school and become college freshmen!

Just as Herman Kahn's *Thinking About the Unthinkable* has forced us to come to grips with such "unthinkable" possibilities as a nuclear decimation of people by the millions, so the "sexplosion" of the modern era is forcing us to do some thinking about the "unthinkable" in sex ethics. If we had to check off a point in modern times when the sex revolution started, first in practice but only slowly and reluctantly in thought, I would set it at the First World War. Since then there has been a phenomenal increase of aphrodisiac literature, visual and verbal, as well as more informational materials. We have seen an unprecedented freedom of expression orally as well as in print, both in ordinary conversation and in the mass media which glamorize sex—the movies, TV, radio, slick-paper magazines.

All of this reflects a new temper about sexual concerns. It is a new mental and emotional attitude, based on a new knowledge and a new frankness. Hollywood personalities are cultural heroes, and they lose none of their popularity or charismatic appeal when they openly engage in sexual adventures apart from the ring and the license. In the movie *The Sandpiper,* even a minister is portrayed as improved and uplifted by a sex affair with an unmarried woman (played by the sexnik, Elizabeth Taylor). The radical psychic ambivalence of the old discredited antisexual tradition, in which women were seen as prostitutes (sexual and bad) or madonnas (angelic, nonsexual, and pure), is not gone yet but its cure is well on the way.

In the great universities of our times, described by Clark Kerr as "multiversities," there is a pluralism or multiplicity of sexual practices and of ethical opinions. We have a sexual diversity that is in keeping with our principles of individual liberty and intellectual freedom. Some of us are quite archaic, some are extremely *avant-garde*, most of us are curious, critical, still cogitating. Undergraduates are often insecure in their sexual views and activities—as in most other areas of responsibility. They tend to despise the hypocrisy with which their elders deal with the "sex question" or evade it. Many of them, of course, profess to be far more confident in their prosex affirmations than they really are. In any case, the older generation has turned them loose, young men and women together in great coeducational communities, with only a few parietal rules to separate them. In the nineteenth century, middle-class parents protected their daughters' virginity with all kinds of chaperonage; in the mobile twentieth century, they've turned it over to the boys and girls themselves.

In what follows we shall focus our attention sharply on one form of unmarried sex—*pre*marital. "Unmarried sex" is a term that covers a wide range of human and infra-human sexuality, as we know. Homosexuality is a part of it, as well as ethical issues about noncoital sex problems such as abortion and sterilization. (For example, few states are as enlightened as North Carolina, which provides voluntary sterilizations and "pills" for unmarried mothers who request them.)

THE SITUATION

Back in 1960, Professor Leo Koch of the University of Illinois, a biologist, was fired for saying that it was ethically justifiable to approve of premarital intercourse. His offending statement was: "With modern contraceptives and medical advice readily available at the nearest drug store, or at least a family physician, there is no valid reason why sexual intercourse should not be condoned among those sufficiently mature to engage in it without social consequences and without violating their own codes of morality and ethics."[4] With due regard for his three qualifying factors—maturity, social concern, and integrity —we can say that Professor Koch's position is the one at which this position paper will arrive. We shall try, incidentally, to demonstrate that the fear of honest discussion revealed by Koch's dismissal is at least not universal. (Professor Koch shared the earlier opinion of Professor George Murdock of Yale that premarital intercourse would prepare young people for more successful marriages.[5] But this paper will not offer any analysis favoring or opposing the Murdock-Koch thesis about marriage preparation.)

The American Bar Association has lately urged the different states to review and revise their civil and criminal laws regulating sex acts. Few have done so—except for Illinois. Serious efforts are under way in California and New York, in the face of strong opposition in the churches. A model code committee of the American Law Institute in 1956 reported some important proposed changes in existing law, all in the direction of greater personal freedom sexually, and calling for a lowering of the age of consent to eliminate unjust convictions for statutory rape. Fornication is a criminal offense in thirty-six of our fifty states, the penalty running from $10 in Rhode Island to $500 plus two years in jail in Alaska. Fourteen (14) states have no law against it, but in six of these states "cohabitation" (nonmarital intercourse consistently with the same person) is a criminal offense.

This is a typical anomaly of our sex laws. It makes the punishment for cohabitation heavier than for promiscuity, thus creating the absurd situation in which a measure of interpersonal commitment between such sexual partners is penalized and promiscuity or *casual* fornication is preferred! In Massachusetts, for example, the penalty for fornication is $30 or ninety days in jail, but for cohabitation it is $300 or as much as three years. On the other hand, while many states outlaw adultery, there are others that allow extramarital sex—as in wife swapping clubs. California is one, for example.

A great deal of both clinical and taxonomic evidence has been gathered showing that sexual activity, or at least sexual exploration, occurs before marriage—unrecognized by the conventional wisdom. The Kinsey findings were that 67 percent of college males are involved, 84 percent of males who go as far as high school, and 98 percent of those who only finish grade school. We can raise these figures for the intervening fifteen years or more, but very probably it is still true that there is a reverse correlation between education levels and nonmarital intercourse. With females the opposite is the case—the higher the school level the greater their frequency of fornication. College women rated 60 percent in Kinsey's studies (1953), but the rate would be discernibly higher for 1966.

In recent years there has been a considerable black market in oral contraceptives. They can be had from "a man on the corner" or from drugstores that just don't ask for a prescription. Five million pills were hijacked in Philadelphia not long ago. Incidentally, local investigators have learned that more pills are sold in the vicinity of colleges than elsewhere. Doctors give unmarried girls and women prescriptions for them even when they do not personally approve of their patients' use of them. They rarely refuse them to applicants, and practically never when the young woman is engaged to be married. A year's prescription costs from $5 to $25 as the fee. In some college health services the medical staff make this distinction, giving to the engaged and refusing the unengaged. Soon we will have injections and vaccines that immunize against ovulation for several months at a time, making things easier than ever. It is even likely that a morning-after pill is coming, an abortifacient.

This will be a blessing because of the increase of unintended pregnancies and venereal diseases, due to the new sexual freedom. The surgeon general has said that fifteen hundred people get a venereal disease every day in the year.[6] Syphilis has increased by 200 percent from 1965 to 1966, among persons under twenty.[7] The rate of illegitimate pregnancies among teen-agers doubled from 1940 to 1961, and it quadrupled among women in the age level twenty to twenty-five. The highest incidence of pregnancy is among those least promiscuous, i.e., those who are least competent sexually. Yet the risks do not deter them anymore. Fifty percent (50%) of teen-age girls who marry are pregnant; 80 percent of those who marry teen-age boys. It is estimated that nearly 200,000 teen-agers are aborted every year.

Sociologists, psychologists, and psychiatrists give us many reasons for the spread of premarital sex. Popularity seeking, the need for a secure companion and dater, the prestige value of full sexual performance, the notion that it achieves personal self-identity, even—but rather rarely —the need for physical satisfaction: these are among the things most mentioned. It is probably still the case that the majority of young women, and some young men, ordinarily and except for an occasional lapse, stop short of coitus, practicing petting to the point of orgasm instead of actual intercourse. Yet from the moral standpoint, it is doubtful that there is any real difference between a technical virgin and a person who goes "all the way." And as for the old double standard for masculine and feminine behavior, it is clearly on its way out in favor of a more honest and undiscriminatory sex ethic.

These changes in attitude are going on even among Christians. The Sycamore Community at Penn State made a survey anonymously of 150 men and women, mostly ministers or professors and their wives, and found that while 33 percent were opposed to premarital sex, 40 percent favored it selectively. Forty percent (40%) of their male respondents reported that they had themselves engaged in it (a low percentage compared to the whole population), and 35 percent of the women so reported. Fifteen percent (15%) reported that they had or had had premarital coitus frequently or regularly. Of the married respondents, 18 percent of the husbands and 15 percent of the wives reported extramarital sex acts, although one third of them said they had petted short of coitus. Yet 40 percent felt it might be justifiable in certain situations.[8]

In order, however, to get a sharp forcus on the ethical problem and a possible solution, let us agree to stay with *pre*marital sex. And let us agree that this term covers both casual sexual congress and more personalized experience with dating partners, "steadies," and a "shack up" friend.

The Problem

In terms of ethical analysis we have, so to speak, *two* problem areas. The first one is the problem of premarital sex for those whose moral standards are in the classical religious tradition, based on a faith commitment to a divine sanction—usually, in America, some persuasion or other of the Judeo-Christian kind. The second area is the "secular" one, in which people's moral standards are broadly humanistic, based on a value commitment to human welfare and happiness. It is difficult, if not impossible, to say what proportion of our people falls in either area, but they exist certainly, and the "secular" area is growing all the time.

As a matter of fact, there is by no means a set or unchanging viewpoint in the religious camp. Some Christians

are challenging the old morality of the marital monopoly
of sex. The Sycamore report declares that "there are no
distinctively Christian patterns of sexual behavior which
can be characterized by the absence or presence of specific
acts." Their report favors a more situational, less legalistic
approach to sex ethics. "Let Christians," they say, "face
squarely the fact that what the body of authoritative Christian thought passed off as God's revealed truth was in fact
human error with a Pauline flavor. Let us remember this
fact every time we hear a solemn assertion about this or
that being God's will or *the* Christian ethic."

Over against this situation ethics or religious relativism
stands the legalistic ethics of universal absolutes (usually
negatives and prohibitions), condemning every form of
sexual expression except horizontal coitus eyeball-to-eyeball
solely between the parties to a monogamous marriage contract. Thus one editorial writer in a semifundamentalist
magazine said recently, and correctly enough: "The new
moralists do not believe that the biblical moral laws are
really given by God. Moral laws are not regarded as the
products of revelation."[9] A growing company of church
people are challenging fixed moral principles or rules
about sex or anything else.

The idea in the past has been that the ideal fulfillment
of our sex potential lies in a monogamous marriage. But
there is no reason to regard this ideal as a legal absolute.
For example, if the sex ratio were to be overthrown by
disaster, polygamy could well become the ideal or standard. Jesus showed more concern about pride and hypocrisy than about sex. In the story of the woman taken in
adultery, her accusers were guiltier than she. Among the
seven deadly sins, lust is listed but not sex, and lust can
exist in marriage as well as out. But even so, lust is not so
grave a sin as pride. As Dorothy Sayers points out scorn-
fully, "A man may be greedy and selfish; spiteful, cruel,
jealous and unjust; violent and brutal; grasping, un-
scrupulous and a liar; stubborn and arrogant; stupid, mo-

rose and dead to every noble instinct" and yet, if he practices his sinfulness within the marriage bond, he is not
thought by some Christians to be immoral![10]

The Bible clearly affirms sex as a high-order value, at
the same time sanctioning marriage (although not always
monogamy), but any claim that the Bible requires that
sex be expressed solely within marriage is only an inference. There is nothing explicitly forbidding premarital
acts. Only extramarital acts, i.e., adultery, are forbidden.
Those Christians who are situational, refusing to absolutize
any moral principle except "love thy neighbor," cannot absolutize Paul's one flesh (*henōsis*) theory of marriage in
I Cor., ch. 6.[11] Paul Ramsey of Princeton has tried to
defend premarital intercourse by engaged couples on the
ground that they become married thereby. But marriages
are not made by the act itself; sexual congress doesn't
create a marriage. Marriage is a mutual commitment,
willed and purposed interpersonally. Besides, all such
"ontological" or "naturalistic" reasoning fails completely
to meet the moral question of nonmarital sex acts between
*un*engaged couples, since it presumably condemns them all
universally as unjustifiable simply because they are nonmarital. It is still the old marital monopoly theory, only
one step relaxed.[12]

The humanists in our "secular" society draw close to
the nonlegalists, the nonabsolutists among Christians,
when they choose concern for personal values as their
ethical norm, for this is very close to the Biblical "love thy
neighbor as thyself." Professor Lester Kirkendall, in a
privately circulated position paper, "Searching for the
Roots of Moral Judgments," puts the humanist position
well:

"The essence of morality lies in the quality of interre-
lationships which can be established among people. Moral
conduct is that kind of behavior which enables people in
their relationships with each other to experience a greater

sense of trust, and appreciation for others; which increases the capacity of people to work together; which reduces social distance and continually furthers one's outreach to other persons and groups; which increases one's sense of self-respect and produces a greater measure of personal harmony.

"Immoral behavior is just the converse. Behavior which creates distrust destroys appreciation for others; decreases the capacity for cooperation; lessens concern for others; causes persons or groups to shut themselves off or be shut off from others; and which decreases an individual's sense of self-respect is immoral behavior.

"This is, of course, nothing new. The concept has been implicit in religions for ages. The injunction 'love thy neighbor as thyself' is a case in point."[13]

On this view, sarcasm and graft are immoral, but not sexual intercourse unless it is malicious or callous or cruel. On this basis, an act is not wrong because of the act itself but because of its *meaning*—its motive and message. Therefore, as Professor Kirkendall explains, the question "Should we ever spank a child?" can only be answered, "It depends upon the situation, on why it is done and how the child understands it."

In the same way, as a *Christian* humanist, Professor John Macmurray declares: "The integrity of persons is inviolable. You shall not use a person for your own ends, or indeed for any ends, individual or social. To use another person is to violate his personality by making an object of him; and in violating the integrity of another, you violate your own."[14] This one of Kant's maxims, at least, has survived the ravages of time. Recalling Henry Miller's book titles, we might paraphrase Kant and Macmurray by saying, "The plexus of the sexus is the nexus."

Both religious and secular moralists, in America's plural society, need to remember that freedom *of* religion includes freedom *from* religion. There is no ethical basis for compelling noncreedalists to follow any creedal codes of behavior, Christian or non-Christian. A "sin" is an act against God's will, but if the agent does not believe in God he cannot commit sin, and even those who do believe in God disagree radically as to what God's will is. Speaking to the issue over birth control law, Cardinal Cushing of Boston says, "Catholics do not need the support of civil law to be faithful to their own religious convictions, and they do not need to impose their moral views on other members of society. . . ." What the cardinal says about birth control applies just as much to premarital intercourse.

Harking back to the report of the Group for the Advancement of Psychiatry in its support of sexual *laissez faire* on college campuses, we could offer an ethical proposition of our own: Nothing we do is truly moral unless we are free to do otherwise. We must be free to decide what to do before any of our actions even begin to be moral. No discipline but self-discipline has any moral significance. This applies to sex, politics, or anything else. A moral act is a free act, done because we want to.

Incidentally, but not insignificantly, let me remark that this freedom which is so essential to moral acts can mean freedom *from* premarital sex as well as freedom for it. Not everybody would choose to engage in it. Some will not because it would endanger the sense of personal integrity. Value sentiments or "morals" may be changing (they *are,* obviously), but we are still "living in the overlap" and a sensitive, imaginative person might both well and wisely decide against it. As Dr. Mary Calderone points out, very young men and women are not always motivated in the same way: "The girl plays at sex, for which she is not ready, because fundamentally what she wants is love; and the boy plays at love, for which he is not ready, because what he wants is sex."[15]

Many will oppose premarital sex for reasons of the social welfare, others for relationship reasons, and some for simply egoistic reasons. We may rate these reasons differently in our ethical value systems, but the main point morally is to respect the freedom to choose. And short of coitus, young couples can pet each other at all levels up to orgasm, just so they are honest enough to recognize that merely technical virgins are no better morally than those who go the whole way. In John Hersey's recent novel, the boy and girl go to bed finally but end up sleeping curled up at arm's length.[16] It is ethically possible, that is to say, to be undecided, conflicted, and immoblized. What counts is being honest. In some cases, decision can be mistaken. Let honesty reign then too. Bryan Green, the evangelist, once said that the engaged but unmarried should thank God for the "experience" and ask his forgiveness for a lack of discipline.[17]

The Solution

Just as there are two ethical orientations, theistic and humanistic, so there are two distinct questions to ask ourselves. One is: Should we prohibit and condemn premarital sex? The other is: Should we approve of it? To the first one I promptly reply in the negative. To the second I propose an equivocal answer, "Yes and no—depending on each particular situation."

The most solid basis for any ethical approach is on the ground common to both the religiously oriented and the humanistically oriented—namely, the concern both feel for persons. They are alike *personalistically* oriented. For example, both Christians and non-Christians can accept the normative principle, "We ought to love people and use things; immorality only occurs when we love things and use people." They can agree also on a companion maxim: "We ought to love people, not rules or principles; what counts is not any hard and fast moral law but doing what we can for the good of others in every situation."

The first principle means that no sexual act is ethical if it hurts or exploits others. This is the difference between lust and love: lust treats a sexual partner as an object, love as a subject. Charity is more important than chastity, but there is no such thing as "free love." There must be some care and commitment in premarital sex acts or they are immoral. Hugh Hefner, the whipping boy of the stuffies, has readily acknowledged in *Playboy* that "personal" sex relations are to be preferred to impersonal.[18] Even though he denies that mutual commitment needs to go the radical lengths of marriage, he sees at least the difference between casual sex and straight callous congress.

The second principle is one of situation ethics—making a moral decision hangs on the particular case. How, here and now, can I act with the most certain concern for the happiness and welfare of those involved—myself and others? Legalistic moralism, with its absolutes and universals, always thou-shalt-nots, cuts out the middle ground between being a virgin and a sexual profligate.[19] This is an absurd failure to see that morality has to be acted out on a continuum of relativity, like life itself, from situation to situation.

The only independent variable is concern for people; love thy neighbor as thyself. Christians, whether legalistic or situational about their ethics, are agreed that the *ideal* sexually is the combination of marriage and sex. But the ideal gives no reason to demand that others should adopt that ideal or to try to impose it by law, nor is it even any reason to absolutize the ideal in practice for all Christians in all situations. Sex is not always wrong outside marriage, even for Christians; as Paul said, "I know . . . that nothing is unclean in itself" (Rom. 14:14). Another way to put it is to say that character shapes sex conduct, sex does not shape character.

As I proposed some years ago in a paper in *Law and Contemporary Problems,* the Duke University law journal, there are only three proper limitations to guide both the civil law and morality on sexual acts.[20] No sexual act between persons competent to give mutual consent should be prohibited, except when it involves either the seduction of minors or an offense against the public order. These are the principles of the Wolfenden Report to the English Parliament, adopted by that body and endorsed by the Anglican and Roman Catholic archbishops. It is time we acknowledged the difference between "sins" (a private judgment) and "crimes" against the public conscience and social consensus.

Therefore, we can welcome the recent decision of the federal Department of Health, Education, and Welfare to provide birth control assistance to unmarried women who desire it. It is a policy that puts into effect the principles of the President's Health Message to Congress of March 1, 1966. If the motive is a truly moral one, it will be concerned not only with relief budgets but with the welfare of the women and a concern to prevent unwanted babies. Why wait for even *one* illegitimate child to be born?

Dr. Ruth Adams, new president of Wellesley College, has said that the college's role is to give information about birth control educationally, but no medical assistance. Actually, birth control for unmarried students, she thinks, is "the function of the student's private physician rather than the college."[21] This is the strategy being followed by most universities and colleges—to separate knowledge and assistance, relegating to off-campus doctors the responsibility of protecting the unmarried from unwanted pregnancies. As a strategy, it obviously avoids a clash with those who bitterly oppose sexual freedom; it is therefore primarily a public relations posture. It bows the neck to people whose attitude is that if premarital sex can't be prevented, then the next best thing is to prevent the prevention of tragic consequences—a curiously sadistic kind of pseudo morality.

But surely this policy of information but no personal help is an ethical evasion by the universities. If they accept a flat fee for watching over the students' health, is not contraceptive care included? If college health services have treatment to prescribe which is better than students can get in a drug store, they *ought* to provide it. They should give *all* the medical service needed except what is too elaborate or technical for their facilities. Nobody is suggesting that pills or IUD's or diaphragms should be sold in the campus bookstore, but they ought to be regarded as a medical resource *owed* to the student as needed and requested. This is the opinion of most physicians on college health services, and I would support it for ethical reasons —chiefly out of respect for personal freedom.

Euthanasia and Anti-Dysthanasia

THE PATIENT'S RIGHT TO DIE

ON HIS WAY to the hospital, a minister stops at a house near his church to say a word of personal sympathy to a couple sitting on the porch with their family doctor. Upstairs the man's mother is in bed, the victim of a series of small cerebral hemorrhages over the last eleven years. Her voice went two years ago and there is now no sign that she hears anything. Communication has ended. Says the son, with a complex question-asking glance at his wife, "My mother is already dead."

Listening to those telltale words the doctor shakes his head sympathetically and helplessly. To the minister, that involuntary gesture seems almost a ritual. Earlier that day another doctor did exactly the same thing when the minister told him about his talk with a family whose twenty-year-old son has been lying in the "living death" of complete coma for four years. An auto crash hopelessly shattered his cerebral cortex. Since then only the brain stem has sustained life. All thought and feeling have been

---

This chapter comprises two essays: "The Patient's Right to Die" (Copyright © 1960, by Harper's Magazine, Inc. Reprinted from the October 1960 issue of *Harper's Magazine*); "Death and Medical Initiative," published in *Folia Medica* (VIII, 30–35, Jan.–Mar., 1962; Tufts University) and reprinted in *The Christian Scholar*, Fall, 1963.

erased, and he hasn't moved a single muscle of his body since the accident. But he is in "excellent health," although he feels no stimulus of any kind, from within or without. Once an angular blond youth of sixteen, he is now a baby-faced brunette, seemingly ten years old. He is fed through an indwelling nasal tube. He suffers no pain, only reacts by reflex to a needle jab. His mother says, "My son is dead."

Later, at the hospital, the minister visits a woman in her early seventies. He had last seen her at her fiftieth wedding anniversary party two months earlier. She has now been in the hospital for a week with what was tentatively thought to be "degenerative arthritis." But the diagnosis is bone cancer. Both legs were already fractured when she arrived at the hospital and little bits of her bones are splintering all the time; she has agonizing shaking attacks that break them off. She turns away from her clerical caller and looks at her husband. "I ought to die. Why can't I die?" It is the living that fear death, not the dying.

The minister leaves, somehow feeling guilty, and goes upstairs to Surgical. An intern and a young resident in surgery grab his arms and say, "Come on, join our council of war." They go into an empty room where two staff physicians and the chaplain are waiting. In the next room, a man is dying, slowly, in spite of their ingenious attempt to save him from pneumonic suffocation by means of a "tracheotomy," a hole cut in his throat through which an artificial respirator is used. The question is: should they take away the oxygen tank, let the patient go? The chaplain is pulled two ways. One of the doctors is against it, the other joins the resident in favor. The intern says he doesn't "like" it. The visiting clergyman says, "I would." They do. The oxygen is removed, the light turned off, the door closed behind them. Then they send the chaplain to comfort the widow out in the alcove at the end of the hall, saying, "We are doing everything we can."

This heartbreaking struggle over mercy death has become a standard drama in hospital novels—most recently in Richard Frede's *The Interns*. Physicians and clergymen struggle constantly in the most vital, intimate, and highly personal centers of human existence. The "primary events" of birth, procreation, and death are their daily fare. Ultimate as well as immediate concerns tax their capacity for creative and loving decisions. Squarely and continually confronting them is death, the prospect of nonbeing which lurks out of sight though never wholly out of mind for most of us. Because most people cannot look it in the eye, they cling to irrational, phobic, and sentimental attitudes about voluntary death and the medical control of dying. They cannot see death as experienced doctors and ministers do—in perspective, a familiar adversary. This is the case even among psychologists. For example, many aspects were discussed in a recent symposium, *The Meaning of Death,* at a convention of the American Psychological Association. But nothing whatever was said about the growing problem of dying in dignity. Bad words such as "euthanasia" were unmentioned.

We are, however, becoming somewhat less irrational than our forebears on this subject. At the level of sheer logic, one of the most curious features of the "theological era" of the past is that most people feared and sought to avoid death at any and every cost, except sometimes for honor's sake. Even though they professed to have faith in personal survival after death, it was their worst enemy. Nowadays, when faith is waning not only in the prospect of hell but even of heaven, there is a trend toward accepting death as a part of reality, just as "natural" as life. Churchmen, even clergymen, are dropping the traditional faith in personal survival after death, just as many unbelievers do. Curiously, it is the skeptics about immortality who appear to face death more calmly. They seem somehow less inclined to hang on desperately to life at the cost of indescribable and uncreative suffering for themselves and others.

But a painful conflict persists. For instance, not long ago a man came to me deeply depressed about his role, or lack of one, in his mother's death. She had been an invalid for years, requiring his constant care and attention. At last her illness reached a "terminal" stage and she had to be taken to the hospital. One Saturday after work when he arrived in her semi-private room, the other patient greeted him by crying out, "I think your mother has just passed away. See. Quick!" His immediate reaction was relief that her suffering, and his, were now ended; so he hesitated to act on the other patient's plea to breathe into his mother's mouth in an effort to resuscitate her. Ever since, he had been troubled by a profound sense of guilt. His "conscience" accused him. This conflict is a "lay" version of what many doctors, if not most, feel when they forgo some device that might sustain a patient's life a little longer. Some are comforted when their action, or inaction, is interpreted to them as a refusal to prolong the patient's *death*.

Vegetable or Human?

In truth, the whole problem of letting people "go" in a merciful release is a relatively new one. It is largely the result of our fabulous success in medical science and technology. Not long ago, when the point of death was reached, there was usually nothing that could be done about it. Now, due to the marvels of medicine, all kinds of things can keep people "alive" long after what used to be the final crisis. For example, there is the cardiac "pacemaker," a machine that can restart a heart that has stopped beating. Turn off the machine, the heart stops. Is the patient alive? Is he murdered if it is taken away? Does he commit suicide if he throws it out the window? Artificial respirators and kidneys, vital organ transplants, antibiotics, intravenous feeding—these and many other devices have the double effect of prolonging life and prolonging dying. The right to die in dignity is a problem raised more often by medicine's successes than by its failures. Consequently, there is a new dimension in the debate about "euthanasia." The old-fashioned question was simply this: "May we morally do anything to put people mercifully out of hopeless misery?" But the issue now takes a more troubling twist: "May we morally omit to do any of the ingenious things we *could* do to prolong people's suffering?"

For doctors, this dilemma challenges the Hippocratic oath which commits them to increasingly incompatible duties—to preserve life and to relieve suffering. This conflict of conscience is steadily magnified by the swelling numbers of elderly people. Medical genius and sanitation have resulted in greater longevity for most of our population. In consequence, the predominant forms of illness are now degenerative—the maladies of age and physical failure—not the infectious diseases. Disorders in the metabolic group, renal problems, malignancy, cardiovascular ills, are chronic rather than acute. Adults in middle life and beyond fill the beds of our hospitals, and the sixty-five-and-over class grows fastest of all. Under these circumstances, many people fear the prospect of senility far more than they fear death.

Unless we face up to the facts with moral sturdiness, our hospitals and homes will become mausoleums where the inmates exist in a living death. In this day of "existential" outlook, in its religious and nonreligious versions, we might think twice on Nietzsche's observation, "In certain cases it is indecent to go on living." Perhaps it is a supreme lack of faith and self-respect to continue, as he put it, "to vegetate in a state of cowardly dependence upon doctors and special treatments, once the meaning of life, the right to life, has been lost."

Consider an actual case, in a topflight hospital. After a history of rheumatic heart disease, a man was admitted with both mitral and aortic stenosis—a blockage of the heart valves by something like a calcium deposit. The arts and mechanics of medicine at once went into play. First open-heart surgery opened the mitral valve. Then—the patient's heart still sluggish—the operation was repeated. But the failure of blood pressure brought on kidney failure. While the doctors weighed a choice between a kidney transplant and an artificial kidney machine, staphylococcal pneumonia set in. Next, antibiotics were tried and failed to bring relief, driving them to try a tracheotomy. Meanwhile, the heart action flagged so much that breathing failed even through the surgical throat opening. The doctors then tried oxygen through nasal tubes, and failed; next, they hooked him into an artificial respirator. For a long time, technically speaking, the machine did his breathing. Then, in spite of all their brillant efforts, he died.

Should they have "let him go" sooner into the Christian heaven or Lucretius' "long good night"? If so, at what point? Would it have been "playing God" to stop before the second operation? Before the tracheotomy? Before the respirator? Only the ignorant imagine that these are easy decisions. In practice, they are complex, even for those who favor merciful deaths in principle. Doctors as responsible ministers of medicine carry an awesome responsibility. Indeed, by their very use of surgical, chemical, and mechanical devices they are, in a fashion, playing God. In this case from the beginning some of the doctors had little hope, but they felt obliged to do what they could. A few insisted that they had to do everything possible *even if they felt sure they would fail.* Where can we draw the line between prolonging a patient's life and prolonging his dying?

The ugly truth is that sometimes patients *in extremis* try to outwit the doctors and escape from medicine's ministrations. They swallow kleenex to suffocate themselves, or jerk tubes out of their noses or veins, in a cat-and-mouse game of life and death which is neither merciful nor meaningful. Medical innovation makes it ever easier to drag people back to "life" in merely physiological terms. Yet when these patients succeed in outwitting their medical ministrants, can we say that they have committed suicide in any real sense of the word? Who is actually alive in these contrivances and contraptions? In such a puppet-like state most patients are, of course, too weakened and drugged to take any truly human initiative.

The classical deathbed scene, with its loving partings and solemn last words, is practically a thing of the past. In its stead is a sedated, comatose, betubed object, manipulated and subconscious, if not subhuman. This is why, for example, one desperate woman is trying to guarantee herself a fatal heart attack to avoid anything like her mother's imbecile last years. It is an unnerving experience to any sensitive person to hear an intern on the terminal ward of a hospital say with defensive gallows humor that he has to "go water the vegetables" in their beds.

Families—and their emotional and economic resources —deserve some reckoning too. And finally, all of us are potential patients. Surely we need to give these questions a fresh look, even though the obligation lies heaviest on leaders in medicine and allied fields.

Medical Morals and Civil Law

It is an oversimplification to think of the issue any longer as "euthanasia" and decide for or against it. Euthanasia, meaning a merciful or good death, may be achieved by direct or indirect methods. If it is direct, a deliberate action or "mercy-killing" to shorten or end life, it is definitely murder as the law now stands. But indirect euthanasia is another matter, the more complicated and by far the more frequent form of the problem. There are three forms it can take: (1) administering a death-dealing pain-killer, (2) ceasing treatments that prolong the patient's life—or death, if you prefer, and (3) withholding treatment altogether.

An example of the first form is the administration of

morphine in doses which are pyramided to toxic, fatal proportions. The doctor has been forced to choose between doing nothing further to alleviate suffering, or giving a merciful dose which kills both the pain and the patient. Usually he chooses the latter course. An example of the second form is the hospital scene described earlier when two doctors, a resident, an intern, a chaplain, and a visiting minister agreed to "pull the plug" and disconnect the bubbling life-prolonging oxygen tank.

To illustrate the third form of indirect euthanasia, we might look at this practical problem. A poliomyelitis patient—a young woman—is struck down by an extensive paralysis of the respiratory muscles. Lacking oxygen, her brain suffers irreparable damage from suffocation. She *could* be kept "alive" for months—maybe longer—by artificial respiration through a tracheostomy. However, is there anything in moral law, either the law of nature, the law of Scripture, or the law of love, that obliges us to use such extraordinary means, such gimmicks? If we forgo their use, and let the patient die of natural asphyxiation, we have "euthanased" in the third indirect form. Both Protestant and Catholic teachers have favored such a course. Or, to take another case, if a patient with incurable cancer gets pneumonia, may we morally withhold antibiotics that would cure the pneumonia and let the patient "go," thus escaping a protracted and pain-ridden death? Roman Catholics are not so sure about this one, but most others are agreed that the best and most loving course would be to withhold the antibiotics.

Some of those who have tried to face these issues—the Euthanasia Societies in America and England, for example —have wanted to restrict both direct and indirect euthanasia to *voluntary* situations where the patient has consented. Such a concept is applicable to people—of whom there are many—who have private understandings with doctor friends and with their families in anticipation of the end. But what of the patient who has never stated his wishes and is past making a mentally competent choice? Under this code, mercy would have to be denied no matter how hideous and hopeless his suffering. Yet in modern medical practice most terminal patients are in precisely this submoral condition. Therefore, many moralists are prepared to approve even involuntary forms of indirect euthanasia. Pope Pius XII, for example, said that in deciding whether to use reanimation techniques, if life is ebbing hopelessly, doctors may cease and desist, "to permit the patient, already virtually dead, to pass on in peace." This decision could be made by the family and the doctor *for* the patient. In the same vein, an Archbishop of Canterbury (Cosmo, Lord Lang) agreed that "cases arise in which some means of shortening life may be justified." Both of these church leaders of the recent past preferred to leave the decision as to *when* in the physician's hands.

This is probably the wisest policy, provided the doctors do not take a rigid or idolatrous view of their role as "life" savers. Medicine's achievements have created some tragic and tricky questions. Margaret Mead, the anthropologist, in a recent lecture on medical ethics at Harvard Medical School, called for an end to the present policy of pushing the responsibility off on physicians. It is certainly unfair to saddle the doctors with all the initiative and responsibility, to create such a "role image" for them, when pastors and relatives might take it. There is some wisdom, nevertheless, in the Pope's injunction to the family of the dying to be guided by the doctors' advice as to *when* "vital functions" have ceased and only minimal organic functioning continues.

The *direct* ending of a life, with or without the patient's consent, is euthanasia in its simple, unsophisticated, and ethically candid form. This is opposed by many teachers, Roman Catholics, and others. They claim to see a moral difference between deciding to end a life by deliberately doing something and deciding to end a life by deliberately *not* doing something. To many others this seems a very cloudy distinction. What, morally, is the difference between doing nothing to keep the patient alive and giving a fatal dose of a pain-killing or other lethal drug? The intention is the same, either way. A decision *not* to keep a patient alive is as morally deliberate as a decision to *end* a life. As Kant said, if we will the end, we will the means. Although differences persist in its application, the principle of mercy death is today definitely accepted, even in religious circles where the pressures of death-fear have been strongest. Disagreements concern only the "operational" or practical question—who does what under which circumstances?

Doctors and laymen have asked lawmakers to legalize *direct* euthanasia, thus far unsuccessfully. While this writer's decision is in favor of the direct method, it may be necessary to settle temporarily for an intermediate step in the law. One distinguished jurist, Glanville Williams, has suggested that since there is little immediate hope of having the direct method proposal adopted, it might be more practical to try for a law to safeguard the doctors in the *indirect* forms of mercy death which *they are now practicing anyway,* and which leading moralists of all persuasions could endorse. Such a measure would provide that a medical practitioner is not guilty of any offense if he has sought to speed or ease the death of a patient suffering a painful and fatal disease. Doctors would then have protection under the law, freedom to follow their consciences. To bring this matter into the open practice of medicine would harmonize the civil law with medical morals, which must be concerned with the quality of life, not merely its quantity.

The Vitalist Fallacy

The biggest obstacle to a compassionate and honest understanding of this problem is a superstitious concept of "nature" inherited from an earlier, prescientific culture. People often feel that death should be "natural"—that is, humanly uncontrolled and uncontrived. Sometimes they say that God works through nature and therefore any "interference" with nature by controlling what happens *to* people in the way of illness and death—interferes with God's activity. This argument has a specious aura of religious force. For example, one doctor with an eighty-three-year-old patient, paralyzed by a stroke and a half dozen other ailments, tells the compassionate family that he will do nothing, "leave it to God." But God does not cooperate; their mother goes on gasping. Maybe the doctor needs a better and more creative theology.

For the fact is that medicine itself is an interference with nature. It freely cooperates with or counteracts and foils nature to fulfill humanly chosen ends. As Thomas Sydenham said three hundred years ago, medicine is "the support of enfeebled and the coercion of outrageous nature." Blind, brute nature imposing an agonizing and prolonged death is outrageous to the limit, and to bow to it, to "leave things in God's hands" is the last word in determinism and fatalism. It is the very opposite of a morality that prizes human freedom and loving kindness.

The right of spiritual beings to use intelligent control over physical nature, rather than submit beastlike to its blind workings, is the heart of many crucial questions. Birth control, artificial insemination, sterilization, and abortion are all medically discovered ways of fulfilling and protecting human values and hopes in spite of nature's failures or foolishnesses. Death control, like birth control, is a matter of human dignity. Without it persons become puppets. To perceive this is to grasp the error lurking in the notion—widespread in medical circles—that life as such is the highest good. This kind of vitalism seduces its victims into being more loyal to the physical spark of mere biological life than to the personality values of self-possession and human integrity. The beauty and spiritual depths of human stature are what should be preserved and conserved in our value system, with the flesh as the means rather than the end. The vitalist fallacy is to view life at any old level as the highest good. This betrays us into keeping "vegetables" going and dragging the dying back to brute "life" just because we have the medical know-how to do it.

Medicine, however, has a duty to relieve suffering equal to preserving life. Furthermore, it needs to reexamine its understanding of "life" as a moral and spiritual good—not merely physical. The morality of vitalism is being challenged by the morality of human freedom and dignity. Natural or physical determinism must give way to the morality of love. Doctors who will not respirate monsters at birth—the start of life—will not much longer have any part in turning people into monsters at the end of life.

Death and Medical Initiative

Television dramas about medicine and doctors and nurses are very popular these days. After all, in life and death in our urban culture medicine plays the key role. Some time ago I saw a television play built around a problem of conscience—the issue whether it is right or wrong deliberately to let a patient go, if there seems to be no hope of recovery and the effect of continued care is both demoralizing and impoverishing for the family and friends.

In this case a man of middle age has suffered extensive brain damage in an accident. In spite of the very best brain surgery, the patient continues in coma for months and months, having to be tended with close care by his wife and nurses. There is too much necrotic tissue and dysfunction to expect recovery, yet the medical opinion is that he could go on "living" in some sense of the word for an indefinite number of months or years. The wife is losing her mind caring for the patient, their only son (near college age) is breaking up emotionally as he watches his mother breaking up. Finally, the patient's brother takes over. He persuades the now almost obsessive-compulsive wife to let *him* administer a scheduled hypodermic—only in order to empty it surreptitiously and deliberately into a kleenex instead, which he pitches into a nearby wastebasket. The patient, of course, dies.

The brother does what he does to keep the wife from losing her mind. The son finds the telltale kleenex and thinks his *mother* was the one who withheld the hypo, and that she has "killed" his father. After much mental turmoil, the boy confesses his suspicion to his uncle, whom he loves and who loves him, and who wants the youngster released from his father's living death in order to go on again building a life of his own. Then the uncle admits that he, not the boy's mother, had been the "killer" or the "not preserver" of his father. In the end a doctor friend of the family finds out what happened and, even though the brother insists he had only "let the patient go," the doctor condemns the act as killing and murder. After a dramatic argument in which the two points of view are debated, they end the play by marching off to the District Attorney's office to confess the whole thing. We are left with the questions, "Will the brother be charged with murder, and is he actually guilty of such a crime?" During the big argument the all-wise Old Man of Medicine at the top of the hospital ladder says piously that preservation of life is the doctor's highest duty. Yet, he adds, "As a human being, I am not so sure."[1]

We need to be clear, at the outset, that this is the problem of "anti-dysthanasia"—entirely different from, even though logically related to, the classical issue over euthanasia. The television episode just outlined is a fictional case of anti-dysthanasia: not of euthanasia. Let's spell out the distinction.

In the past I have tried to distinguish between "direct" and "indirect" forms of euthanasia. On the one hand are all *direct* acts to end a life—as, for example, by introducing air into a patient's blood or circulatory system to cause a fatal embolism, or the much more common practice of leaving with the patient or actually administering a fatal overdose of morphine. On the other hand is "indirect" euthanasia, i.e., mercifully hastening death or at least mercifully refusing to prolong it. This latter form is different from the classical concept of euthanasia because it is a procedure whereby, even though death is brought about quite rationally and deliberately, it is accomplished only indirectly through omission rather than directly by commission. It is, in short, a procedure by which death is not induced but only permitted. In some kinds of Christian ethics and moral theology an action of this kind is called an "indirect voluntary."[2]

I have decided, therefore, to turn over the label "euthanasia" altogether to the practice of directly inducing death when carried out in order to end demoralizing and incurable suffering. And I am now using the term "anti-dysthanasia" for the indirect form, i.e., refusal to prolong an ugly or painful state. The goal, motive, and foreseeable consequences in both forms, the direct and the indirect voluntary courses of action, are the same: i.e., the death of the patient.

Given the term anti-dysthanasia, then, or indirect euthanasia, we might note that it can take any one of three subforms: (1) administering a death-dealing pain-killer, (2) stopping treatment altogether, simply not doing anything to prolong the patient's dying, and (3) withholding treatment altogether, simply not doing anything first or last to keep the patient alive. The first form is seen in the decision to give a dose of narcotic which by continued graduations is known to have reached a toxic, fatal power even though it can be claimed that the actual "intention" is only to relieve pain, not to kill. The second form is used if and when, for example, intravenous or oxygen is stopped, or a kidney machine is disconnected. The third form is followed when a defective baby is not respirated at birth, or when a highway accident victim is found so late that no attempt is made to reverse the loss of vital function.

One more remark is in order, to make sure we are "setting up" the problem as carefully as it deserves. Anti-dysthanasia, like euthanasia, can on the patient's part be either voluntary, or involuntary. In an earlier day when medicine had not yet found so many marvelous methods of analgesia by pharmacy and surgery, and all kinds of even mechanical devices to maintain vital functions in the terminally ill, those who favored euthanasia in cases of intractable pain usually held to the opinion that it should always be *voluntary*—i.e., employed only if the patient asked for it or had already consented in an earlier understanding or agreement. But what about the patient who has never stated his wishes and is now past making a true choice or giving competent consent? Under the old rubric of patient-chosen release, mercy would have to be denied no matter how hideous or pointless the patient's condition. Yet it is precisely this incompetent, postvolitional state, morally speaking, which most terminal patients have reached when the issue arises. Anti-dysthanasia, for this reason, has to be defined to mean a course of action or inaction whereby the patient's death is indirectly achieved, deliberately and voluntarily by the patient's attendants, whether the patient has ever expressed a wish for it or not. (If the patient has ever expressed his *opposition* to it, that would alter the case altogether.)

There are so many issues in which various kinds of Christians and Jews are not agreed, either within their own households of faith, or between and among them. It is cause for rejoicing, therefore, that Roman Catholic, Anglican, and Protestant moralists have a fairly extensive consensus or common mind about anti-dysthanasia, justifying it—and probably most Jewish moralists do, too.

My fellow Anglicans often do not agree with my ethical analyses, but in the matter of what I am calling anti-dysthanasia I enjoy, I am happy to say, a fairly wide support among Episcopalians. A representative Anglican treatment is my own chapter, "The Patient's Right to Die," in a symposium edited by Marion Sanders called *The Crisis in American Medicine.* I know of no thorough or systematic treatment by a Protestant writer. Rabbi Immanuel Jakobovits, an Orthodox scholar, allows that Jewish moralists might argue for "the legality of expediting the death of an incurable patient in acute agony by withholding from him such medicaments as sustain his continued life by unnatural means."[3] It is my guess that Conservative and Liberal Jews would justify anti-dysthanasia more plainly and firmly, and that they would do so on wider grounds than "acute agony."

It is important to understand that most Christian moralists only conclude that, given certain conditions, anti-dysthanasia is licit or permissible; they do not hold that it is mandatory or an obligation of conscience. Catholic writers, who almost always present a "united front" in these matters, insist that while there is an obligation to use all ordinary means to preserve life, there is *no* absolute obligation to employ "extraordinary" means. So said Pope Pius XII in an allocution to physicians, November, 1957, and earlier (in February of that year), when he even went so far as to defend the knowing and witting use of a pain-killer which ends the patient's life.[4]

In my personal opinion, the most lucid, carefully constructed discussion of this problem of medical conscience published to date was written by the Jesuit moral theologian, Gerald Kelly, a chapter entitled "Preserving Life" in his volume *Medico-Moral Problems.* Father Kelly defines an "extraordinary" treatment as one which (1) "cannot be obtained without expense, pain, or other inconvenience," and (2) "offers no reasonable hope of benefit."[5]

The thing that is *decisive,* surely, is what Father Kelly calls "reasonable hope." Where that hope is groundless it makes no difference whether the treatment which keeps the patient "alive" is ordinary or extraordinary. And anyway, these are only relative terms, since medicine's exciting advances are constantly adding new resources to the weaponry of health. For example, penicillin, once a fairly extraordinary medicine, and machines such as the electronic pacemakers, have become quite ordinary resources in a very short space of time.

Here, then, is a problem of conscience in medical care around which there is a basically united front of moralists, not only the religiously oriented ones, but a front broad enough to include naturalistic and humanistic ethics too, united *against* the publicly professed opinion of the medical profession! (We are aware that privately and clandestinely there are lots of doctors who *practice* both euthanasia and anti-dysthanasia; but we are concerned here only with formal and candid opinions, not with professional hypocrites, whether medical, ecclesiastical, or academic!)

There is room for differences of opinion among the moralists, but in spite of some rather sophisticated differences we are agreed, at least, that there is no absolute obligation to preserve a patient's life simply because it is medically manageable to do so.

I would agree with Pope Pius XII, and with at least two Archbishops of Canterbury (Lang and Fisher) who have addressed themselves to this question, that the doctor's technical knowledge, his "educated guesses" and experience, should be the basis for deciding the question whether there is any "reasonable hope."[6] That determination is outside a layman's competence. But having determined that a condition is hopeless, I cannot agree that it is either prudent or fair to physicians as a fraternity to saddle them with the onus of alone deciding whether to let the patient go. Here is a point at which, if the patient is beyond competent consent, the family and friends must accept their share of the responsibility of loving relationship, just as they would for a child, or a psychotic, or a patient in coma.

The *legal* position is not clear. No doubt one of these days a critical legal research agency such as the American

Law Institute will offer us a model code providing some legal clarification, but meanwhile doctors (perhaps because of their mounting dread of malpractice suits) engage in the most radical and irrational protestations of absolute loyalty to the "vital spark," unqualified by any consideration of the patient's personal integrity or ability to continue living as a person.

At a recent meeting of the American Cancer Society, Dr. David Karnofsky of the Sloan-Kettering Institute spoke out against anti-dysthanasia, which he said is "urged and supported by state planners, efficiency experts, social workers, philosophers, theologians, economists and humanitarians." This wild throwing together of such an unlikely *omnium gatherum* of people is symptomatic of the almost paranoid and embattled mentality of many medical men! Dr. Karnofsky's main *professed* reason for preserving life by any and all means as long as medically possible was that old saw and statistical absurdity about something new possibly turning up at the last moment to save the patient, like the last-minute arrival of the Marines in a Richard Harding David novel.[7] He cited an actual case which is as good as any other to illustrate the pros and cons involved.

A patient with cancer of the large bowel required a colostomy to relieve an intestinal obstruction. A recurrence of cancer nearby was relieved by X-ray treatment. When the abdominal cavity began to fill with fluid, radioactive phosphorus checked the process. Bronchopneumonia was cured by an antibiotic. The cancer metastases spread to the liver, and as X-ray failed to stop it, liver function declined. At that point a host of miraculous devices of pharmacy and technology came into play. The patient, said Dr. Karnofsky, might have died in a matter of days or weeks. They kept him alive for ten months. But we still have to ask ourselves whether it was right or wrong to add ten months to the patient's life, or perhaps more accurately expressed, to his death.

It is necessary, however, to assert rather bluntly that doctors and nurses are making a grave moral or ethical mistake when they absolutize the principle of the preservation of life. A part of the cause for such uncritical, practically superstitious absolutism seems to be the Hippocratic Oath. Doctors swear to Apollo, Aesculapius, Hygeia, Panacea, and all the rest of the gods of health, that "so far as power and discernment shall be mine, I will carry out regimen *for the benefit of the sick* and will keep them from harm and wrong." There is nothing in the Oath about making the preservation of life the *summum bonum,* the highest good. Indeed, to the contrary effect, Hippocrates was a case-minded medical man who refused to bind himself unreflectingly to generalities and absolutes: one of his maxims was, "Life is short and art is long, the occasion fleeting, experience fallacious and judgment difficult." He knew the relativity of decision and made no attempt to escape its difficult demands by escaping into arbitrary and irresponsible absolutes. Even the vow in the Oath never to give a deadly drug was only meant to repudiate taking part as a conspirator in poison murders; some of his disciples actually engaged in direct medical euthanasia.

The tragic error in conventional medical thought is the notion that life as such, the vital or biological principle, is the highest good. This is vitalism. It is worlds apart from the personalism of the Judeo-Christian outlook, in which, as any brave or loyal man can testify, there are many things more important than mere existence; for example, justice in society, human integrity, self-possession in one's own case. Who wants to be one of those tended by the intern or nurse whose task is to "water the vegetables" on the terminal ward or floor? If I may be forgiven for coining a second term, let me say that along with medical vitalism goes another, cognate ethical error: "salubrism," the notion, i.e., that health (psychophysical well-being) is a first-order value, just as hedonists hold pleasure to be.

But hedonism, salubrism, and vitalism, all three, fall short of the beauty and spiritual potential of human persons, and short, too, of freedom. Freedom and personal integrity are the things that come first in a mature value system, with the body as a means, not an end in itself. What I am doing here is challenging the morality of salubrist vitalism in the name of a morality of freedom and personalism.

The problem of anti-dysthanasia is, like most of our truly important conscience-questions, a problem of medical success, not of medical failure. Our most searching problems are usually success problems.

The predominant forms of illness are now degenerative, the maladies of age and physical failure, not the infectious diseases. Disorders in the metabolic group, renal problems, malignancy, cardiovascular ills, and others, are chronic rather than acute conditions which fill our hospital beds with middle-aged and over sixty-five patients. Sensitive people have more fear of the prospect of senility than of death.

Anti-dysthanasia is a perplexing, disturbing, difficult problem of conscience, but we have to face it and try to deal with it as creatively and courageously as we can. It is a problem with a vast amount of technical know-*how* as well as ethical know-*why* at stake, and the moralists cannot even begin to explain it without turning fully and openly to the medical people for their insights and judgments. Many studies will have to be made, and no one ethical analysis will ever do the issues full enough justice.

I claim for my own analysis of anti-dysthanasia only that it is not superficial or petty. My assurance of this I find in the striking coincidence that an Anglo-Catholic writer in an American magazine some time ago called me "an apostle of death" and "a merchant of murder," while a Soviet writer in the Communist journal *Trud* called me "a barbarian" and "a cannibal" and a degenerate of "bourgeois morals."[8] I must be striking close home to something!

X

Situation Ethics for
Business Management

WHEN THE "IDEAL" and the "practical" combine forces, creativity follows. E. J. Hodges of Guild, Bascom and Bonfigli, a San Francisco advertising firm, recently offered a striking example of "the ethical posture" in business policy-making, in an address to the Hollywood Advertising Club. He explained that from the point of view of sales promotion most of the "prime time" on television networks is "like Oscar Wilde's dead mackerel in the moonlight—it glitters but it stinks."

Hodges' firm had found that it is hard to convince people that the television programs attracting the most viewers are not necessarily doing the best sales job, and that "an audience viewing a violent, bloody, or sexy suspense show is simply not attuned to listening carefully and happily to a commercial intrusion."[1] High-powered blood-letting and sentimentality are too stultifying—too shocking and bemusing. Handling a line of dry cereals for the Ralston Company, Hodges and his associates were able to achieve

---

This was an article in a series in the *University of Washington Business Review* (Seattle, October, 1960). The series dealt with issues of ethics and business goals, in the years 1960 to 1963.

a 34 percent increase in sales as against a 5 percent increase for the industry as a whole by spending most of their budget for such nonsensational, modestly rated travelogue programs as John Gunther's *High Road*.

High-order cultural values and hard-headed considerations of gain merged here, and both interests were served. One lesson we can draw, no doubt, is that "idealism" is often more "practical" than a superficial either-or conception ever recognizes. Our American business system could use more of the experimentalism and second-look intelligence advocated by Ernest J. Hodges. Closely tied in to this kind of self-examination are the merits of various new theories of business behavior based on principles such as viability and balanced aspirations rather than profit maximizing.[2]

But we may not leave the problem of relating our value ideals to reality factors to rest comfortably in this happy harmony of cereal sales and broadening travel films. The Ralston Purina case obviously fails to reflect the bitter truth that what we *ought* to do and what we *can* do very often will not coincide, often cannot form a creative merger. It is this problem, the problem of frequent conflicts between our ideals and the far from ideal ways and means available to us, which is the context for questions in ethics in business management.

THREE CORRUPTIONS AND THEIR IMAGES

In our attempts to bring our ethical standards to bear on decision making in business enterprise, far too much intellectual interference or cultural static is generated by certain folk attitudes. There are three characteristic corruptions or distortions of religion and ethics in our culture. They illustrate the old maxim, *corruptio optimi pessima,* for each of these distortions throws a desirable culture element out of focus.

Pietism

One, *pietism,* tends to corrupt religion by separating faith and society; it reduces religion to religiosity by making it a personal and internal or private mystical affair irrelevant to economic or political matters. It encourages the notion that "religion ought not to 'interfere' with politics or business," as if they were divorced dimensions of life. Pietism, in Biblical language, discards the prophetic role of faith and action, allowing a social side to religion only in the sect's or in-group's common concerns, if even that, and frowning upon all religious involvement in questions of economic, racial, or political justice. Thus last spring a Philadelphia oil company director told a United Presbyterian Men's meeting that the church has no right "to meddle in secular affairs." Pietism gives aid and comfort to the secularization of culture and society.

Moralism

A second distortion, *moralism,* tends to trivialize our ethics. It is a form of microethics comparable to the "microeconomics" described in Galbraith's *Affluent Society.* Moralism makes the moral life a matter of petty discipline; it frowns upon dancing, card playing, Sunday recreation, and the like, but never shows much concern for great issues of justice or makes significant and daring demands upon men of good will. Jesus' phrase about straining out the gnat and swallowing the camel fits moralism perfectly, as does his remark about the Pharisaic opposition who paid tithes of mint and anise and cummin but ignored the weightier matters of justice, mercy, and faith. (Matt. 23:23–24.)

Pettifogging morality is the issue in N. Richard Nash's play *The Rainmaker,* when the father of the family defends the love affair of his spinster daughter with a rascal passing through town, because it promises to renew her confidence in her womanly qualities. To his self-righteous and violent older son who wants to stop it at once, he points out that he is so fiercely concerned with what is "right" that he cannot see what is good! Yet another feature of moralism's triviality, in addition to its petty ethics, is its *easy* ethics. Moralistic people tend to be perfectionists who assume that we can be righteous and fulfill the requirements of "the moral law" if we sincerely want to. This is, of course, a tragic failure to see how complex righteousness can be or become in concrete situations. Any business manager compelled to shape decisions involving conflicts of interest between investors, customers, workers, and competitors is bound to see the moral myopia of any ethical viewpoint which supposes that selfishness ("sin") is easily transcended. Moralism's distortion of morality reduces it to petty ethics—easy ethics—mostly irrelevant to the actual decision-making pressures of business management.

Legalism

Legalism is the third cultural corruption. The distortion of law and legality into "legalism" is closely allied to pietism and moralism, especially to the latter. Legalism is at bottom a rigid adherence to the letter rather than the spirit of law, and the law it obeys tends to be statutory or code law, fixed and spelled out. In Memphis recently, for example, a long court battle was opened up around the claim that Supreme Court integration rulings about bus transportation do not apply to streetcars as specifically provided in the city's ordinances. Here is a typical instance of legalism; and business administration could provide innumerable cases of its own. The motive and purpose behind all law is to *minimize obligation,* to define and distribute the costs and burdens and restraints of justice and social order. This in itself is only fair and constructive; law as such is a necessary and even creative feature of all community life; but when the motivation of the law observer is to hide behind the letter of the law in order to escape the higher demands of its spirit, we have legalism.

Legalism is "formal" obedience, "material" avoidance— to use terms from the archaic glossary of classical philosophy and theology. In more contemporary language, it is technically legal but ethically it is only legalistic. It shuts its eyes to the fact that in some situations what is legally right is morally wrong, when the total context and consequences are weighed. Last March an Episcopal minister in New York hacksawed off the utility company's locks on gas and electric meters in a tenement of poor people, to prevent accident, illness, and exposure. Here was a clear case of contralegalism. He broke the letter of the laws on trespass and burglary to prevent the unjust victimization of tenants whose landlords were scofflaws in arrears on Consolidated Edison's bills.

Neighbor-concern or social conscience, or what is called "love" in Christian ethics, *maximizes* obligation. Legalism minimizes it. Legalism would have urged the Episcopal pastor to "stick to the law." Moralism would have encouraged him to be complacent or even self-righteous in having done so. Pietism would have insisted, to begin with, that the landlord's economic practice and the company's legal rights and the city's public health policies are no concern of the minister anyway, as a "spiritual servant" of his people![3]

So widespread have these corruptions, this pattern of the *Triple Travesties,* become that they have created role images to conform to them. The minister of religion and the moralist, whether he be a school teacher or public official or anything else in the culture-function line, is looked at and stereotyped in terms of these travesties of authentic piety, morality, and legality. Clergymen and all others who concern themselves with ethics and moral ideals are quite generally "seen" and "heard" as pietistic, moralistic, and legalistic. This means, of course (and, given the folk image, quite rightly), that they are prototypically discounted as well-meaning people who do not live in "the real world" because they do not do full justice to the relativities and complexities of life and of the difficult choices that "men of affairs" have to make daily. Pietism, pettifoggery, puritanism—these are the cultural hallmarks of the "idealists" as seen by the "practical" men of business and public affairs.

AN ETHICAL PROBLEM IN BUSINESS

An illuminating episode out of the business school world occurred a year or so ago in a class taught by the present writer. It was a course for theological students in Contemporary Literature and Christian Social Analysis, using current novels and plays as "mirrors" of our cultural and social problems, including business organizations and personalities. At one session we were visited by four graduate students from the School of Business Administration (Harvard). They role-played a case of industrial espionage, on which they had done research in the automotive industry, in which certain information about a competitor's plans for new models was gained first by misrepresentation in a telephone call (posing as the officer of a new design-engineering company), and then by "planting" a spy. The usual elements of threatened disaster to the payroll, to dividends, to subcontracting companies, and the like, were shown as reasons for the espionage to counteract various condemnations of the practice in the industry's ethical codes.

Once it was thrown open for general class discussion, pro and con, the theological students asked questions instead of giving answers—to the evident surprise of the business students, who expected them to be moralistic, with easy and pat answers and right-or-wrong judgments.

They were failing to behave according to the image of moralism that was *a part of the businessmen's own conceptual apparatus!* The surprise of the business students was compounded, as the discussion developed, by the churchmen's refusal to be legalistic. None of them came forward with a rigid, let-the-chips-fall-where-they-may copybook maxim. On the contrary, they appeared to the businessmen to repudiate all "codes" and to subordinate law to "love" by asking, "What, in the situation, is the most constructive decision to make, as measured by a primary concern for people, and not for profits alone nor only for the one company's sake?" Here again the role image of the minister failed to be enacted, and it was felt by many in the class that the visiting business students were to a degree *disappointed* as well as surprised, that they *wanted* to be reassured somehow by a legalistic ruling from the ministers (e.g., "it is always wrong to deceive") even if they had no intention of accepting it as practical.

THREE DIFFERENT ETHICAL DECISION METHODS

The business students were prepared to conclude that a "religious ethic" and a "business ethic" cannot be reconciled, because the former is "idealistic" (meaning, of course, absolutistic and prefabricated) and the latter is "practical" (i.e., relativistic and situational). Fundamentally, their surprise and discomfiture lay in the discovery that a religious ethic could be elastic and as fully "contextual" in its realism as their own method of making value choices. They saw that their image of Christian morals did not fit all Christian moralists anymore than it fitted the decision-making practices of their own world. In short, they ran into sophisticated and trained Christian analysts and learned that there is an alternative, in religious life and thought, to the pietistic-moralistic-legalistic syndrome. This alternative may not yet be as normative in our culture as the Triple Travesties are, but it is here—and growing.

What exactly is the alternative? There are various names for it: situationism, contextualism, occasionalism, circumstantialism, even "existentialism." These labels indicate, of course, that the core of the ethic to which they are attached is a healthy and primary awareness that "circumstances alter cases"—i.e., that in actual problems of conscience, the situational variants are to be weighed as heavily as the theoretical constants, so that circumstances alter not only cases but rules. This antilegalistic temper is joined to antimoralism, for inherent in situationism's empirical, let's-look-at-the-facts approach is an appreciation of the frequent complexity of situations. It is neither simplistic nor perfectionistic. It is casuistry ("case centered") in a constructive, nonpejorative sense.[4]

In the development of Western morals, much influenced by the Biblical, Judeo-Christian world view, there have been three basic methods of ethical decision distinguishable.

Legalism

The major method has been *legalism,* in Judaism, Catholicism, and Protestantism. The Jews have lived by the Law, Torah: a code of precepts with an increasingly complicated mass of Mishnaic interpretations and applications. Statutory or code law inevitably piles up, ruling upon ruling, because the complications of life and the claims of mercy and compassion combine to establish—in code legalism—an elaborate system of rules for the breaking of rules!

Any web thus woven sooner or later defeats itself; so much that Reformed and even Conservative Jews have been driven to extricate themselves from orthodoxy. Something of the same elaboration and contraversion may be seen in Christian history. With the Catholics, it has taken the form of a fairly intricate and systematic moral theology which, as its involutions have increased, resorts more and more to a casuistry which appears to be evasive (as, to its credit, it really is!) of the very "laws" of right and wrong laid down in its textbooks and manuals. Casuistry is the homage that legalism pays to love of persons and to realism.

Protestantism has perhaps never constructed intricate codes and systems of law comparable to Catholicism's, but what it has gained by such simplicity it has lost through rigidity. Indeed, the very lack of casuistry and complexity, once any company of people is committed to even the bare principle of legalistic morality, is itself evidence of their blindness to the complications and contradictions in human experience. Or, what may be worse, no casuistry at all may reveal a punishing and even sadistic use of law "regardless of circumstances," putting law, not love, first. In the language of classical ethics and jurisprudence, the more statutory the law, the greater the need for equity. For, as statutes are applied to actual situations, something has to give; some latitude is required for genuinely doubtful or perplexed consciences. Questions inexorably arise as to whether in a particular case the law truly applies, or which of several more or less conflicting laws is to be followed. The effort to deal with these questions is exactly what casuistry is. When law listens to love it rises above legalism, and, paradoxically enough, the development of Catholic casuistry is some evidence of less legalism in the Catholic fold than the Protestant.

Legalism in the Christian tradition has taken two forms. In the Catholic tradition it has been reason legalism based on nature or natural law. Catholic moralists have tended to adumbrate their laws of morality by applying human reason to the observable facts of nature, of historical existence, and by this procedure they claim to have adduced universally perceived and therefore valid moral *laws*.

Protestant moralists have tended to take as their laws of morality the words and sayings of "the law and prophets" and the evangelists and apostles of the Bible. With them the rules of conduct are *revealed* rather than reasoned. The one is rationalist, the other Biblicist. Yet both are methods of legalism. Even though Catholic moralists deal also with revealed law (e.g., "the divine positive law of the Ten Commandments") and Protestants have certainly used reason in interpreting the sayings of the Bible ("hermeneutics"), still both have been by and large committed to a law-ethic, or legalism.

Antinomianism

Over against legalism we can put its polar opposite, *antinomianism*. While legalists are preoccupied with law and its stipulations, the antinomians are so opposed to law—even in principle—that their moral decisions are unpredictable and spontaneous, and often quite anarchic. They are not only "unbound by the chains of law" but actually irresponsible, perpetrators of confusion worse confounded. Paul, who struggled against the legalism of the Jewish Christians in the primitive church, nevertheless had also to stand firm against the antinomians who took his strictures against law too literally. They were prepared not only to subordinate law's provisions to the principle of "edifying" or constructive love in the situation (what Paul called "expediency" and the Greeks called "prudence"), but they went far beyond that and threw law, as such, entirely overboard.[5] This was the issue he fought with the *pneumatikoi* or spirit-guided converts at Corinth and Ephesus, who repudiated any and all law and relied in every decision-making situation solely upon the leading of the Spirit. It was a form of ethical intuitionism or guidance doctrine, a kind of "radar theory" of moral choice. It died out fairly quickly in that particular context, but has always persisted in certain sectarian and peripheral

forms of conversionism—to be seen, for example, in some
of the pentecostal and holiness sects on the cultural fringe
of our contemporary American religious life. Antinomianism of a nonreligious kind is to be seen in the "dread-
ful freedom" of the atheistic existentialism of Jean-Paul
Sartre and Simone de Beauvoir and their disciples in the
café cliques.[6]

The Alternative—"Situationism"

Legalism and antinomianism, as methods of approach
to value choices or ethical decisions, are therefore polari-
ties. To change from one to the other is to jump from the
frying pan into the fire. Somewhere in the middle ground
is another method of approach which will avoid the petri-
fying effect of legalism and the random, inchoate nature
of antinomian subjectivism. There are, of course, various
kinds of attempts to provide a norm (value standard) along
with a free and responsible application of the norm according to circumstances—as in hedonism, utilitarianism,
and the like.[7] In this paper attention will be focused upon
one specific ethical method, already pointed to under the
banner of "situationism" or "situational ethics." It will be
further pinpointed by putting it in its Christian form.

SITUATIONISM

It starts with the elemental faith proposition that "God
is love," a starting point in New Testament theology,
from which it follows that love is good—the highest good,
the *summum bonum*. The situational ethic holds, furthermore, that love and *only love* is intrinsically, inherently
good, always and forever, regardless of circumstances.
This is the same, logically, as saying that only God is absolute and unconditional; that all else, all creatures and
conditions, are relative—relative to their total situations
and shifting contexts. The value or worth of anything

or any action, on this view, depends upon its circumstances. What is good or right in one context could be evil or wrong in another. *Value is extrinsic* or contingent, not intrinsic or inherent or given. It only exists according to the situation. This is, therefore, a highly relativistic conception of value, and because of its insistence on the contexual facts as the determining factor, it is also an empirically tempered and fact-finding philosophy—not fundamentally legalistic or dogmatic at all!

But if, on the other hand, the Christian moralist were to hold that the good or evil, the righteousness or viciousness, of our actions is given, that some things are intrinsically or inherently right or wrong, then the situation, the fact-context, loses its significance. The ethic then becomes dogmatic and leans toward legalism. If it is always wrong to deceive or mislead, for example, then it makes no difference what is at stake in war or business enterprise or even in family affairs, it will always be wrong. Espionage, "white lies," merciful misrepresentations are *ipso jure* evil! If a merchant tells a lie to divert "protection" racketeers from their victims or to betray them to the police, he has, according to the intrinsic view of value or moral quality, chosen to do evil.

Classical Catholic and Protestant moralists, holding to the law-ethics of "nature" or Scripture, have been intrinsicalists by and large. They have, to use another illustration, usually forbidden as unlawful any deliberate act of taking life even if it is the "life" of a monster born in a delivery room at the hospital. Similarity, they have forbidden any act of suicide, even if it be by a captured soldier who would take his own life to avoid betraying his comrades under torture. Some Protestants, it is true, have been willing to justify "intrinsically evil" actions as sometimes unhappily the lesser of two evils between which a choice must be made. To this the consistent situationist replies that whatever is the most loving action *in the situa-*

tion is the good and right thing to do, not merely excusable. The situation *makes* it good. The merchant's lie or the obstetrician's death-dealing act or the soldier's self-destruction are, in their contexts, good and righteous—not merely evil things for which excuses or "extenuating circumstances" can be found. The idea of "greater good" makes sense, but the concept of "the lesser evil" in its ordinary form has no place in a situational ethic. It recognizes no intrinsic evil except ill will or "malice" and no intrinsic good except good will or love.

In the same vein, just as God is love and love is therefore good, so God is a person—he to whom we bend our knee and bow our head—and persons (made in his image) are therefore important. Love is the highest good, personality is of prime importance. Indeed, since love is a personal matter, not given or received by things—from, for, between and to persons, starting with him who is love—*all values are such in relation to persons.* Apart from persons who appreciate or value things, things are empty and worthless.

This "personalist" proposition about the nature of value lies behind the commonly asserted opinion in Christian ethics that people are more important than profits. It is a doctrine which can lead to a real clash with those "business philosophers" for whom the maximizing of profits is the first law![8] Kant's second maxim, with its insistence that we always treat people as ends, never as means, is consistent with Paul's "law of love" and its personalist implication. Nothing has any worth (value) except as it helps or hinders persons—God, neighbor, and self.

When Kant held that the only inherently good thing is a good will, he meant exactly what the New Testament means by neighbor-love. It is not an emotion or a passion, but an attitude—a "disposition of the will." Romantic love (*eros*) and friendship or brotherhood love (*philia*) are not the love of the New Testament, but *agape*—concern for the good of the neighbor—is. This love is critical, careful, even calculating; it is not sentimental or impulsive. As Søren Kierkegaard once put it, to imagine that love is a feeling or anything of that kind is an unchristian conception of love.[9] This is why it can be commanded, as in "love thy neighbor," as romantic love could not be commanded. Affection cannot be turned on and off at will, like water from a faucet, but kindness and generosity and constructive concern *can*.

Loving and *liking* are not the same thing. To suppose that we can like all of our neighbors is either hypocritical or superficial. But Christian love is possible for the deserving and the undeserving alike; it is required of us for every neighbor, friend and foe alike. It is to be like God's rain falling upon both the just and the unjust. It is a matter of loving even the unlikable. In Christian situationism, this "law of love" is the only law that holds always in all contexts; every other law is relative and expendable.

This situational approach is based upon a monolithic law of love, which is nearer in a way to antinomianism than to legalism. It shoulders aside all codes, all statutory and prescriptive and absolutistic laws or rules. This is why Jesus was willing to ignore Sabbath observance rules, and why Paul was so permissive about circumcision that it resulted in his arrest and possible execution. The whole New Testament stoutly defends the spirit of the law while at the same time it flouts letter-law without compunction. Jesus even boldly told his disciples that they could, if hungry, not only pluck and eat grain on the Sabbath in spite of legal prohibitions, but that in such circumstances they could follow David's translegal precedent and even eat the showbread, the very "reserved sacrament" on the altar! This approach casts aside "natural laws" of procreation; it is prepared to tie off the tubes of a cardiac mother in delivery, or to utilize "artificial" means of birth control out of loving concern for her health or the size of her family. It "resists steadfast in the faith" all legalistic prohibitions and exhortations, whether they be of drink or food or profits or sex or recreation or worship or anything else. It refuses to absolutize (idolize) any law, positive or negative. Christian situationism's highest good and only law is love, neighbor-concern, and it decides or chooses its course of action accordingly. (In all ethical approaches the *first* question is never "What shall I do?" but "What do I want?" The values we live by, our high- and low-order values, are the crucial factor, and the "top value" is the kingpin in every moral choice. It is interesting to observe how many people do not know what *wants* make them tick, and how often they even hide their real values from themselves, repressing them and dressing them up in neon-lit disguises of a pious or patriotic kind.)

One of the main reasons for this situationist insistence on the relativity of ethical decisions is the realization that love rarely, if ever, has only one neighbor or one set of interests to serve. Doing the "right" thing in any situation would be a simple matter if it was only a question of being concerned to help *a single neighbor,* one at a time! But how rarely that is the case. Who lives like Crusoe, alone on a desert island with one man Friday? Living in society means having many, many neighbors. The Christian maxim is really "love thy neighbors [in the plural] as thyself." This complex and pluralistic involvement is faced by any industrial personnel manager who has to choose between letting an illness-weakened supply clerk keep his job, on the one hand, or on the other playing fair with output workers whose piece-rate pay is being cut down by the clerk's delays. Any businessman faces it who must somehow balance costs and quality in pricing a product made for a low income market.

Justice is indeed "giving to each man what is his due," as the classical notion has expressed it ever since Aristotle, but in the Christian situational ethic what is due is *love—*

not some posited "natural law rights" which are unverifiable outside the perennial philosophy. The problem, then, is to distribute love's favors among many beneficiaries. And this is, of course, *justice*—love distributed. This is why law in principle—the principle of order and justice—is so basically sound. Law, as such and apart from any of its statutory "fixes," is the means justice employs to deal with the ambiguities and conflicts of interest in community life. Justice and its steward, law, are love (or "grace") facing the fact that absolute love has to be served relatively, shared and balanced among many neighbors. Justice is love being prudent. Justice is love using its head, facing *all* of the facts, refusing to be sentimental or myopic.

The radical relativism of this situational method of ethical analysis may make some people uneasy. The business students who visited our class with their problem about industrial espionage were certainly surprised by it; probably they were also uneasy. Nothing is gained by running away from the warning that the situationist contributes to and invites the anarchy of "*absolute* relativism" —true antinomianism or a sheer acceptance of *de gustibus non est disputandum*. If the slogan, "What's one man's meat is another man's poison," is literalized, the result is, admittedly, the autistic ethics of secular existentialism. In that case situationism's alleged middle ground between legalism and antinomianism has disappeared, and lawlessness takes over.

For whatever it is worth to the classical moralists, with their intrinsic values and "objective" moral laws, it must be confessed that—just as piety is distorted into pietism, morality into moralism, and legality into legalism—the situationist's danger is that he will slip over into the antinomian trap as he is trying to extricate himself from the snares of the Triple Travesties. Nevertheless, there is always this vital and determinative difference between antinomians and situationists: *the antinomian enters into his situations with no presuppositions nor prevenience whatsoever,* and makes his decisions "out of the blue" and out of his own self-center, whereas *the situationist enters into his situations with principles, but no laws,* able and willing to be infinitely elastic in their application and even to ignore any abstract principle at all, except the "law of love" itself.

"Sin Bravely"

On the other hand, we need to be protected fully as much, and perhaps more, against the danger in our contemporary cultural moralism and legalism. There is a kind of infantile dependence upon "laws" and "systems" of morality, widespread among us. It reveals the presence of a considerable spiritual insecurity. People feel that they have to lean on prefabricated "directives" in their moral life, just as the "policy books" of lower-echelon management in business and plant departments are getting fatter and fatter with detailed directives. They minimize and finally cast out the initiative and responsibility that make up freedom. Contextual, situational, clinical, circumstantial decision making is obviously too full of variables, too lacking in constants, for anxious personalities. Our ordinary, traditional "fundamentalist" morality, "prefab" code morality in either the Catholic or Protestant forms, is a kind of neurotic security measure to bolster up timid souls who prefer to wear blinders and follow a "line" laid down for them. They want to fit reality to the rules, while situationists reverse their procedure! As Bruckberger, a French priest and student of American culture, puts it, "Fanatic love of virtue has done more to damage men and society than all the vices put together."[10]

Legalism always emphasizes order and conformity; situationism emphasizes freedom and responsibility. The situationist sees that prescriptive morality falsifies reality situations by oversimplifying them or actually twisting the facts. Prescriptive morality does this whether it is the Scripture legalism of Protestantism or the nature legalism (natural law) of Catholicism. Like all existentialists, situationists in their own way are in revolt against the cultural stodginess of "respectable" and traditional ethics. They rebel against the reigning ethics of American culture because of its ambiguous "high, firm" demands on the one hand and its evasive shilly-shallying on the other, often described as "the leap" from Sunday to Monday. Nothing in the world causes as much confliction in conscience as the continual, conventional payment of lip service to moral "laws" that are constantly denied in practice because they are too petty or too rigid to fit the facts of life!

Is Payola Always Wrong?

The "payola" scandal in television and the entertainment industry recently aroused us to a fresh ethical awareness. The resentment and self-examination it brought out was pretty solid evidence that we are not by any means a nation of fast buck boys with split-level minds and gray flannel hearts. Still, for all of its evil quality and demoralizing influence, we could not condemn every act of that genre out of hand, if we followed the call of the situational ethics. It *could* be constructive, at least hypothetically. If desecration of the tabernacle on an altar *could* be justified in some situations, then payola is certainly not subject to proscription by any absolute, negative law!

Kickbacks, grafts, bribes, payola in all manner of forms, is an old story in business—the story of embezzlement. In 1957, according to the FBI, $479 million was stolen by professional crooks in America, but more than twice as much ($1 billion) was "lifted" by white-collar crooks through violations of trust in legitimate business. The amount of such graft going on among union organizers is small potatoes compared to business payola.[11] Candid students of the American business system know this perfectly well, having observed how kickbacks can be ingeniously indirect in payments for call girls, gambling accounts, contributions to favorite charities, loans never repaid, lavish entertainment, putting a buyer's relatives on the payroll, and gifts. The case against these practices is a familiar one, and possesses strong merits. The consumer pays the cost at the end of a chain reaction: each enterpriser in the series from producer to consumer trics to get the kickback back, by markups in a kickback spiral similar to passing on wage increases to the ultimate buyer. It sours the "original sinner," the briber; and the embezzler who takes the bribe is demoralized by violating a trust. Both suborner and bribee muddy the waters of relationship within their organizations. It spreads like a disease.

But can we, in all seriousness, absolutize the prohibition of gratuities? Are we to literalize the usual laws which, like Section 429 of the New York State penal code, outlaw "any gift or gratuity whatever"? If a general manager for a garment manufacturing company employing most of the wage earners in the community is faced with a choice of paying a kickback on a big order from a chain-store clothing firm, big enough to keep his plant in operation, or of losing the business to a big competitor and cutting wages and salaries, making layoffs, even closing up shop—should he pay it? Would this be an "altruistic" (neighbor-loving) bribe? Would that change anything?

The manager here would not be like the banker in a New York town who came to grief trying to juggle the books in order to provide overdrafts needed to keep a small paper mill and a hotel going. The banker tried to play God, balancing a great network of interests on a hairline—three thousand depositors' funds against a payroll of two hundred employees.[12] His was a mystic faith in his own business ability to pull it off in spite of the obvious risks. Nor would the mill manager be like the embezzlers whose motives are private greed, or pressing medical bills, or egoism, or fear of future personal poverty, or desperately

trying to hang on to his job against inside competition from
fellow salesmen or fellow purchasing agents.

Factors in a Moral Decision

In the classical ethics of the past it has been held, first,
that there are four factors to be weighed and ethically
evaluated in every moral decision—the end sought, the
means used, the motive at work, and the foreseeable consequences; and second, that all factors have to be right, none
of them wrong, to make any action a good or righteous one,
but that if any *one* of them is wrong, the action is wrong
in toto. On this basis, if he paid the kickback, the mill
manager would be doing an evil thing because his means
(bribery) is forbidden by both moral and civil law, even
though the motive, the end sought, and the foreseeable
consequences are good. In order to do full justice to this
kind of legalism, however, it is necessary to point out that
some would argue that means which are evil always, in
actual fact, corrupt any goal however good in the abstract,
and that there are "remote" as well as immediate consequences to be taken into account, such as character cor-
rosion. Legalists thus argue that one consequence of dis-
obeying law, moral or civil, is that it weakens law and
order and that the ultimate consequence is anarchy, no
matter how attractive the immediate foreseeable consequences might be. An English court recently gave the
lightest possible prison sentence to a father convicted of
ending the life of a Mongolian idiot son, on the ground
that although the judge might have done the same thing in
those circumstances, to let him escape the law and penalties of murder would encourage others to commit murder,
and weaken the social fabric.

Situation Ethics

To all of this the situationist replies: each of the
factors of a moral decision has to be weighed and judged

within the situation, in the total context; none of them (the means, for example) can be predetermined to be good or evil. He would claim that the justification for bearing arms in warfare and police controls, for example, depends entirely upon a situational ethic; that a simpleminded protest that "the end does not justify the means" is legalistic nonsense and falsifies reality. He would say that in some situations lying and bribery and force and violence, even taking life itself, is the only righteous and good thing to do *in the situation.* Depending upon the case, he might even tell the mill manager to pay the kickback.

An Ethic of Responsibility

Finally, in a situational approach, the decision must be made not only *in* the situation but also *by* the decider in the situation! It is an ethic of deliberate responsibility, based on the need for stoutly embracing "the burden of freedom" like men, not mice. The burden is only added to, not lightened, by the understanding that the decisions we make will rarely if ever be "correct." Its very relativism compels it to acknowledge that finite men will never fully foresee all of the consequences, never "objectively" assess all of the motives and means and ends at stake.

The Human Margin of Error

The situationist, cutting himself loose from the dead hand of prefabricated and unyielding law, with its false promises of relief from the anguish of decision, can only determine that as a man of good will he will live as a free man, with all of the ambivalences and ambiguities that go along with freedom. His moral life assumes the shape of adventure, ceases to pretend to be a blueprint. In all humility, knowing that he cannot escape the human margin of error, he will—to use Luther's phase—"sin bravely."

XI

Wealth, Taxation, and Stewardship

I WENT BACK into the stacks of one of America's topflight theological libraries where they had arranged together all the general works on Christian ethics and moral theology published in the last hundred years. I wanted to see how much attention had been paid to stewardship as a category of Christian concern and moral obligation. The search resulted in a nearly *nil* finding.

THE CUPBOARD WAS BARE

There were thirty-eight of these general surveys of Christian ideals and problems of conscience. There was not one single index reference to stewardship in thirty-five of the thirty-eight volumes. And of the three that did refer to it in the index, I found that there was only a single reference in each case. Furthermore, in only one of these three was there anything more than an incidental reference to the concept, only an incidental use of the term. In short, only one treatise on Christian ethics has even *one* paragraph on the subject of stewardship as such! Of the most influential works—whether Protestant or

A chapter in *Stewardship in Contemporary Theology*, edited by T. K. Thompson (Association Press, 1960), in a symposium treating both historical backgrounds and present-day questioning.

Catholic—I found none that mentioned it. For example, there was none in Brunner's *Divine Imperative;* Beach and H. R. Niebuhr's selected readings from the tradition, *Christian Ethics;* Dorner's *System of Christian Ethics* (1887); Kirk's *Some Principles of Moral Theology;* Cronin's *Science of Ethics;* Reinhold Niebuhr's *Interpretation of Christian Ethics;* Mortimer's *Elements of Moral Theology;* Garvic's *Christian Ideal for Human Society;* Ramsey's *Basic Christian Ethics;* Henry Davis' *Moral and Pastoral Theology;* George Thomas' *Christian Ethics and Moral Philosophy*. The three books in which stewardship was mentioned at all are Protestant works—none Catholic.

What, then, of special treatments or narrower works dealing with economic problems in particular, such as the ethics of property or ownership? Here, as we might expect, the question of Christian stewardship receives some attention in nearly all of them. But—it must be noted—none of these Christian economic studies treats stewardship analytically or developmentally as a concept or category of Christian ethics, subject in any way to change or reconception according to changes in cultural context. It is always a high-order abstraction. And it is never discussed in relation to vocation, as I shall do in this chapter.

There is, of course, any amount of reference to it in the "promotional" literature of church finance and money-raising for ecclesiastical enterprises. Yet even here the treatment is largely one of moralistic insistence on the individual's obligation to "share" his "good things" with his "less fortunate" neighbor as a "duty" owed to God who wills him to do so. This kind of rationale for stewardship is entirely familiar to most of us in the American religious-cultural pattern of both Protestant sectarianism and church Christianity, but its lack of depth and its moralism —as this paper attempts to show—may well account for its separation of stewardship from vocation, its neglect in serious works of basic Christian ethics, and the further fact of its *total absence* from any professional or technical works on fiscal policy, investment problems, business management, or economic theory in general. Finally, to drive the point home, there is even no reference whatsoever to stewardship in any standard work on business *ethics*—a negative fact which may seem to indicate how post-Christian is the shape of contemporary thought forms.

It is reasonable to suspect, therefore, that the concept has somehow been impoverished or lost its relevance, or (as I shall suggest) even fallen into pettiness.

The Concept: A Biblical Story

Concept forming is basic to all problem solving and decision making, including whether to share our resources with others, and if so, with whom and how much. Every ethical value judgment, every moral approval or disapproval, rests upon hidden or perceived *preethical* considerations. Put slightly differently, there is a theological or philosophical frame of reference for every moral choice we make, every spiritual decision. For Christian ethics in particular there is certainly a primary dependence upon Biblical bases, and of all the things that bear upon stewardship in the Bible there are three New Testament matters that I have chosen to highlight: the story of Ananias and Sapphira; what is said about "detachment" from "wordly goods" in the seventh chapter of I Corinthians; and the concept of "poverty" so much idealized in the Gospels.

Let's not be too squeamish about mooted matters. There is always some controversy over the Ananias-Sapphira story in Acts 5:1–11, even though it is hard to see how there can be any serious exegetical or hermeneutical debate possible. Ananias and Sapphira as members of the Christian fellowship, the *koinōnia,* sold their property— as Barnabas and the others had sold theirs—to distribute it as a liquid asset "as any had need." But then they kept back some of it, or as Kirsopp Lake said, "embezzled part of the price," and when they were found out, Peter faced them with it and accused them of "lying" to or "tempting" the Holy Spirit. The radical solidarism of these early Christians, a fellowship in material as well as in spiritual resources—sometimes called "religious communism"—is plainly set out in the preceding verses, ch. 4:34–37, as well as earlier in ch. 2:44–45.

The Ananias-Sapphira story is clearly part of the whole section chs. 4:34 to 5:11. I have heard and read commentaries in which it was contended that the fault of this man and woman was their dishonesty and not their selfishness. Frankly, I cannot imagine any contention any more vulnerable to ethical attack! In the first place, selfishness is sin in greater depth than deceit. Their crime was their *cheating* on the Holy Spirit—i.e., on the community of believers and sharers that was the Spirit's temple. Some will argue that Peter asked, "And after it was sold, was it not at your disposal?" in order to suggest, "Was it not still up to your own choice whether to keep it or share it?" But he would have said so, in that case. What Peter's question meant, surely, was that after it had been sold it was *disposable* and dispersible. The man and his wife had violated the sharing principle—the story is not a moralistic tale about telling fibs! I agree heartily with George Bernard Shaw who said in his *Farfetched Fables:* "They let the narrative stand but taught that Ananias and Sapphira were executed for telling a lie and not for any economic misdemeanor. This view was impressed on me in my childhood. I now regard it as a much graver lie than that of Ananias." Apart from describing their deaths as an "execution," Shaw has gone to the heart of the matter.

DETACHMENT VS. BIBLICAL ETHICS

The second of the New Testament factors I would like to bring into view is the so-called "detachment" from "worldly" things in chapter seven of Paul's first letter to

Corinth. The chapter as a whole sets forth a rather pragmatic view of sex, marriage, and divorce and is not aimed at all at the question of a balanced view of material and spiritual values. However, interspersed through it are three remarks that are quite often made to bear the weight of a somewhat Stoic-Manichaean-Buddhist interpretation. They are: (1) v. 24, which asks "in whatever state each was called, there let him remain with God"; (2) v. 31, which asks those who "deal with the world" to act "as though they had no dealings with it"; and (3) the plea in v. 35 for their "undivided devotion to the Lord." This indifference to things of the world, whether it be property, or status and role, is not in the least typical of the rest of the New Testament. Paul's apparent indifference here to material goods, to sex and marriage and reproduction— an indifference not found elsewhere—is apparently a prudent time-schedule preview of the immediate future and a desire to put first things first, in the belief (which he seems to have shucked off later) that the Kingdom was about to arrive as *parousia* at any moment. Indeed, he makes this apocalyptic eschatology quite explicit by warning in v. 29 that "the appointed time has grown very short" and in v. 31, "For the form of this world is passing away."

Nowhere else in the Pauline letters do we find this combination of "detachment" and a parousian expectation. Indeed, it seems to be precisely in the *combination* that the explanation lies—i.e., without the belief that the world order was about to be brought to an end, the detachment advice never shows itself. Since most of the rest of the New Testament takes history and the social process seriously, there is no consistent or coherent doctrine of detachment, not even implicitly. On the contrary, the *Biblical ethic takes material goods seriously,* giving approval or disapproval according to their *use* and assigning no inherent or intrinsic value to them at all. None of the Persian dualism, making material things evil and false while holding spiritual things good and real, entered into the New Testament ethic. It was largely Hebraic in its assumptions about man and the world. The dictum, "You must serve God or wealth: you cannot serve both" (see Matt. 6:24), is in no possible twist of meaning a detachment saying; it points to the *use* and priority problem, not to wealth itself. Dualism only crept in later with Hellenistic influences, but that was considerably after New Testament times.

As in the Bible, so in church history. This is not to say that Christianity is without its own form of asceticism—but it is not dualistic and it is not antimaterial. In the first place, Christian ascetics soon ceased to be eremites or hermits, like St. Anthony in his cave and Simeon on his pillar, and joined together socially as cenobites or monks. Thus they forsook private or *individualistic* wealth, but wealth as such they certainly did not repudiate or condemn—only its greedy or exploitive *uses* were condemned. The monastery was a community enterprise in property and production. As social or corporate wealth, to be well shared, they endorsed worldly goods. Monastic "poverty" was personal poverty *plus* common wealth and social security! And in the second place, the most telling evidence that Christian asceticism was never "detachment" is found in the ethical character of Christian *mysticism!* Whereas oriental mystics have commonly sought to break the barrier of human limitations by some sort of cognitive or supermental purification, the Christians—even Meister Eckhart with his "disinterestedness"—have turned from the Gnostic "way" and tried instead to achieve *ethical* purification, *including a loving use of wealth* rather than detachment from it. From this point of view it is necessary to challenge the opinion of Walter Meulder, in the symposium *American Income and Its Uses* (p. 317), that "detachment" and "non-possessiveness" are spiritual values which go with stewardship.

POVERTY, NOT PENURY

The third and last of these New Testament matters is the notion of "poverty" which we find held up in such high esteem in the Beatitudes, and in various parables and numerous ethical sayings in the Gospels. Nevertheless, it is vital to understand that this is no *mystique* of nonpossession, any more than Christian asceticism is a *mystique* of detachment! Not at all. We can see this in the parade of both good and bad rich men through the Gospels, and of poor men in both character categories; sympathetic figures such as Zacchaeus, Lazarus, and Joseph of Arimathea, all men of wealth, as well as unsympathetic rich men such as the one who wanted Jesus to divide an inheritance (Luke 12:13), and the one who let a begger lie neglected at his gate (Luke 16:19–31). The story of the rich young man (Mark 10:17–27) points at possessiveness, not at possessions, which is precisely the import of the saying about treasure and the "heart" in Matt. 6:21.

Perhaps the simplest way to phrase it is to say that the gospel principle is poverty but not destitution—modest possessions but not penury or pennilessness. The Gospels do not distinguish the Haves from the Have-Nots but the Have-Too-Muches from the Have-Enoughs. The poverty they idealize means only a lack of luxuries, while destitution would be a lack of necessities. Jesus was of the poor, the modest, the minimum-income *am haaretz*. But Jesus was not one of the beggars. His people lived modestly but not desperately. St. Francis and the mendicant orders tried for a while to embrace destitution; it was not poverty, as Jesus proposed. Lady Poverty for the Franciscans was really Dame Destitution. Jacques Le Clerque, the Roman Catholic writer who sees this vital distinction quite clearly, reminds us in his *Christianity and Money* (p. 56) that once when a friar was given some alms and saved it for future needs, St. Francis ordered him to throw it in the dung on the road. Obviously, this deliberate pennilessness does not fit the dominical injunctions about laying gifts before the altar, making loans, giving good things to children, offering hospitality, teaching a careful use of possession, tending one's flocks, feeding the hungry, the thirsty, and clothing the naked. Nor does it fit the advice to the rich in I Tim. 6:18–19 to be "liberal and generous"— but still without any hint that they should liquidate their possessions or impoverish themselves.

The ethical insight here is that, on the score of character, the possession of material goods has a kind of built-in danger that we will idolize them. *Sometimes* wealth corrupts its owners, and sometimes poverty produces piety! We also know, of course, that sometimes wealth is used by saintly people, and sometimes poverty produces aggression and greed. Poverty as distinct from destitution is, therefore, for *some* a privilege, because it is spiritually *safer,* but the deeper ethical insight is that material wealth is a necessary means to loving the neighbor and an obligation of stewardship. The only issue is *who* is to have the *"means"* of wealth and to whom he is to minister it. If the factors of an ethical act are four—motive, end, means, and consequences—then the motive of "voluntary poverty" is self-surrender and, as such, a good one. But on the other three scores of end, means, and consequences, it is clear that the resources of neighbor love are radically reduced or subverted by the lack or rejection of material means.

It is an interesting observation that there is practically never any reference to the financial basis of Jesus' ministry! This is partly due to a lack of attention to the question in the Gospel accounts, of course, even though it peeps through such episodes as the anointing at Bethany and the protests against the involved "waste" of three hundred denarii (Mark 14:3–9). The only reference seems to be in Luke's Gospel (ch. 8:1–3), but we are merely told that the disciples' company was followed and subsidized by "some women" (e.g., Mary, Joanna, and Susanna) "who provided for them out of their means." Nevertheless, this in itself is a clear enough indication that Jesus knew that somebody has to foot the bills! Chuza was Herod's steward, in the sense of a functional role in a rich man's service, but his wife Joanna in Jesus' company was fulfilling the "stewardly" role on another level and in another way. She was not, like her husband, handling another man's wealth on his behalf; she was acting in faith as a steward of God on *God's* behalf.

THE CHRISTIAN COMMONWEALTH

There is a rock-bottom difference between being stewards of wealth because it is God's and we are acting on his behalf, on the one hand, and being stewards of wealth because it is *ours* and we are acting on behalf of our own charity. I have already pointed out, in my *Christianity and Property* (p. 186), how easily stewardship is perverted into a sub-Christian idea. The creationist doctrine is that "the earth is the Lord's and the fulness thereof" (I Chron. 29:14; Ps. 24:1), and therefore stewardship is on God's behalf—he is ultimately the only landlord or owner. Furthermore, God's creation—his material wealth—is, under the divine *patrimonium* of a heavenly father, provided for his children on earth on a familial basis, intended for all and not just for some. These principles of divine ownership (men have possession but not the ultimate title) and of social equity or "commonwealth" are fundamental in the Christian world view. This is why almsgiving in Christian ethics and moral theology has always been treated under the heading of justice, *not of mercy*. In some measure, then, to give to a neighbor in need—to share with him—is actually *giving him what is his own*. We all have an inalienable equity in God's patrimony, so that contributing to a community fund or paying taxes for social security is not *largesse* or *noblesse oblige* but simple, obligatory stewardship.

The sub-Christian twist comes when we begin to think of our giving and sharing as *our* mercy to the less fortunate, instead of seeing that it is a stewardly handling of God's wealth to fulfill God's purposes. We are not our own stewards, being generous to our neighbors out of our greater wisdom and wealth; we are God's stewards, acting for God in the distribution of *his* wealth to his family on earth. There is no ground here for the hypocrisy or pretension of self-congratulation because we may be trying to share the wealth on one scale or another—for example, by one or more tenths. To grasp this point about the total claims of Christian stewardship, as against the notion of merely granting something out of our superfluity, makes it possible to see without confusion why stewardship is a "stewardship of *ten* tenths" as they express it in the Church of England's *Christian Stewardship of Money* (p. 30), and not a mere calculation of one tenth or "tithing." Tithing is a part but only *a part* of stewardship, and it is definitely not the subject of this discussion. Any tendency to reduce stewardship to church tithes is a perversion of Biblical theology.

As a concept or category of Christian faith, "stewardship" stands or falls with "vocation"—they go together like love and marriage. Stewardship does not stand alone, nor is it just a hyphenated conception. In a way, I should like to suggest, stewardship is, as vocation is, a synonym or equivalent term to what is meant by "the ministry of the laity." It is a dimension of every Christian's ministry of work and witness in the world as we distinguish that ministry from the *ordained* ministry of the Word and Sacraments. The lay ministry is our "vocational stewardship" of our talents, time, and money. Again, we might call it a "stewardly vocation," for all of those who "having this ministry" are "ambassadors"—to use Paul's words for it in his second letter to Corinth (chs. 4:1 and 5:20). But the main point here is not that stewardship is vocation in the sense of being paired with it, but in the sense of being *merged* with it. Just as society has been guilty of separating work from vocation, so has the church been guilty of separating stewardship from vocation, as if it were something in addition to or alongside of our working role in the world!

Here then, using the language of present-day social analysis, is a role definition of the Christian—a faith proposition or a theological inference, in terms of personal obligation, from the doctrines of creation, God's sovereignty, human agency, the incarnation, sacramentalism, redemption. In short, Christian economics is applied theology.

Consider the relevancies of these doctrines. A God of love who is a heavenly father creates (provides) for all without discrimination or favoritism—since a father provides for the weaker as much if not more than for the strong children. Being the Lord of his creation, the Landlord of Ultimate Title, whatever any of us holds by whatever rules of acquisition and ownership, we use under the Landlord's judgment. What we hold, we hold for him and administer only the usufruct, nothing more. His sovereign will obtains. It is both our glory and our humility that we are God's agents through whom he works out his plans and purposes in the world.

By becoming material and earthly himself—since the Word was made flesh and dwelt among us—all dualism between the material and spiritual is once and for all discredited. No longer may "religion" betray us into a false "spirituality" that regards the material goods and values of life, its economic assets, as somehow inferior or morally suspect. So, too, Christian sacramentalism continues to act out the "materialism" of the incarnation by the ministration of spiritual grace through material, economic means —through bread and wine, as Christ ordered it. The Lord's Table is as obvious as any denial could be of the material-spiritual dualism. It is, finally, through our reemployment of the material goods of the world, of the economic resources of the world, that God redeems his creation—through our use of his whole material order as a "sacramental" order. And thus it is, although expressed in only a few stark phrases, that the stewardship of our talents, time, and money—all three—is our vocation, the means or method by which the ministry of the laity (i.e., of the people of God) is fulfilled.

THE CONTEXT: AN ECONOMICS OF PLENTY

We have now indicated that the Biblical ethic contains the principles of *sharing*—even in the radical, primitive version of the Jerusalem congregation, of *concern for* rather than detachment from material values, and of *modest possessions* or moderate wealth. However, we cannot elaborate such theological abstractions and high-order ideals without taking a very empirical and down-to-earth look at the concrete situation, at the living context in which our stewardship is to be exercised. In the contemporary milieu, things in America are radically, almost unbelievably, advanced over the picture of even fifteen years ago. Our new "people's capitalism" has developed an "affluent society" far beyond the dreams of the past, and even beyond anything imagined by much of the world in our own day outside the North Atlantic community. Most of the classical concept forming for the doctrine of Christian stewardship was carried out in the past era of widespread poverty in the agrarian and low-energy societies of the Biblical and European worlds, not in the mid-twentieth-century comparative opulence of America with its gross national product of over 375 billion dollars!

This is a new world we have, with a median family income of $4,000. We have moved from scarcity to plenty, even though there is still a lot of moving to be done!

As a result of ten or fifteen crucial technological "breakthroughs" in the last two hundred years, and the policy innovations and researches of business enterprise, combined with collective bargaining and corporate organization, we have an unprecedentedly high standard of living. All of this is being achieved with fewer and fewer so-called "productive workers" working at it. Managerial, professional, and technical employees already outnumber production-line workers. But we can also be sure that it is only a matter of time until the rest of the world catches up; its capital accumulation will grow as its technical organization grows. The United States and Canada just now have only 10 percent of the world's people but they have 75 percent of the world's income, while about 75 percent of the world's people have only about 10 percent of its income. Yet this won't remain the case. There is a dynamic movement everywhere abroad and its direction is toward the American standard.

This "Twentieth Century Capitalist Revolution," as Berle called it, or "permanent revolution" in Russell Davenport's phrase, has come about through an empirical, nondoctrinaire, experimentalist mixture of both managed and competitive enterprise. The almost anarchic *laissez faire* of the classical Private Enterprise System has been modified in the last quarter century by the corporation, as well as by Keynesian fiscal policy, graduated income tax, collective bargaining, and a host of other innovations in business management and practice. Most of our history has been one of poverty in both individuals and nations. The revolution in economic ideas has overthrown the Economics of Poverty as we can see it in Ricardo's gloomy "iron law of wages," and Marx's reapplication of it in his prediction of the proletarianization of all but a shrinking group of capitalists at the top! These things simply have not happened. Our revolution in a nonideological spirit has embraced the Economics of Plenty, and on the record has successfully ignored both orthodox capitalist and orthodox socialist doctrine. We cannot continue to think any longer in the scarcity terms of pretechnical culture, and one of the major Christian categories to be shaken by the new milieu of the postmodern era is stewardship.

An "affluent society"—so John Galbraith names it in the title of his important book—presents new problems for stewardship. Peter Drucker has put his finger on one of them in his *Landmarks of Tomorrow* (p. 103) when he says, quite correctly, that although the "poor" have not disappeared, they no longer represent the "masses"—rather "they constitute isolated special-problem groups." He refers to hard-core poverty groups that suffer from discrimination, such as racial minorities like the Puerto Ricans, Negroes, Indians, and Mexicans; to scattered groups of small farmers on worn-out submarginal land; to old people or widows with children. These are for the most part nonemployables, either through prejudice, accident, or debility.

This is no attempt, by any means, to make believe that the poor are no longer with us—that there are no neighbors who need our help. We cannot rely on the old trick, "Close your eyes and the bad thing will go away." Harry Emerson Fosdick used to say that "the basic test of any society is what happens to the underdog," and that still applies because we still have underdogs. The achievements of a high-energy economy must not blind us to the continued presence of claims upon us for stewardship in terms of physical human needs, as well—as we shall see—as broader social and cultural needs in the fields of public health, education, the arts, and similar common "goods," which can only be met by a *stewardly* concern for them and willingness to pay the necessary freight!

ORGANIZATION AND STEWARDSHIP ETHICS

If this chapter has any central thesis it is this—that Christian stewardship must keep step with the collective structures and the increasing "organization" of modern society. Technology raises the standard of living, and also technology has a built-in principle of organization. Technology's division of labor and necessary interdependence creates more and more *association:* associated work, management, marketing, entertainment, policing, government —associated everything. Kenneth Boulding rightly calls it the "organizational revolution." Prosperity and organization go together. Individual small-scale production, marketing, and ownership management are being replaced by corporate enterprise. The same will have to become true of stewardship; it cannot remain a private, small-scale, individualistic affair—in the form of purely voluntary and private "tithing" or anything of that kind. Postmodern man is going to have to exercise his stewardship, his social use of wealth, in forms that fit the way he gets it—i.e., in social planning and public welfare, in corporate or community giving. In a way this will be returning from modern individualistic attitudes and mores to the essentially social or corporate character of stewardship at its Biblical source in the Old Testament—when it was a "role" assigned to and accepted by the whole covenant community of Israel, and not a private or individual election. We appear to have forgotten that the tithing of Biblical stewardship was neither merely voluntary and spontaneous, nor solely an ecclesiastical "contribution." On the contrary, Biblical sharing was a matter of *the law of the whole "secular" community,* and the tithe was used for vastly more than "church" costs—it was a stewardly support of all the things that the modern, nontheocratic *government* has to do! In the spectrum of stewardship, *ecclesiastical claims upon us are only a small part,* one sector only!

I have already indicated that even though the destitute are by now only a marginal claim on our stewardship, there are other claims and other human needs—for health, for education, for the arts and the spiritual life, even for simple beauty. Our generation must be needled into facing the ominous gap between our *private opulence* and our *public poverty!* Closing this gap is the basic task of stewardship. Christian stewardship has the crucial task of witnessing to the dangerous imbalances of opulence. For example, more automobiles create more highways, call for more engineers and maintenance workers, scarify more green countryside, require more policing and planning, maim more people and increase the demands upon already overburdened hospital facilities. Increased private consumption increases public costs and adds to public needs. These new costs created by the increase in our private or personal wealth are all, in their nature, in public facilities. Stewardship—a redemptive, creative use of wealth as God's agents would use it—has to come to grips with the postmodern situation. And to use Galbraith's neat analysis, the *social balance* between private goods and services and public goods and services will have to be established by an *investment balance* between investing in material goods and investing in human and cultural values—in things like smoke abatement, urban renewal, the battle against juvenile delinquency, reforestation, educational grants and scholarships, art centers, church support, scientific research. The agenda will be constantly lengthened and revised.

Galbraith (*The Affluent Society,* p. 104) speaks of small-scale patchwork devices in economic and management practice as "microeconomic," and pleads for "macroeconomic" procedures adequate to the importance and dimension of our modern needs. Using his neologism slightly turned, I would claim that to think of stewardship in terms of individual giving to human needs, straight from the private pocket or wallet, is *microethics;* whereas to see stewardship in terms of Christian support for increased taxation and funding, aimed at a wholesome investment balance and socially sensitive social balance—this would be *macroethics!* It would be true social ethics. This would be stewardship reconceived in its new economic context. Admittedly it wouldn't be easy—we shall have to contend against the "conventional wisdom" of the superseded medieval and modern eras in which taxation was a dirty word. The hatred of taxes is something we inherit from the past ages of scarcity when want and famine always hovered, and often it was the rich who greedily taxed the poor. This prejudice is out of date; we will have to outgrow it. For stewardship *is* taxation, local or federal, whether as a voluntary discipline privately exercised or a corporate and civil matter. Stewardship, vocation, and Christian citizenship coincide.

Christian stewardship confronts more than mere anachronistic hatred of taxation, which never seems to abate, even though it is plain that Democrats and Republicans alike increase tax rates and at the same time raise both the national debt and its legal limit. Stewardship also has to wrestle with blocked thinking, of which the basic block may be the myth of production—the fixed notion that production is the central and vital economic problem—perfectly true in the Scarcity Era but not in this Plenty Era when the main question is *distribution!* And distribution is, of course, the question of stewardship.

Our preoccupation with *producing* wealth, inherited from the Scarcity Era of the past, has the psychological effect of focusing our values in material goods. We slide steadily into a greedy consumerism. There seems to be no limit to the assumed need for production of consumer goods, to the disregard of the social balance between private and public needs, between material and cultural investments. Could it be that because we can supply consumer needs with a work force far below the level of "full employment," we are caught in an orgy of consumerism to stave off unemployment? A real question of macroeconomics and macroethics is how we can be stewardly enough to solve the problem of distributing purchasing power in creative ways other than salaries and wages paid out for goods production! As the productivity of automated manufacture and work proceeds, this becomes crucial. At present we are still depending on material things alone for prosperity, and therefore we are having to *create* demand by creating desires. Of the basic economic roles today, the persuaders are almost kingpin among the owners, managers, makers, fixers, and users. High-pressure advertising is becoming a form of forced feeding!

THE THREAT OF SHEER GREED

Vance Packard speaks in his *Hidden Persuaders* (p. 262) of "the larger question of where our economy is taking us under the pressures of consumerism. That, too, is a moral question. In fact I suspect it is destined to become one of the great moral issues of our times." And he is right. High-pressure advertising, want creation, is the powerful foe of the investment balance that stewardship must somehow establish. The challenge of stewardship boils down to whether it can alter the prevailing value system and change the high-order goal from consumption of material things to their most *redemptive* use. Think upon Galbraith's sharp remark (p. 223): "In a free market, in an age of endemic inflation, it is unquestionably more rewarding, in pecuniary terms, to be a speculator or a prostitute than a teacher, a preacher or policeman. Such is what the conventional wisdom calls the structure of incentives."

Let's put it this way. Christian stewardship faces us with a "success" problem—i.e., we have learned how to overcome the historic evil of naked need. But now we have to learn how to handle our opulence. Maynard Keynes (*Essays in Persuasion,* p. 365) foresaw that our real problem was not the production of enough goods, but the production of peace and the restriction of population. Yet in stewardship terms he underestimated the success problem, the question whether we will be able to do something constructive with our plenty. He did not illuminate the issue of the social and investment balances. We are still in the old *consumer* mentality. To quote Galbraith only once more (p. 140), we have managed in our affluent society to "transfer the sense of urgency in meeting consumer need that once was felt in a world where production meant more food for the hungry, more clothing for the cold, and more houses for the homeless to a world where increased output satisfies the craving for more elegant automobiles, more exotic food, more erotic clothing, more elaborate entertainment—indeed, for the entire modern range of sensuous, edifying and lethal desires."

This is the point at which the schools and churches must function—to reconceive and reinterpret the value system and priorities of the economics of opulence. Without some such ethical reorientation in our culture, we are headed for a disastrous imbalance between material and moral values, and between private and public needs. And the practical issue is whether we are prepared to go along with a taxation on our opulence, public or private or a combination of both, which will redress the balance. The sales tax principle, whether self-imposed or a civil measure, with its automatic private-public balance of investment, seems about the only quantitatively adequate way to instrument the principle of stewardship. The sales tax policy automatically strikes the social balance and investment balance at the point of private consumption, just as the graduated income tax applies the principle of "ability to pay" to the distribution of the costs of public administration. To date, local use of the sales tax has been too primitive and unfair to lower-income groups. It can be refined by freeing basic necessities, "graduating" it to balance as between a Ford and a Cadillac, and other such adjustments.

Now, in this postmodern world emerging without as yet a name, those of us who are serious about stewardship at the "macroethical" level will need to consider a policy based on the sales tax principle (combined, of course, with the graduated income tax and others such as excise and import). Private self-taxation at the level of grace, as in tithing, is too little and too spotty. While Christian people will certainly fulfill love's call to share and avoid indulgence, it is necessary to *administer* stewardship also at the level of *law*, as a civil or social discipline. Wealth so corporately produced and enjoyed must be corporately tithed.

Conclusion: A New Economy, A New Ethic

All of this can be put bluntly in the question: "How is Christian stewardship to be reconceived and reoriented in an economy which has succeeded in shifting from scarcity to plenty?" My answer is also, on reconsideration, a simple one: "Let Christians who seek to work out their ministry in the economic world, who want to fulfill their vocation of stewardship, face the facts of the new era and follow the realistic policy of a social remedy for the social ills of opulence."

Thanksgiving baskets and Christmas coal bags are gone with the horse and buggy. There are always a few hard-core underdogs, yes, and alert public as well as private volunteer agencies will always be on hand to help. But the work done by the churches and the money given by the churches will always be a drop in the bucket. The claims of neighbor love in the new world are cast in the much broader terms of the public good—terms too broad as yet for the imagination of many church people unless Christian stewards help them to grasp their meaning. This is the high hurdle of social understanding (i.e., stewardship realism) in a high-energy, large-scale, organization economy. The new economy needs desperately to be buttressed by an organization ethic. We cannot fulfill our stewardship any longer in the outmoded terms of scarcity or by any classical policy of sharing on a private offering basis. The human needs that cry aloud for stewardship are on the social scale and require socially structured and socially administered forms of response—chiefly, I suggest, a tax on opulence. Anything less than this is microethics, petty moralism.

XII

The Ethics of Stewardship
in a Changing Economy

THE ECONOMIC CONTEXT

WHEN A GROUP OF Dutch laymen came to Hendrik Kraemer during the Nazi occupation of Holland and asked him what they should do—collaborate or resist by subversive activity—his answer was: "I will not tell you what you should do, but I *will* tell you who you are." They say that this episode was the start or germ of his classic modern study *A Theology of the Laity.* In any case, when those Dutch Christians heard who they were, their resistance movement began to take shape! Kraemer's starting point or line of approach is, I believe, the correct strategy and the true task of a Christian or theological ethics.

Following that strategy, I won't try to tell you what stewardship requires you to *do,* but I will tell you what stewardship *is.* And then, if you are still listening, I will suggest one vital thing stewardship *might* do—among others.

The very first thing required of us in any serious scru-

Read to the national assembly of the United Church of Christ in French Lick, Indiana, in February, 1965, this paper later became a debate document for UCC stewardship councils in Philadelphia, Hartford, and other places.

tiny of stewardship is to be contextually or situationally realistic and sensitive, to make sure we are seeing our key concept ("stewardship") in a meaningful and actually live *setting*, the setting of contemporary history. If we give it a merely abstract shape, in some sort of timeless intellectual tidiness remote from where we are and when we are and who we are, then it's not very likely that we'll ever get to the heart of the matter. In any case, an idealistic conception of stewardship will never succeed in being down-to-earth, which is precisely what Christians believe God himself is—incarnate in the man Jesus, present in the church, and seeking acceptance in and by the world he so loves.

The setting of our question today—what our German brethren would call *Sitz im Leben*—is, using President Johnson's slogan coined for the new administration in Washington, "The Great Society." Under the push of hot and cold war and the breakthrough success of science and technology in the past quarter of a century, we have come a long way from the old economy of poverty or scarcity to a new economy of plenty or abundance. We are still on the way, but we are coming strong—far faster and surer than any nineteenth-century dreamer ever imagined we would. The doctrinaire predictions in the early 1930's of capitalist breakdown (and I once made my share of them) have been discredited beyond repair.

With this greater wealth and prosperity, however, has gone a significant increase in the sheer size or magnitude of the structures in which we live together. Government, industry, education, scientific work, businesses, communities—all have grown Leviathan-like. These mass structures are what make our plenty possible, but they mean that we can no longer leave to private choice a lot of things we did in times past. This frightens the timid. There is a lot of nostalgia for the older, simpler order of things—it was still strong enough among us to have won over twenty million votes for an avowed conservative in a presidential election. But the radical right only offers archaic solutions for surrealist fears. The world we have lost was no paradise. I for one am willing to wave it good-by. Let's not forget that the liberal individualism of the laissez-faire era, the pretechnical society, produced John Locke's dictum that the children of the poor must begin work for some part of every day when they reach three years of age! We just do not and cannot *think* that way any longer.

Our own country's economic picture, and others' chasing after it, presents a pattern of plenty—and this is the bony structure of the culture we have created by the science and learning and exploration searched for and gained so successfully. In the year 1964 we produced $235 billions in goods and $165 billions in services, a total of $400 billions of consumer spending by and for 191 million people. That meant a per capita average income of $2,400 for the nation as a whole, with an average of $6,300 per household. Our political and economic leadership achieved this with a remarkable degree of wage-price stability. There was only a 1.1 percent rise in the cost of living index.

By now, monetary and fiscal manipulation, labor-management contracts, retail and wholesale price agreements, budgetary planning—a hundred and one things have worked so well that the old-fashioned, cycle-ridden theory of "automatic" or market adjustment is dead. At the same time, for the sake of the cautious, we should note that the ratio of the national debt to the gross national product has fallen by more than half in the last eighteen years. And besides that, in 1964 America had a favorable balance of trade, with $25.1 billions of exports over against $18.3 billions of imports. And to cap all this, corporate profits in the past year alone rose by $7 billion, with a tax cut at the same time!

THE AMERICAN SCENE

When I was born over sixty years ago, the world of the West was of another kind—we still worried about having enough. The worry that plagues us nowadays, in the mature economies, is not that—now we worry about having enough consumers with enough purchasing power to keep inventories cleared out to make way for fresh and continuous production. This is the basic need of a "people's capitalism" using a technical tool system.

In this connection, one of the most serious and searching issues in economic morality is the policy of so-called "planned obsolescence," whereby consumer goods are deliberately made of inferior stuff and design in order, by artificial scarcity, to keep production going. This is the "answer" to "full employment" followed by those whom Vance Packard has called "the wastemakers." They are pushed into it because it is only through productive employment that people can get the "right" (i.e., the *money*) to consume our growing pile of wealth. I personally have no doubt whatsoever that in the end technology, especially when it is coupled with harnessed nuclear energy, will have so increased the productivity of our capital that, in order to distribute enough purchasing power, we shall have to pay a "citizen's salary" to all who are not criminals —in the style already forecast by the Ad Hoc Committee in its Triple Revolution report. The old wages-salaries-dividends mechanism of the so-called "wage system" of the past is a scarcity device that rapidly ceases to be "in phase" with our actual and potential plenty. When I had my first paying job, labor represented 65 cents in the cost dollar; now it is less than 25 cents!

But we cannot start down that interesting side road now, important as it is for the understanding of our system of distribution. Let us just say that our basic ethical problems now arise in distribution, not in production. The main thing is that we cannot go on thinking about our problems and policies in the scarcity terms of a pretechnical culture—and one of the major Christian categories that have been shaken to their foundations by this postmodern world is *stewardship*. In the language of John Galbraith, we must tackle stewardship by breaking out of the "conventional wisdom" of classical economic thinking. We have to try to catch up with ourselves.

Stewardship is a principle of the Christian ethic that has a range wide enough to cover our time and talents as well as our treasure. To reduce it solely to money giving turns a true steward into a mere patron. But it is upon the material and money side that I am fixing here. An important preethical Christian faith proposition is what we call "Christian materialism," the sacramental belief that spiritual or moral values are expressed in and through and by means of material things, not above or around or in spite of material goods. This "dialectic" is the theological meaning of the doctrines of creation, providence, incarnation, the Lord's Supper, the Biblical psychosomatic view of man as a person—who is no more to be seen as "a ghost in a corpse." Spirit and matter are different "sides" of one reality, one "ground" of being. Christian ethics in the postmodern era has given a death certificate to the old idea, the "religious" idea, that we owe an obligation to people's "souls" apart from their material well-being. In nontheological language, we know now that energy is matter and matter is energy, the difference being only a temporary state (like steam and ice). As somebody said lately, good-by to all that "holy gas and gross stuff" dualism!

In trying to say what stewardship *is*, I think we must point directly to two first-order requirements of any definition that is adequate to the realities of wealth in an economy of plenty-by-technology.

First, our definition must recognize that in such a job-replacing system there are "losers"—and we haven't yet found a solution for this human breakage. Our distribution of income, as I have already suggested, must find some other nexus than job employment—whether for the skilled or unskilled, manual or managerial work, in production or services. All such roles and functions are in jeopardy. Our present level of unemployment (5 percent) will go up, as the President has candidly admitted in his economic reports to Congress. This is a new economy, in which *we not only have greater prosperity in spite of greater unemployment but because of it!* Here is the simple clinical pattern: in the past decade our gross national product rose by 40 percent, our employment force by 12 percent— an increase ratio of more than three to one in favor of capital improvement over labor need.

Then we have to face the additional factor of hard-core poverty groups, such as racial minorities victimized by prejudice, some scattered farmers on worn-out submarginal land, and old people or widowed mothers. There is an ethical imperative in Harry Emerson Fosdick's saying, "The basic test of any society is what happens to the underdog." Yet without being callous we must also recall Peter Drucker's remark several years ago that although the "poor" have not disappeared, they are no longer the "masses"—they are "special problem" people. In its main features, our new society is one of mass production, mass finance, and mass merchandizing, i.e., mass consumption.

Second, our definition of stewardship must aim at an ethical corrective for consumerism—the Macy-mindedness of the reigning secular culture. All around us we see, and enjoy prosperity by virtue of, a consumeristic orientation that is obviously more and more want spending rather than need spending. Who needs Macy's iguanas at $21.49, or a heart-shaped mattress, or fresh Beluga caviar? Regular paying jobs no longer yield enough consumer dollars; hence, widespread moonlighting and jobs for married women (one third of whom are working). The average motorist now buys a new car every three years, not four; and often there is a second or third car in the family, like a second or third television set.

Jack Strauss of Macy's, which is probably as near a cathedral as anything in the eyes of our devout consumerists, says: "Our economy keeps growing because our ability to consume is endless. The consumer goes on spending regardless of how many possessions he has. The luxuries of today are the necessities of tomorrow." There are, he says, no "hicks" anymore among the consumers. Under the onslaught of high-pressure, mass-media advertising propaganda, whimsy and impulse buying reign supreme at self-service racks instead of by choices discussed over a counter. In 1964, Americans spent 93 cents of every income dollar, three fourths of it through the relaxed fingers of the ladies.

The Concept of Stewardship

This, then, is the situation in which we must define stewardship and act it out. It seems to me that the essential feature of stewardship as an abstract concept is well enough stated by Nels Ferré: "All property [i.e., wealth] belongs to God for the common good. It belongs, therefore, first of all to God and then equally to society and the individual. When the individual has what the society needs and can profitably use, it is not his, but belongs to society, by divine right."

Here we have a specifically and sharply *theological* statement. On any other basis, it would be only a kind of idealistic moralism, hopelessly abstract and arbitrarily oversimple. Ferré should not have said wealth is "equally" society's and the individual's, for he promptly and properly denies it by giving society's claim a higher order than the individual's. I say he does this "properly" because the subordination of private to common wealth is the *theological* logic of Biblical monotheism, with its patrimonial principle. Let me say something now about what I have called the principle of the divine *patrimonium*.

Stewardship is easily perverted into the sub-Christian idea of *noblesse oblige*. Lots of naïve Christians suppose that stewardship means being generous or merciful to the less fortunate. But the theology of stewardship asserts something very different from that—it says that all wealth is God's and he has given it to his children *corporately as a family* (a *patrimonium*), the community and not its individual members being God's steward or warden or bailiff, so that we are acting on his behalf, we are *not* acting as our own stewards on behalf of our own love or charity! The creationist doctrine is that "the earth and the fulness thereof" is the Lord's: God is the only landlord and owner of both our natural resources and their products. He turns it over to us for our use (ours the possession, his the title) on a familial basis—for all, not just for some. Social equity and "commonwealth" are elemental features of Christian economic ethics. This is why almsgiving in Christian moral theology has always been treated as *justice,* not as mercy! Helping the neighbor in need is only *giving him what is his own.* Every time we give a dime to a community fund or pay a tax for social security, we are doing *stewardship,* not philanthropy or citizenship.

There is no place in this ethic for self-congratulation, because we are sharing "what is our own" through some "goodness of our hearts" in a supererogatory spirit—for example, by one or more tenths. The total claim of stewardship covers ten tenths, not a moralistic calculation of one tenth—as in "tithing." Any attempt to reduce stewardship to tithing is a perversion of Biblical theology and of the Christian ethic that leans upon it. Both philanthropy and tithing can be said, without elaborating it here, to be (1) historically passé, appropriate to an ancient nomadic-agrarian economy but not to a high-energy technical society; (2) theologically fallacious, since they presume to give both the initiative and the preference to the individual wealth holder rather than the community; and (3) ethically ambiguous, since their motive is merely merciful rather than justice, or at best only based on Greek "prudence" rather than the nonpreferential "love" of the New Testament. By Christian norms, philanthropy and tithing are exercises in microethics, and the outmoded scarcity thinking behind them is only microeconomics. They do not fit the size and dynamism of The Great Society. We cannot go on thinking of stewardship as a private, small-scale, and voluntary affair.

Updating the Concept

Postmodern man is going to have to exercise his stewardship of wealth in forms that fit the way he gets it—i.e., in social planning and public welfare, corporate and community-wide giving. We shall be returning, strangely enough, to the social or corporate stewardship *of the whole people* in ancient Israel, when "tithing" was *taxation,* and the money given was not merely for "church" costs but *a stewardly support of government and the whole community's needs.* In terms that fit our twentieth century A.D. situation, yet strictly parallel to the twelfth century B.C.—*taxation is stewardship!* In a highly interdependent urban-industrial society like ours, stewardship cannot safely be left to private impulse and personal preference: it must be a civil agreement, a matter of distributive and contributive justice, for this is not so much the "century of the common man" as of the *corporate* man.

Those who resist taxation falsely assume it is evil on four counts. (1) They complain that it is based on compulsion. Yet it is not "voluntary" self-taxation which is ethically desirable, but its being *willingly* paid. (2) They argue that it is an invasion of private rights. This attitude, of course, completely misunderstands or rejects the Biblical patrimonial belief about property. (3) They declare that it is impersonal, not direct, warm, interpersonal. As an objection this is sentimental and unimaginative, since a rational sharing is as real as a turkey-basket handout and often far more sympathetic, less humiliating. (4) They claim it is inefficient because indirect. This is probably based on a naïve distrust of "bureaucrats," a premodern, small-scale liberal notion that "the best government is the least government" appropriate to an 1865 society but not to one in 1965.

We have practically no destitute people anymore, due to welfare services and social security. We *do* have poor people still—and will have marginally until we finally rid ourselves of the wage and loan system of access to wealth —i.e., access established only through work and investment. In the meantime, there will be increasing pressures: in 1964 we felt the first great shock of the postwar birth rate (not, mind you, the permanent and increasing pressure of population explosion) when 7.3 million young people reached job age with no jobs and no skills—one million more than in 1963.

The core of the stewardship question in our times is the ominous, shameful gap or disparity between our private prosperity and our public poverty. Closing this gap is the task of stewardship. Our unchecked consumerism is the demon to be tamed. It must be forced to share its money with the public sector of our economy, to correct the imbalance of opulence. More cars, for example, call for more highways, more engineers, more patrolmen, more planners—and also, alas, more doctors, nurses, and hospitals. Increasing private consumption *increases public costs, adds to public needs*. To use Galbraith's neat formulation, the "social balance" between private and public expenditures must be established by an "investment balance" which puts back an adequate share of income into nonconsumption or nonmaterial values—such things as reeducation, urban renewal, smoke abatement, medical care, reforestation and conservation, scholarship grants, school aid, scientific research and development, arts centers, and neighborly help to underdeveloped countries. The agenda can be lengthened or shortened pragmatically —and in the list "church support" has some proper proportionate place.

Christian stewardship is faced with a "success" problem. We have learned how to overcome the historic evil of naked need. Now we must transcend the old consumer mentality (greed is nine tenths fear, fear of famine), and learn how to strike the social and investment balances— to balance our private with our public or common needs, and the consumption of material goods with our provision for cultural and spiritual goods.

We seem to be caught in an orgy of consumerism to stave off unemployment. Christian stewardship must wean our people away from their dependence on material things alone as the way to prosperity, and resist the pressure to create demand by creating desire. Among the economic roles of today, the "persuaders" are almost kingpins over the owners, managers, makers, fixers, and users. High-pressure advertising is an unethical form of forced feeding.

A Serious Suggestion

In order to give point and specificity to this analysis, permit me to propose that stewardship through taxation will most effectively correct consumerism in the form of a sales tax. This proposal always is greeted with either orchids or onions. I know that labor always opposes a sales tax, on the ground that it unjustly puts the burden on those who can least afford to pay it. But this argument fails to make any kind of practical distinction between general and *selective* sales taxes. The latter could certainly be shaped to shift the burden away from the lower-income groups. Necessities can certainly be exempted. It offers us an automatic balance of both the private-public investment, and the material-cultural tension.

Thirty-seven of our states already have a sales tax in one form or another. I predict that other states soon will join their company. As a category in point, I turn a tax-greedy eye on a 17.8 percent increase in transatlantic travel in one year, all of it on jet planes. In the nineteenth century, the sales tax was condemned because it conceals itself by collecting only a few pennies at a time. In the twentieth century, this "painless" feature is a recommendation. In my own state, Massachusetts, our people are ninth among the states in per capita personal income, tenth in personal expenditures for retail goods, but only forty-third in taxes paid on personal retail purchases! This exemplifies the absence of stewardship.

Conclusion

To sum up, here is what I have been saying. The question: "How is Christian stewardship to be reconceived and reoriented in an economy which has graduated from scarcity to abundance?" The answer: "Let Christians in their economic ministry to God's world face the facts of the new era, as their stewardship using a social remedy for the social ills of opulence. That remedy is corrective taxation."

Politicians have a morbid fear of imposing new taxes, but the old saw is unrelentingly true: death and taxes are inevitable. The Christian comment is, of course, that there is a theological—i.e., faith based—interpretation that finds a redemptive meaning in them, and converts both death and taxes into a spiritual victory.

PART THREE

A STYLE OF LIFE

XIII

Discontent and Self-renewal

WE ARE IN THE beginning of the end of the Era of Common Sense. But too many of us do not know that common sense has little or nothing to do anymore with *who* we are and *what* we do. In the fashionable jargon of these days, our "self-images" and "ego ideals" are very apt to presuppose laissez-faire or open-ended structures in life and society that have, in fact, gone with the wind. It is in this hiatus or lack of phase between the structures of life and our inherited ideals which is the source of paralyzing conflicts in the lives of young people trying to look forward, and of older people trying to understand why "things" are so "mixed up" even though we never before "had it so good."

C. P. Snow, the English scientist-novelist, in essays such as *The Two Cultures* and novels such as *The New Men,* has been warning us about the schizoid separation between our men of science and our humanities people. Some of us don't know the plot of *The Merchant of Venice,* while others can't describe the second law of thermodynamics. That is, we cannot talk to each other. Now add to that schism the additional, looming fact that research

A lecture in the annual Duke University Symposium, November 10, 1964, in Page Auditorium, with John Roche and Norton Long as fellow panelists. It was announced as "Leviathan Society and Lilliputian Men."

and development are piling up knowledge to proportions that are personally or individually unmanageable. The ordinary, well-educated person as such has no competence for the social roles and functions of the new era. College arts degrees are a dime a dozen—only "background" for professional or special training.

Harold Laski recognized as early as the 1930's that "the day of the plain man has passed." Taking its place is what the Spanish historian-philosopher Ortega y Gasset used to call, in a somewhat reactionary temper, "the barbarism of specialization." Already the sophisticates of science and technology are speaking of ordinary people as "finnegans"—from an old word *finnikin,* meaning (according to Webster) a minor person or domestic pigeon. We will have to discover, however reluctantly, that ours is the day of the *periti,* the experts—indeed, of the *peritessimi!*

During the great depression of the 1920's and 1930's, a lunatic fringe group calling themselves "technocrats" offered us "technocracy"—rule by experts—as the solution for all our social ills. We laughed them out of court then, but they were only a little premature in making a virtue of necessity, and our laughter was myopic. Now we know that "expertise" is here to stay—that it is an irreversible trend. Oscar Wilde once said of Bernard Shaw that he had no enemies but his friends all disliked him, and perhaps we could say the same thing about our technocratic culture—i.e., it is disliked, distrusted, and disparaged by most of its beneficiaries. Too many of us, in relation to "the new man," are like the last-ditch householder who sneers condescendingly at the urban renewal man who comes knocking at his door.

Science and its practical results, which we call technology, has to keep up a running fight with supposedly "revolutionary" forces as well as with conservation. Only recently was a cybernetics society formed in Warsaw with a grudging stamp of approval from the commissars of culture; and as recently as its 1954 edition the Soviet Encyclopedia described cybernetics as a "pseudo science." Nevertheless, the Communists too have now started down the path of computers and data processing. Like our new men, their experts are busy reproducing and improving upon the human nervous system in their mechanico-electronic innovations. The IBM, Remington-Rand ethos is on the march in the world, with its new structures of life and work. Those that don't know it or can't believe are "dead" to the world. History has passed them by.

This technico-scientific culture in our postmodern era carries and creates a new hierarchy of pneumatic and charismatic figures. They are postreligious high priests— the theoretical physicists and chemists. Their monastic orders enclose and discipline the research and lab man. Their secular clergy are the engineers. They rule in all the structures of our common life—in industry, government, the military apparatus, in outer space, education, medicine, transport, in everything. To illustrate their ascendancy, we need only consider how helpless the old, outmoded elites—the business tycoons and government— would be if they had to program their own mechanical brains or even only read the outtapes. Yet no market analysis, paycheck process, or tax-record system can be operated anymore without electronic computing. *This is what happens of necessity to leadership and executive roles in a mass society.*

Now, in all of this, the key word is "expertise." When any function, anything from baking a cake to tripping a stamping machine to a surgical sympathectomy, becomes a matter of competence based on special knowledge and practical skill, it has been "professionalized." There is little today that isn't a profession. It is nearly already true that to be employed is to be a professional. The educated untrained are unneeded and unemployable. Common sense no longer gets us a work badge, even though it helps us to keep it once we get it. The idealists of democracy at the end of the Second World War called this the Century of the Common Man, but nothing could be farther from the truth. In our American tradition, we have always supposed that experts are only consultants—that the ordinary person is the decision maker. This is simply not true any longer. Some sociologists still talk about "social control of the professions," but the *real* problem is the reverse—professional control of society!

Since 1954, there have been more white-collar than blue-collar workers employed in America. Less than 5 percent—think of it! only 5 percent—of the gainfully employed are classed as "unskilled" people. Special information and know-how have *sophisticated* our vocations altogether past the rubrics of common sense. Even business managers are professionalized, trained in business schools. So with nursing, market analysis, teaching, welding, filing, library research—nearly anything you can find on the Help Wanted page. In the old days the professions and professionals were few—the ministry, law, and medicine were the main ones. Now there are the proliferating sciences, and a hundred and one engineering specialties based on them.

In the 1950's, there was a 40 percent increase in professional, technical, and service jobs. In the 1960's, there is a more rapid increase. The traditional simple muscular workingman is the vanishing American. The unions are declining in number and power and interest. Labor used to represent 65 cents in the cost dollar—but by 1961 it was only 25 cents, and we can be sure it will shrink to less and less. The United Mine Workers, for example, has found that dues-paying members are a liability, not an asset. They get 40 cents a ton for all coal weighed out at the tipple—paid into the union's health and retirement fund. But mechanization and automation have reduced the men needed from three thousand to three hundred in a typical shaft mine, so that the union gets the same amount of fund payments, the company gets the same amount of coal, and there are fewer miners to complicate things for either the union or management!

Business, government, and defense—the garrison sciences—to take only three important structures, are recentralizing controls and initiatives. That is, they are now collective processes. Top management is doing to middle management what middle did to the workers—squeezing it out. For example, Chrysler is putting private telephone lines between its forty plants to send automated production orders. They now carry fifty thousand calls daily and will soon carry encoded instructions to activate digital computers by set tonal variations. Who needs branch plant managers? Some Monsanto, Texaco, and B. F. Goodrich plants are already fully automated.

We have moved from mechanization (using machines instead of muscles) to automation (using set cycles instead of human control of machines) to cybernation (using computers instead of human initiative to set cycles instead of human controls of machines doing the work instead of human muscles and skills). From 1945–1950, electronic research pioneered automatic control of machines, using thousands of vacuum tubes. From 1950–1955, we saw electronics applied to scientific and engineering research. From 1955–1960, it reached clerical and commercial operations. Since 1960, we have seen digital computers using a few transistors hooked to *physical* process controls. Top management is left, and some bottom management—supervisors, shop foremen, line leaders, straw bosses—a grinning company of button pushers. And behind all of this is the prospect of nuclear energy. For the time being its high cost and waste hazards block its use, but it will come fairly soon, and when it does, it will multiply the human energy potential manifold. The amount of purchasing power we distribute for employment rewards, and prices based on supply-and-demand principle, is already nearly irrelevant to the activities of scientific-technical affluence. The coming economic revolution packs a mental shock for the old-fashioned Communist revolutionaries of the postautomated era.

All of this adds up to one thing—each one of us knows more and more about less and less. Our understanding of our total life situation is shrinking. Not to know is to be powerless, to be in somebody else's power. This is what being professionalized means—it means that in our *personal existence* we are more vulnerable and less self-contained. Just as the men of power based on money and votes find themselves more and more helpless in the hands of the men of know-how, we are all "involved" or "engaged" in this new postmodern web of interdependence. Specialism entails mutual dependence. The scientific revolution has ended all individualism. *Science* has done this, not leftist ideology.

Individual initiative and private enterprise and personalized performance are being left behind. The culture context in which our ethos and moral values were shaped on the eighteenth- and nineteenth-century frontiers is dead. We are conflicted because our social and ethical ideals are bogged down in a "culture lag"—and therefore we suffer in depths more than we realize or could tolerate if it was altogether a conscious pain.

It is impossible in this era of specialism and the organizational revolution to declare ourselves simply socialists *or* individualists. We can no longer set freedom over against planning or an "open" over against a "managed" society. In a world of radical, technical interdependence, our only choice is between good and bad planning—but planning it must be. If personal liberty is to be saved in any authentic measure, if we are to keep it at all, it will only be by planning for it—making freedom the number one item on the planning agenda. Our huge corporations and huge government agencies are, both of them, creatures of technology's built-in principle of interdependence and collective integration, the web of specialism and expertise.

The collective process can be illustrated in big business and the rise of its mass production and mass finance and mass merchandizing. These massive structures come along as science is applied to serve a mass population in the mass concentrations of industrial urbanism. Then big business brings big unionism, with nationwide agreements between nationwide alliances for nationwide markets. Then big government is needed to referee them—fulfilling the old maxim in political science that agencies of control have to be as extensive as the activities they seek to control. There is nothing more ironical than the big businessman's complaints about the growth of big government. This is the Leviathanism that is also at work in community organization and the social welfare agencies, in city and regional planning, in military programs and national defense, in education, medicine, and the mass media of communication.

What happens to *people* in such a culture context—in such a society of mass organization? They become organization people, of course! Their interdependence and integration shape them to fit their world. Their values, their preferences and priorities, are altered accordingly. It is foolish to expect anything else but that young men and women will feel and think and value what surrounds and dazzles and motivates them. Ours is an organization society because of science, technology, and specialization. Therefore, we are organization people.

Many of our social analysts and mass-culture critics in recent years have remarked on the American people's interest in mirror gazing. They say we like to examine ourselves and criticize what we see—that there is even a faint tinge of culture neurosis or psychic masochism in it,

because we are most fascinated by the most negative accounts. I doubt it—in more than a year spent in Asian
universities, I found the practice of social self-criticism
going on there. In Japan, for example, as much as in
America, the core concern is to recover or discover *values*
—the things we prize, what makes us tick motivationally.
From one vantage point we can call it psychology, from
another *ethics*. I am speaking, I think, from both perspectives.

We could, if we had time, draw up a fairly imposing
list of ethical issues raised around new situations in our
mass society. In my own view, one such issue is of great
importance, namely, "consumerism"—which is posed by
our high productivity and affluence and leads to materialism in the *ethical* sense of greed and self-indulgence at the
expense of growth and discipline. Another such moral
problem is the fact that technology's rapid dysfunctioning
of human labor is throwing too many good people on the
junk heap and keeping too many from ever finding a productive role. We are still operating with a competitive social system in which "losers" are a built-in part of it, at
the same time that science (not the loser's incapacity) is
increasing their numbers. All investigators agree that one
out of four or five Americans does not share in our prevailing abundance. We are going to have to do something
about this—if not out of neighbor-concern, then out of
enlightened self-interest, and for our sale's sake!

However, space is limited; and having painted in the
background, I want now to draw a picture of three deep-
seated, very pervasive factors in our mass society—what
I will call "the three A's," anger, anomie (or valueless-
ness), and alienation. They are, perhaps, factors of morale
more than of morals, but the motivations behind behavior
cannot be separated from its norms and standards—and
in any case, we shall see that these three A's run strong
and deep as culture dynamics in the American character.
They help us to see what makes us tick.

It is within these structures of the mass society—(1) functional interdependence and (2) Gargantuan collectivities or incorporations—that human beings in their own personal existence have to discover themselves, identify themselves, and relate themselves. The problem of being *who* we are and *what* we are in the simple social situations of the old pretechnical world was child's play compared to the complexity and subtlety of our postmodern search for individual integrity and individual creativity. On all hands we see that the search is a failure—sometimes tragically plain to be seen in mental and emotional disorders, sometimes in antisocial behavior.

May I suggest that there is a pattern of failure, that people are defeated by our new society's specialties and magnitudes in a reactive progression from anger to anomie to alienation? It runs something like this:

1. First people feel angry, as they sense a twofold loss of utility (i.e., of functional neededness and ability) and identity (i.e., of the self-recognition that dies without social recognition). Losing out in the race for expertise combines with the loss of one's name, increasingly replaced by a number in big organizations, to stir up anger, the fury of frustration. It may not always be conscious, but it is nonetheless powerful, because we cannot detect it or will not admit it. Some analysts have insisted that precisely this driving force could have led Lee Harvey Oswald to assassinate President Kennedy.

2. Next comes anomie—apathy, listlessness, indifference—in which value interests or concerns are dropped as false and futile hopes. Such people "couldn't care less." I have no case to make for the term itself. In Greek, its literal meaning is "lawlessness," but some European sociologists have given the term a little currency in America, especially Émile Durkheim and Max Weber. It seems to carry the meaning of listlessness and indifference to values or norms. Fairchild's *Dictionary of Sociology* defines it as "demoralization" and *Webster's Third New International*

Dictionary describes it as a state "in which normative standards of conduct and belief have weakened or disappeared."

Apathy follows anger because anger is too intense to tolerate very long. Even apart from frustration, overshadowing of the humanities by the sciences in our educational system itself tends to minimize values, to demoralize our culture and ways of thinking. Our new generations are strong on *de*scription, weak on *pre*scription! Fifty years ago, Josiah Royce anticipated C. P. Snow's warning by distinguishing between "worlds" of appreciation and observation; the latter—the radically empirical temper—is in control. When, on top of the basic cultural orientation to quantities rather than qualities, widespread failures and losses of individual integrity and of personal initiative develop, defeat and apathy are bound to follow.

3. But there is a third level or stage of the process. Anger and apathy do not stop there. They often end in actual alienation. Consciously or unconsciously, the victims of technology and magnitude go on to *withdrawal*. In anger they say, "I have been thrown aside and ignored"; in apathy they say, "I don't give a damn"; finally, in detachment and self-alienation they say, "The hell with it." This reactive alienation sometimes takes a personal, pathological form—as in schizophrenia and involutional melancholia—and sometimes it is a more social and "existential" phenomenon.

In its existential form, alienation may be sophisticated —as with the so-called "beatniks" or "holy barbarians" of the beat generation and in the protests of the "theatre of the absurd." Again, it may be quite unsophisticated and brutal—as in the subcultures and lumpen societies of the gangs, the dope addicts, and the riot prone among the poor, or in the politics of the hatemongers among the rich. We cannot appreciate the dynamism of the radical right or of the forces of reform by reaction, unless we understand the pattern of the three A's and its source. It is true, of course, that we cannot turn the clock back, to restore the small-scale structures of nineteenth-century individualism. The "conscience of a conservative" is only dangerous moralism. But it is equally dangerous to ignore or misunderstand how profound, in human terms as well as structural, is the revolution carried by our new technical civilization.

What I have here distinguished as pathological and existential alienation are parallel to Tillich's pathological and existential forms of anxiety. Anxiety is a universal feature or phase of human experience, resulting from our awareness of our finitude and limitedness in the face of the magnitude of the universe and the ultimacy of God. The three A's, which come into play as a by-product of collectivism and Leviathanism and because of technology's built-in principle of interdependence, are perhaps the most tragic culture expressions of human anxiety. Sometimes it is experienced as a dread of death, of nonbeing, as the fear of *nothingness.* This was anxiety's dominant form in the Middle Ages and Reformation periods. Sometimes it comes as a dread of isolation, of rejection, of *loneliness.* This was its dominant form in the era of *laissez faire,* pre-technological capitalism and its radical individualism, which Erich Fromm has analyzed in his *Escape from Freedom.* But in our own era, in my opinion, anxiety's dominant form is a dread of insignificance, of the undiscrete, in short, of meaninglessness. The fear that our very existence has no real meaning, that we cannot make any "sense" of it—a fear that always lurks at the edge of our awareness—is only multiplied and aggravated by our double loss of function through technology and of identity in the mass structures of the organizational revolution.

How much easier and authentic it was to see meaning in one's life in frontier or agrarian or even early industrial societies, when we were obviously needed to prepare food, shelter, and clothing; when we lived in a single hut or home, not in a high-rise, multiple dwelling; when we made a shoe with our hands instead of setting a cycle for a line of machines; when—as was true only a short time ago—if we were lucky enough to be in a university, there were fifty at a lecture, not five hundred; and if we went to work instead, we wore our own face to get to our bench instead of a badge with a number.

Well, the plain truth is that those days are gone forever. Our task now, in terms of personal freedom as well as of social policy, is to "be our age" in the sense of "getting with it"—with life as it is in a mass society.

There are those who take the dark view, who agree that the personality damage of our mass society is something that goes inevitably with technical civilization. They declare that it obliterates individuality and destroys the creative powers of the independent personality. To this I can only oppose my own conviction that the opposite is true, and that we are slowly but surely learning that the antimachine mentality is only a pathetic case of culture lag. If anything, there is too much rather than too little creativity and innovation, pioneering in depth.

We have more variety, experiment, originality, and self-expression than this country has ever had before, but we fail to see it because it cannot be expressed in the familiar forms of the past. Ingenuity and invention are being devoted to the mechanisms of our common life rather than to private "self-realization"—but think of how many "selves" now share in their creation and their fruits! One of our big growing pains will be to learn the strategies and sentiments of group leadership, as the old individualists and top-dog forms of leadership, research, and pioneering take second place. Groups and teams can and do achieve individuality. Identity and distinction are no longer the privilege of a minority of outstanding persons—it is distributed and shared as never before. More people, not fewer, are finding ways to realize their potential, because in a mass society most people—not just a minority—are given a break by mass education, mass communication, mass merchandizing, mass entertainment, mass lots of things. After all, mass production of anything means a wide distribution of the benefits.

Henry A. Murray in *The American Style* (edited by Etting Morrison) puts the present place of identity and self-regulation in our new mass society this way: "Instead of a dozen isolated peaks rising from a flat plain of commonplaceness, we see a great number of hills and a few mountains, something like the Alleghenies." Remembering a few rare wonders such as Thoreau, or Melville, or Whitman, we "forget the enormous incubus of conventionality" in their day. "Today we have fewer snow-capped Matterhorns of individuation, but we have a multitude of Snowdons and Mt. Washingtons." We are, I believe, entering upon an era in which personal success is something *shared* with our neighbors, and no longer gained at the expense of everybody else: success is no longer destructive of others as it was in the precollective, preorganizational social order.

If, however, our mass society can actually extend and increase the chances of our people to realize who they are (identify) and what they are (genuine role and function), then why—as we have seen—is there so much danger of failure, of the three A's? Any separate answer to this question in depth, surely, requires us to take note of how many people lack a *positive faith*. The faith they lack is a believing trust in God, man, history (i.e., the social process); and in logical consequence, they lack faith as well in themselves. If a person is without a basic commitment and living faith in the social process and its new technical, mass structures—if he is without great expectations—he is obviously a candidate for anger, apathy, and alienation.

Speaking for myself, I do not believe that we can possibly escape the three-stage descent into despair unless we have a faith conviction that (1) interdependence is good and creative, better and more growth potent than an individualistic culture, and (2) that the same claim can be made for the mass or corporate structures of our common life.

But I cannot leave the matter at that level. Faith in ourselves or in our society or even more broadly in the total course of world history does not make much sense if such forms or ranges of faith are held arbitrarily, as if confidence in man or history were self-validating and self-explanatory. They are not. To "justify" such faith commitments there must be some kind of transcendent sanction or assurance. To put my point bluntly, without a "religious" basis, or, as Tillich has expressed it, an "ultimate" concern and thrust, to "believe" in man or history is naïve and too much like brave whistling in the dark. Only an ultimate faith can underwrite our immediate and proximate assurances.

What we are dealing with in this question is the "tone" or "style" or *posture* with which we encounter the structures of mass society. To use the language of the classical Judeo-Christian tradition, we must understand that our "solution" lies in meeting the experiences of anxiety with the armory of I Cor., ch. 13—that is, to face nothingness and emptiness with the virtue of hope, so that it will lose its sting; to face loneliness and isolation with the power of love; to face doubt and the threat of meaninglessness with the strength of faith. Faith, hope, love, these three. But this is not a sermon. What has to be made clear in a quite pragmatic temper is that the so-called "theological virtues" have the most fundamental, practical importance for successful living in a mass society.

XIV

Moral Responsibility

H. Richard Niebuhr's *The Responsible Self* (1963)[1] pointed to *four* elements in the notion of responsibility. Of these the second was that it includes our interpretation of the demand being made upon us in every decision-making situation. The third was that our response looks forward to the reactions of others, and the fourth was that it takes account of the givenness of our social solidarity—our continuing membership in an interactive community of existence. But the *first* element is the one I want to focus upon here; the factor of *response* as the real key to responsibility.

All four of these elements combine to make up what Niebuhr called "fitting action," a concept of situational sensitivity already set out by A. C. Ewing in *The Definition of Good* (1947). "The first element in the theory of responsibility," said Niebuhr, and I would have said "first" in importance as well as cognitively, "is the idea of *response*" (p. 61).[2] He meant, of course, response to God as well as to men. Some people, scholars, are annoyed by Niebuhr's novelistic way of putting familiar things, such as calling the follower of deontological or duty-centered law morality "man the citizen," and calling the one who is teleological and a doer of goal-centered morality "man the maker," but I see no point in fussing about it—it's a harmless conceit. In any case, I want to hail and praise his third and different kind of decision maker—"man the *answerer*." (The factor of *freedom* in any ethic based on response to situations is not fully treated in Niebuhr's essay as he might have done if he had lived to complete it himself. But he knew its importance, and would have found no fault with the emphasis I gave it in 1966 in *Situation Ethics*.[3])

RESPONSE IS TO PERSONS

This way of understanding responsibility as response has had an interesting history in modern theological ethics, running through the Big B's—Buber, Brunner, Barth, and Bonhoeffer. (Another Big B is Berdyaev; see his *Solitude and Society*, 1938.[4]) Apparently it was the Jew Buber who first effectively set it out in 1922 in his *I and Thou*,[5] and then the Protestants took it up. The core of his concept was *relationship* ("real life is meeting," as J. H. Oldham expressed it), the conviction that to be authentically personal we have to be in "dialogue" with others. Friedrich Gogarten put it bluntly, with both humanistic and theistic meanings, by saying, "The 'I' comes from the 'Thou.'" James Sellers is hardly correct in his *Theological Ethics* (1966)[6] to speak of Niebuhr's concept of responsibility as a "new dimension" in ethics, but he is altogether on course in pointing to it as a particularly appealing version of the concept.

Buber as early as his *Events and Meetings* (1917) speaks of "the loving man" as one who is responsible, i.e., capable of responding in encounter and dialogue. He always insisted that to be responsible means to respond, to hear the call or claim of others, and furthermore that (in Maurice Friedman's words, in *Martin Buber: The Life of Dialogue*, p. 145) "responsibility cannot be laid down according to any set principles but must be ever again recognized in the depths of the soul according to the demands of each concrete situation."[7] We could express the same thing this way: that morality, like the Sabbath, is made for man, not man for morality.

To Brunner goes the credit for the first adequate Christian theological construction of the Buberian concept, even though earlier uses were made by Gogarten,[8] Karl Heim,[9] and the radical existentialist ethicist, Eberhard Griesbach.[10] (Barth's discussion in his *Church Dogmatics,* III/2 in 1948[11] was also beamed in the same direction.) In *The Divine Imperative* (1932),[12] Brunner speaks of the ethics of relationship or response as Christian humanism (p. 191), and declares that the meaning of human existence as responsible ("reciprocal") existence is precisely love, Christianly understood (p. 296). But even Brunner failed to see that for authentic existence mere coexistence is not enough—that it must be genuine interexistence, a radical "socialism" or solidarism. To express what I mean in theological language I can only say that our response to others, *to persons in situations,* must be as radically "dialogic" as the incarnation, in which God makes *all* of mankind one in and with himself!

Harvey Cox suggests in his *God's Revolution and Man's Responsibility* (1965)[13] that for today "sin" can best be understood as *apathy* (pp. 39 ff.). Sociologists (for example, Max Weber) have had much to say about the social evil of "anomie," just as the classical moralists condemned *acedia.* They are all referring to the same thing —indifference, neutrality, not caring, ir-responsibility or *not responding.* I can only repeat again and again: The opposite of love is not hate but indifference. However, let us make this point even more sharply by saying that while the essence of moral guilt lies in the failure or refusal to respond to the needs or call of others, *it does not lie in the failure to obey an abstract rule or principle!* It is indeed impossible to be responsible, i.e., responsive, to any principle. We can only respond to the calls and claims of others who, like ourselves, are persons rather than things, subjects and not objects. We may follow or obey or submit to rules and principles, if the situation calls for it, but true *responsibility* is always a response to a call from others, an answer. Or, again to use Buberian language, responsibility is responding to an I or Thou, whereas all principle-bound law morality is enslavement to an *it*. Like material objects, abstract principles are *its,* no matter how moral or pious. Situation ethics is close in temper at least to the existential norms of love, freedom, and openness which are described, for example, by John Wild in his *Challenge of Existentialism* (pp. 250–272).[14]

The trouble is that responsibility is too much thought of in a forensic way, as answerability to laws or rules rather than as a response to people's calls and needs. *The Dictionary of Social Sciences* says that the core meaning of moral responsibility is answerability or *accountability* for failure. (This is not "answering" in Niebuhr's sense of responding to persons but in the sense of obeying rules and meeting standards.) Thus H. L. A. Hart in jurisprudence has always insisted that responsibility means blameworthiness. The *Dictionary* also has an entry on "response" but draws no connection between response and responsibility. (The term "responsibility" is absent from Bible dictionaries, e.g., Hastings' *Dictionary of the Bible, The Interpreter's Dictionary of the Bible,* and the *New Bible Dictionary.* It is not a Biblical term, even though its *content* may be adduced from both Testaments.) But in classical philosophical ethics and moral theology, responsibility has been forensic or law-tied, meaning imputability and culpability—a matter of assessing guilt, related to vincibility and invincibility in a "forum of conscience" where response to law rather than to need is required of the agent. This legalism has always been at the heart, in Christian ethics, of "seminary" or "manualistic" ethics, whether drawn from a literalistic bibliolatry or from "natural law" and church canons.

In Situations

In every situation the probing question is not so much, What shall I *do?* as What shall *I* do? Responsibility is response, and only the decision maker in his personal being and autonomy can make a response. Certainly no prefabricated moral rule or law can respond. Law excludes response because it attempts to obviate the vital dimensions of freedom and openness, and therefore it frequently, if not constantly, cuts straight across true loving concern. After all, by its very design law aims at being *im*personal and uniform. In spite of a metaethical quarrel with Kant, situationists must confess that he (Kant) was close to their own posture or style of action because he tried to part company with the theological moralists (his phrase) and their heteronomous reliance upon a morality of law prelegislated by some authority other than "the morality of the will" of the decision maker himself. Like Kant, the situationist puts the burden or the onus of decision on the action taker, rather than upon prefabricated directives —even though he does not try, as Kant does, to "universalize" his decisions as if what is right in one situation will always be right (e.g., truth telling). On the contrary, the situationist says to both Kant and to the classical theological moralists whom he sought to undermine that it is a moral mistake to ask *whether* a thing such as lying is right or wrong universally and in the abstract; that the correct question is *when* it is right and *when* it is wrong. He agrees with Chekhov who prayed to God to defend him from generalizations, usually professed by people who have never been in trouble. For in *Christian* situationism there is only one thing about which the question "when" is never asked. That one thing is love, or justice, or *concern*. It is always in order.

In my view the analysis that comes closest to the bone is Bonhoeffer's discussion of the "structure of responsibility" in his *Ethics* (pp. 224–262). He perceives that

responsibility is "essentially a relation of man to man."
By reason of his faith in Christ he calls this "deputyship"
or discipleship. Therefore he can say, "The conscience
which has been set free is not timid like the conscience
which is bound by law, but it stands wide open for our
neighbor and for his concrete distress" (p. 244), the
decision maker being conformed to Christ "the man for
others" and therefore himself for others, since Christian
responsibility does not serve "the ends of an abstract ethic"
(p. 230). Let me quote Bonhoeffer's own words more
fully:

> The question of good is posed and is decided
> in the midst of each definite, yet unconcluded,
> unique and transient situation of our lives, in the
> midst of our living relationships with men, things,
> institutions and powers, in other words in the
> midst of our historical existence. (P. 214.) [What
> sociologists call "defining the situation."—J.F.]
> The responsible man is dependent on the man
> who is concretely his neighbor in his concrete
> possibility. His conduct is not established in ad-
> vance, once and for all, that is to say, as a matter
> of principle, but it arises with the given situation.
> He has no principle at his disposal which possesses
> absolute validity and which he has to put into
> effect fanatically, overcoming all the resistance
> which is offered to it by reality, but he sees in the
> given situation what is necessary and what is
> 'right' for him to grasp and to do. . . . It is not an
> 'absolute good' that is to be realized; but on the
> contrary it is part of the self-direction of the re-
> sponsible agent that he prefers what is relatively
> better to what is relatively worse and that he per-
> ceives that the "absolute good" may sometimes be
> the very worst. . . . All ideological action carries
> its own justification within itself from the outset
> in its guiding principle, but responsible action does
> not lay claim to knowledge of its own ultimate

righteousness. When the deed is performed with a responsible weighing up of all the personal and objective circumstances and in the awareness that God has become *man* and that it is *God* who has become man, then this deed is delivered up solely to God at the moment of its performance. Ultimate ignorance of one's own good and evil, and with it a complete reliance upon grace, is an essential property of responsible historical action. The man who acts ideologically sees himself justified in his idea; the responsible man commits his action into the hands of God and lives by God's grace and favour. (Pp. 227–234.)[15]

Here, apart from its Christian faith based in *pecca fortiter,* is the honest relativism of the modern man. It is found all the way from the pragmatic temper of scientists to the "openness" of existential philosophers. Thus, among the latter, Sartre says in his foundational short essay *Existentialism and Humanism*[16] that "man is always the same, that is, facing a situation which changes, and choice is always a choice in a situation." In the same mood the psychiatrist Eric Berne, author of the best seller *Games People Play,*[17] is quoted in *Life* (August 12, 1966) as saying that what we "have to do about problems is make decisions. But people want certainty. You cannot make decisions with certainty. All you can do is compute likelihoods. People don't like that." (The situationist would amend Berne's statement, "*Faithless* people don't like that," because they are not free to be responsible.) I might add here that it seems to me quite plain how to put it in the language of depth psychology. Libertinism is control by the id, legalism is control by the superego, and situationism is ego control—which is what all analysis and therapy aim at. Ego control is responsibility. The superego must function for the love of law, but the ego at least has the possibility of serving the law of love. Legalism is a heteronomy, spontaneism is sheer subjectivity and infantilism, situationism is self-control, autonomous and acting by the "reality principle."

We can hardly do better than to quote Helmut Thielicke's *Theological Ethics*[18] to reinforce what is said here. "Robinson Crusoe would not be a good example for the ethical situation. For the consistent solipsist—let us say, someone who has lived in lonely isolation from early childhood and grown up without any real human communication— would simply not exist as an ethical person, or ever know himself to be such a person. I learn who I am in encounter with the Thou. Only here does it become apparent that I love and hate, act and am acted upon, fulfill my obligations or fail in my responsibilities" (p. 468). Thielicke, further, explains that since "there can be no legalistic preformed decisions, decision must be made within the framework of each existing situation. The ethics of Law is replaced by a kind of 'situation ethics' (*Situationsethik*)" (p. 650).

Let it be noted, however, in all God-talk by Christians that there is only one way to be responsible in practice, and this is in the form of responsiveness to men. In "deputyship" we may be responding to a call *from* God, but the only way we have to respond is to and with men. This is the incarnational meaning, in terms of responsibility, of the saying that "the dwelling place of God is with men." We validate our response to men in every situation by our faithful response to the God-man. Gerhard Ebeling of Zurich, Brunner's successor, in his *The Nature of Faith* (1959)[19] explains how the responsible self (the I of faith) responds to God's offer of his love in faith or trust, so that self-love is no longer necessary and thus freedom for others is born in us, which freedom is the capacity to respond to the moral claims of our neighbors— the ability to be "responsible" both to God and to men (pp. 132–137). This is the *process* of responsibility in Luther's observation, "Faith is the doer, love is the deed."

And this, in an arresting way, is close to Sartre's deliberate reduction of sin to bad faith and virtue to good faith.

All of this comes down to the "personalistic" nature of responsibility. Impersonal laws and principles may and often do in some situations have a validity and claim, but this is true when it is true only for the sake of persons. Christians, in any case, are commanded to love people, not principles. But a final limiting consideration is of the greatest importance. We are all members one of another, and cannot play favorites, are not "respecters of persons" in Paul's sense of *favoritism* out of obsequious or sentimental impulses. Personalism, to parody Sartre's way of speaking, is a solidarism, not a special interest exclusion or selection of some rather than others or of the few rather than the many. The political principle of the responsible man who heeds the call of others is "one man, one vote." This is the agapeic dimension of Christian responsibility, its social or nonsegregationist nature. And this radical universalism of response is what makes agapeic responsibility a constant threat and judgment to all claims of unique interest.

It is because Sellers, in the book mentioned above, makes the error of supposing that love is selective and interpersonal, thus distinguishing and separating it from justice, that he finds himself (p. 55) saying that love should be *a* means and not the end of Christian living. He thereby cuts across what Jesus and Paul plainly declare, by narrowing love's outreach, but at least when he makes this mistake of separating love and justice (as so many others have done) he has the courage to reach the practical conclusion, in consequence, that what really counts is *justice* (p. 163)!

THAT WORD "LOVE"

Love is all of a piece, no doubt, *psychologically* speaking. But social love or justice is what the New Testament is talking about most of the time. Friendship and romance are valid and real and creative, but they have to be kept in their place. Ralph Harper's *Human Love* (1966)[20] distinguishes rightly between "human" and "mystical" love, the former existential and experiential, the latter a faith commitment. Harper rejects Anders Nygren's radical opposition of the two, arguing (I think successfully) that they can both be encompassed in a responsible human being. But what *I* want to insist upon is that there is a third dimension or kind of love—the *social,* and that this is the key to the New Testament's agapeic principle.

Many will be sure to say that all of this is just a further push toward secularization—toward what Bonhoeffer called "man coming of age" in the sense of living and responding and acting without any God-talk and God-thought. It may very well do so, but just the same, secularization goes on quite apart from what any Christian says. When Margaret Mead says she believes people in modern urban-technical culture need temporary or "student" marriages, as did old Judge Ben Lindsay in the 1920's when he called for "companionate" marriages to the outrage of conventional legalism, Christians may disagree with her ways and means, but she is at least *responsible.* (See *Redbook,* July, 1966, and her proposal of "parental" marriages afterward, to cut down divorce.) Modern education is shifting to freedom, openness, choice, constructiveness rather than imitative practice, away from authoritarianism, rules-bound thinking, answers whether a question is being asked or not! All of this is a shift to *responsibility.* It also reflects the relativity of situation ethics, which while it crystallizes out of legalism nevertheless confronts mere intuitive spontaneity and subjectivity with a rational No.

Let me close with a little embroidery on the story of Solomon and the two harlots who claimed the same baby (I Kings 3:16–28). He ordered the child cut in half, divided between them, and just as the soldier's sword was about to descend one woman (the true mother) cried, No, let the child be given to my antagonist! That was loving concern of a sacrificial order. But now, let us suppose that Solomon had insisted that since each woman *claimed* to be the mother each should have at least part of the child. This poses another issue than sacrificial love, as in the story. It raises the issue of the claim of a moral principle, about truth telling. And suppose that she then said, telling an outright lie: "Oh, no. I confess that I have falsely testified. The child is really hers, not mine." Would she be doing *right*? Do you, gentle reader, want to know whether you are or are not really a situationist? Do you want to know whether your sense of responsibility is agapeic or forensic? Then answer: Would she have done right?

If this essay, or the book as a whole, seems to be more antilegalistic than antiexistential, rather more "down" on impassive principles than on spontaneous or impromptu decisions, it is because in this age it is more strategic to keep the old morality off balance than it is to try to give balance to the often wild reactions against it. Law ethics is still the enemy, by far. Daniel Bell may speak bravely of "the end of ideology," but straightjacket principles are still stifling creative moral conduct and social policy. This suffocation is bad faith, and irresponsible.

Notes

Chapter I.   The New Look in Christian Ethics

1. William Temple, *Nature, Man and God* (London: Macmillan & Co., Ltd., 1934), p. 211.

2. Emil Brunner, *The Divine Imperative*, tr. by Olive Wyon (The Westminster Press, 1947), p. 194.

3. Maurice S. Friedman, *Martin Buber: The Life of Dialogue* (The University of Chicago Press, 1955), p. 20.

4. Edgar S. Brightman, *Nature and Values* (Abingdon Press, 1945), p. 62.

5. John C. Bennett, in *Christianity and the Contemporary Scene*, ed. by Randolph C. Miller and Henry H. Shires (Morehouse-Barlow Co., 1943), p. 119.

6. Cf. *The Clergy Review*, Sept., 1955, 40.9.

7. Charles Benton Eavey, *Principles of Christian Ethics* (Zondervan Publishing House, 1958), p. 246; and Kenneth Moore, O. Carm., *American Ecclesiastical Review*, 135. 1 (July, 1956), 29–38.

8. Augustine, *Ep. Joan.* vii. 5 (MPL 35.2033).

9. Gerald A. Kelly, S.J., *Medico-Moral Problems* (Catholic Hospital Association of the U.S. and Canada, 1958), pp. 149–167; and Thomas Slater, S.J., *Cases of Conscience* (1911), I.341.

10. R. W. Gleason, *Thought*, 32.127 (Winter, 1957–58), 533–558.

11. *Morals of the Catholic Church*, p. 26.

12. Paul Ramsey, *Basic Christian Ethics* (Charles Scribner's Sons, 1950), p. 347.

13. Count Leo Tolstoy, *On Life* (London: Oxford University Press, 1934), pp. 97–98.

14. Henry Davis, S.J., *Moral and Pastoral Theology* (Sheed & Ward, Inc., 1943), Vol. I, p. 310.

15. Oliver Chase Quick, *The Doctrines of the Creed* (Charles Scribner's Sons, 1938), p. 54.

16. "Love," by C. E. B. Cranfield, in Alan Richardson, *Theological Word Book of the Bible* (The Macmillan Company, 1951), pp. 131–136.

17. Quoted in Frederick Donald Coggan, *The New Testament Basis of Moral Theology* (London, 1948), p. 8.

18. *Journals of Søren Kierkegaard*, tr. and ed. by Alexander Dru (Oxford University Press, Inc., 1938), entry 932, p. 317.

19. C. H. Dodd, *Gospel and Law* (Columbia University Press, 1951), p. 42.

20. Immanuel Kant, *Critique of Practical Reason*, tr. by T. K. Abbott (London: Macmillan & Co., Ltd., 1923), p. 176.

21. Theodore Roosevelt, *The Strenuous Life* (New York, 1900), quoted in advertisements of the Container Corporation of America.

22. Kenneth Escott Kirk, ed., *The Study of Theology* (Harper & Brothers, 1939), p. 383.

23. Lynn White, ed., *Frontiers of Knowledge in the Study of Man* (Harper & Brothers, 1956).

24. Brunner, *The Divine Imperative*, p. 132.

25. W. Burnet Easton, Jr., "Ethical Relativism and Popular Morality," in *Theology Today*, 14.4 (Jan., 1958), 470–477.

26. *Acta Apostolicae Sedis*, 44 (1952), 413–419.

27. Reinhold Niebuhr, *Moral Man and Immoral Society* (Charles Scribner's Sons, 1932), p. 277.

28. Edward LeRoy Long, *Conscience and Compromise* (The Westminster Press, 1954), *passim*.

29. The situational approach to ethical decisions has at least a parallel in the classical tradition—in the *"epieicheia"* or equity discussed, e.g., by Aquinas in *Summa Theologica* ii.2, Q. 120, a.1. Kenneth Kirk (*Some Principles of Moral Theology*, p. 208n; London: Longmans, Green & Co., Ltd., 1921) calls it "a just interpretation of the law with due reference to the circumstances of the particular case." Henry Davis (in *Moral and Pastoral Theology*, Vol. I, p. 187) quotes Aristotle's definition: "Equity makes allowance for human weakness, looking not to the law but to the meaning of the

law giver, not to the act but to the intention, not to the part but to the whole." However, many *Christian* legalists will not apply equity to "natural" or "divine" law, holding that God is their author and has foreseen every situation!

Chapter III.   Love and Justice Are the Same Thing

1. *Esquire Magazine,* October, 1959.

2. Anders Nygren, *Agape and Eros,* tr. by Philip S. Watson (The Westminster Press, 1953).

3. Denis de Rougemont, *Love in the Western World,* tr. by Montgomery Belgion (Pantheon Books, Inc., 1956).

4. Martin D'Arcy, *The Mind and Heart of Love* (Henry Holt & Company, Inc., 1947).

5. Reinhold Niebuhr, *An Interpretation of Christian Ethics* (Harper & Brothers, 1935); Reinhold Niebuhr, *The Nature and Destiny of Man* (Charles Scribner's Sons, 1943), Vol. II, pp. 245 ff.

6. Cf. Emil Brunner, *Justice and the Social Order* (London: Lutterworth Press, 1945), pp. 114–118, 125; and William Temple, *Christianity and Social Order* (London: SCM Press, Ltd., 1950), p. 75.

7. Gustaf Aulén, *Church, Law and Society* (Charles Scribner's Sons, 1948).

8. G. Ernest Wright, *The Biblical Doctrine of Man in Society* (London: SCM Press, Ltd., 1954), p. 168.

9. Oliver Chase Quick, *Christianity and Justice* (London: Sheldon Press, 1940), p. 25.

10. Paul Tillich, *The Theology of Culture* (Oxford University Press, Inc., 1959), pp. 133–145.

11. Paul Tillich, *Love, Power, and Justice* (Oxford University Press, Inc., 1954), p. 79.

12. Nicolas Berdyaev, *The Destiny of Man* (Harper & Brothers, 1960), pp. 106–107, 187–192.

13. Albert Schweitzer, *The Philosophy of Civilization* (The Macmillan Company, 1960), p. 311.

14. Cf. esp. Karl Barth, *Church Dogmatics* (Edinburgh: T. & T. Clark, 1961), III/4, and II/2, p. 719.

15. Cf. Jacques Maritain, *Moral Philosophy* (Charles Scribner's Sons, 1964), p. 81; and Bernhard Häring, *The Law of Christ* (The Newman Press, 1963), Vol. II, pp. 98 ff.

16. C. H. Dodd, *Gospel and Law* (Columbia University Press, 1951), p. 42.

17. Immanuel Kant, *Critique of Practical Reason,* tr. by T. K. Abbott (London: Macmillan & Co., Ltd., 1923), p. 176.

18. Herbert Waddams, *New Introduction to Moral Theology* (London: SCM Press, Ltd., 1964), p. 122. His view is refined in his *Life and Fire of Love* (London: S.P.C.K., 1964).

19. Kenneth Kirk, *Some Principles of Moral Theology* (London: Longmans, Green & Co., Ltd., 1921), p. 43n.

20. Robert Mortimer, *The Elements of Moral Theology* (London: Adam and Charles Black, Ltd., 1947), p. 137.

21. Rudolf Bultmann, *Jesus and the Word* (Charles Scribner's Sons, 1958), p. 117.

22. Alan Richardson, ed., *Theological Word Book of the Bible* (The Macmillan Company, 1951), p. 134.

23. Millar Burrows, *Outline of Biblical Theology* (The Westminster Press, 1946), p. 163.

24. Waldo Beech and H. Richard Niebuhr, eds., *Christian Ethics* (The Ronald Press Co., 1955), p. 438.

25. Reinhold Niebuhr, *An Interpretation of Christian Ethics,* p. 210.

26. Martin Buber, *I and Thou* (Charles Scribner's Sons, 2d ed., 1958), p. 14.

27. Martin Buber, *Two Types of Faith* (The Macmillan Company, 1952), pp. 69 ff.

28. Thomas Edmund Jessop, *Law and Love* (London: SCM Press, Ltd., 1940), p. 144.

29. Paul Tillich, *Morality and Beyond* (Harper & Row, Publishers, Inc., 1963), p. 39.

30. Buber, *I and Thou;* Martin Buber, *Between Man and Man* (Beacon Press, Inc., 1955).

31. See note 6.

32. Cf. Joseph Fletcher, *William Temple: Twentieth-Century Christian* (The Seabury Press, Inc., 1963), pp. 48, 308.

33. Brunner, *Justice and the Social Order*, p. 116.

34. Emil Brunner, *The Divine Imperative*, tr. by Olive Wyon (The Westminster Press, 1947), pp. 328–329.

35. Two works here are illuminating: Will Herberg, ed., *Four Existentialist Theologians* (Doubleday & Company, Inc., 1958), and Paul E. Pfuetze, *Self, Society, Existence* (Harper & Brothers, 1954).

36. William Blake, *Jerusalem*, 55:59.

37. Quoted by Brunner, *Justice and the Social Order*, p. 117.

38. *Morals of the Catholic Church*, p. 26.

39. Leo Tolstoy, *On Life* (London: Oxford University Press, 1934), pp. 97–98.

40. Stephen Toulmin, *Examination of the Place of Reason in Ethics* (Cambridge: Cambridge University Press, 1950), esp. pp. 10–64.

41. H. Richard Niebuhr, *Christ and Culture* (Harper & Brothers, 1951), p. 15.

42. Henry Davis, S.J., *Moral and Pastoral Theology* (Sheed & Ward, Inc., 1943), Vol. I, p. 310.

43. Tillich, *Morality and Beyond*, p. 39.

44. *Ibid.*, pp. 39 ff.

45. Jeremy Taylor, *Ductor Dubitantium*, III. Cf. also Ch. III in his *The Rule and Exercise of Holy Living* (1650).

Chapter IV.   The Ethics of Natural Law

1. Richard Hooker, *Ecclesiastical Polity*, I. viii, 9.

2. William Paley, *Works*, ed. by D. S. Wayland (1837), Vol. I, p. 41.

3. Bishop Butler, Sermon 3, *Sermons* (New York, 1858).

4. Jeremy Taylor, *Ductor Dubitantium*, II.i.1.

5. Isa. 55:8.

6. Karl Barth, *Church Dogmatics*, II/2.8.

7. William Temple, *Thomism and Modern Needs* (London: Blackfriars Publications, 1944).

8. Cf. Joseph Fletcher, *William Temple: Twentieth-Century Christian* (The Seabury Press, Inc., 1963), esp. pp. 147–163 and notes. .

9. *Malvern, 1941,* Proceedings of the Archbishop of York's Conference (London: Longmans, Green & Co., Ltd., 1941).

10. Vigo Demant, *Theology of Society* (London: Faber & Faber, Ltd., 1947).

11. J. Fuchs, *Le Droit Naturel* (Paris: 1960).

12. A. R. Vidler and W. A. Whitehouse, eds., *Natural Law: A Christian Reconsideration* (London: Macmillan & Co., Ltd., 1946).

13. Eng. trans. (St. Louis, 1957).

14. Kenneth Kirk, *Some Principles of Moral Theology* (London: Longmans, Green & Co., Ltd., 1921).

15. Denys Lawrence Munby, *Christianity and Economic Problems* (London: Macmillan & Co., Ltd., 1956).

16. There are a few elliptic references in the two Books of Homilies associated with the Articles.

17. A joint statement based on a fifteen-year inquiry by the Convocations of Canterbury and York.

18. *Canadian Journal of Theology,* I.3 (1960), cited p. 60.

19. Cf. p. 44.

20. Nathaniel Micklem, *Law and the Laws* (London: William Green & Son, Ltd., 1952).

21. Jacques Ellul, *The Theological Foundation of Law* (Doubleday & Company, Inc., 1960).

22. Paul Tournier, *The Whole Person in a Broken World* (Harper & Row, Publishers, Inc., 1964). (*Désharmonie de la Vie moderne;* Neuchâtel, 1947.)

23. *Contra Celsum,* V. 37.

24. John C. Bennett, *Christians and the State* (Charles Scribner's Sons, 1958), p. 16.

25. Walter George Muelder, *Foundations of the Responsible Society* (Abingdon Press, 1959).

26. Ronald Preston, in *Theology,* Jan., 1961.

27. Edward Duff, S.J., *The Social Thought of the World Council of Churches* (Longmans, Green & Co., Inc., 1956), p. 93.

28. Emil Brunner, *Justice and the Social Order* (London: Lutterworth Press, 1945), pp. 80 ff. Also *The Divine Imperative* (*Das Gebot und die Ordnungen*), tr. by Olive Wyon (The Westminster Press, 1947), esp. note, p. 269.

29. William Temple, *Church and Nation* (London, 1915), p. 134.

30. C. H. Dodd, in *Theology*, May–June, 1946.

31. Werner Elert, *The Christian Ethos* (Muhlenberg Press, 1957).

32. Cf. Helmut Thielicke, *Theologische Ethik*, I. 1001 ff., 2010 ff., 2144 ff.

33. James Pike, *A Time for Christian Candor* (Longmans, Green & Co., Inc., 1964), pp. 41–50.

34. Samuel Miller and Ernest Wright, eds., *Ecumenical Dialogue at Harvard* (Harvard University Press, 1964), pp. 264–270.

35. Edward Schillebeeckx, in *De Linie*, Brussels, Dec. 20, 1963.

36. R. O. Johann, "Natural Law and the Person," American Society of Christian Ethics, Jan. 21, 1965.

37. F. E. Flynn, "Natural Law and Overpopulation," in *What Modern Catholics Think About Birth Control*, ed. by W. Birmingham (The New American Library of World Literature, Inc., 1964), p. 167.

38. Eric D'Arcy, *Conscience and Its Right to Freedom* (London: Sheed & Ward, Ltd., 1961), p. 138.

39. Lynn White, ed., *Frontiers of Knowledge in the Study of Man* (Harper & Brothers, 1956).

40. Brunner, *The Divine Imperative*, p. 132.

41. Joseph Sittler, "The Structure of Christian Ethics," in *Life and Community*, ed. by H. C. Letts (Muhlenberg Press, 1957).

42. *Acta Apostolicae Sedis*, 44 (1952), 413–419.

43. E.g., cf. Karl Rahner, "On the Question of the Formal Existential Ethics," in *Theological Investigations* (Helicon Press, 1963), Vol. II, pp. 217 ff.

44. Cf. Erik Routley, *The Man for Others* (Oxford University Press, Inc., 1964); Canon Douglas Rhymes, *No New Morality* (London: Constable & Co., Ltd., 1963); A. R. Vidler, ed., *Soundings* (Cambridge: Cambridge University Press, 1962), esp. H. A. Williams; and *Objections to Christian Belief* (London: Constable & Co., Ltd., 1963), esp. D. M. MacKinnon; J. A. T. Robinson, *Christian Morals Today* (The Westminster Press, 1964).

45. Two works may be cited: Albert Terrill Rasmussen, *Christian Social Ethics* (Prentice-Hall, Inc., 1956); and less succinctly a kind of subtype, Paul Lehmann, *Ethics in a Christian Context* (Harper & Row, Publishers, Inc., 1963).

46. William Temple, *Nature, Man and God* (London: Macmillan & Co., Ltd., 1934), p. 416.

47. Cf. P. T. Coffee, "Moral Systems and a Defense of Compensationism," *Anglican Theological Review*, July, 1959.

Chapter VI. Sex Offenses: An Ethical View

1. Morris Ploscowe, *Sex and the Law* (Prentice-Hall, Inc., 1951), p. 271.

2. Edmond Cahn, *The Moral Decision* (Indiana University Press, 1955), p. 89.

3. Alfred C. Kinsey, Wardell B. Pomeroy, and Clyde E. Martin, *Sexual Behavior in the Human Male* (W. B. Saunders Company, 1948), p. 392.

4. Morris Ploscowe, "The Place of Law in Medico-Moral Problems," 31 *N.Y.U.L. Rev.* 1238 (1956).

5. Walter Lippmann, *A Preface to Morals* (1929), p. 286.

6. See J. Kenneth Galbraith, *The Affluent Society* (Houghton Mifflin Company, 1958), pp. 7–20.

7. Bertrand Russell, *Marriage and Morals* (1929), p. 88.

8. Glanville Williams, "The Reform of the Criminal Law and of Its Administration," 4 *J. Soc'y Pub. Teach. L.* 217, 221 (1958).

9. City of Milwaukee v. Milwaukee Elec. Ry., 173 Wis. 400, 406, 180 N.W. 339, 341 (1920).

10. American Banana Co. v. United Fruit Co., 213 U.S. 347, 356 (1909).

11. Cohen, "Judicial Ethics," 12 Ohio St. L.J. 3, 10 (1951).

12. D. H. Lawrence, *Pornography and Obscenity* (1930), p. 13.

13. Adultery in certain circumstances, especially of the wife, is punishable; but it is punished as an offense against the marriage contract, not as a sexual act in itself.

14. *Model Penal Code* art. 207 (Tent. Draft No. 4, 1955; Tent. Draft No. 9, 1959).

15. British attitudes and policies, as reflected in sex offender legislation, are treated more extensively elsewhere in the symposium "Sex Offenses." Hall Williams, "Sex Offenses: The British Experience," *infra* pp. 334–360.

16. See Ploscowe, *Sex and the Law,* p. 151.

17. *Ibid.,* p. 281.

18. John McPartland, *Sex in Our Changing World* (Rinehart & Co., Inc, 1947), p. 145.

19. Va. Code Ann. § 18.82 (Cum. Supp. 1959).

20. W. Va. Code Ann. § 6058 (1955).

21. R.I. Gen. Laws Ann. § 11–6–3 (1956).

22. Ariz. Rev. Stat. Ann. § 13–222 (1956).

23. N.D. Rev. Code § 12–2208 (1943).

24. Ploscowe, *Sex and the Law,* p. 157.

25. *Ibid.,* p. 281.

26. H. C. Lea, *History of Sacerdotal Celibacy in the Christian Church* (1932), pp. 244, 260 *et seq.*, 445, *et seq.*

27. Geoffrey May, *Social Control and Sex Expression* (1930), p. 105.

28. 25 Hen. 8, c. 6 (1953).

29. Offenses Against the Person Act, 1828, 9 Geo. 4, c. 31 § 1, as amended, Criminal Law Amendment Act, 1885, 48 & 49 Vict., c. 69, § 11.

30. N.Y. Pen. Law § 690.

31. Nev. Rev. Stat. § 201.190 (Supp. 1958).

32. Ky. Rev. Stat. § 436.050 (Supp. 1955); La. Rev. Stat. § 14:89 (1950); N.H. Rev. Stat. § 579.9 (1955); S.C. Code § 16–412 (1952); Wis. Stat. § 944.17 (1957).

33. Ariz. Rev. Stat. Ann. § 13–651 (1956); Idaho Code Ann. § 18–6605 (1948); Mont. Rev. Codes Ann. § 94–4118 (1947); N.C. Gen. Stat. § 14–177 (1943); S.C. Code § 16–412 (1952); Tenn. Code Ann. § 39–707 (1956).

34. Ind. Acts 1905, ch. 169, § 473, at 584.

35. Augustine, *De Ordine* II. iv. (12).

36. Thomas Aquinas, *Summa Theologica* ii.2, Q.10, a.11.

37. Williams, *loc. cit.,* p. 224.

38. *Ibid.,* p. 197.

39. Pitirim A. Sorokin, *The American Sex Revolution* (Porter E. Sargent, Inc., 1957), p. 131.

40. Dersch, "Chastity Is Not Outmoded," 18 *Child-Family Dig.* 3, 5 (1959).

41. Committee on Homosexual Offenses and Prostitution, "Report," Cmnd. No. 247 (1957) [hereinafter cited as Cmnd. No. 247].

42. D. S. Bailey, ed., *Sexual Offenders and Social Punishment* (1956).

43. *Ibid.*, p. 38.

44. *Ibid,* pp. 17, 62.

45. Eustace Chesler, *Live and Let Live* (Philosophical Library, Inc., 1958).

46. Albert Ellis, *Sex Without Guilt* (L. Stuart, 1958). Complete promiscuity (short of coercion) is also defended by Rene Guyon, *The Ethics of Sexual Acts* (Alfred A. Knopf, Inc., 1934); Norman Haire, *Hymen or the Future of Marriage* (1928).

47. Ellis, *op. cit.*, p. 190.

48. Cmnd. No. 247, para. 61.

49. *Ibid.*, para. 257.

50. *Model Penal Code* § 207.11, comment at 151 (Tent. Draft. No. 9, 1959).

51. Cf. Frey, "Freedom of Residence in Illinois," *Chicago Bar Record,* Oct. 1959, p. 4.

52. Edvard Westermarck, *Christianity and Morals* (The Macmillan Company, 1939), p. 374. Cf. Havelock Ellis, *Sex in Relation to Society* (London: William Heinemann, Ltd., 1937), p. 207.

53. *Model Penal Code* § 207.11, comment at 150 (Tent. Draft. No. 9, 1959).

54. George Frazer, *Man, God and Immortality* (1927), pp. 191–92.

55. Holloway v. United States, 148 F.2d 665, 666–67 (D.C. Cir. 1945).

56. *Time,* Nov. 30, 1959, p. 44. The Earl of Winterton has remarked that if the Archbishop's wish to outlaw adultery were realized, a good many members of the House of Lords would have to go to prison. *Ibid.,* Jan. 4, 1960, p. 23.

57. F. J. Boland and J. A. Ryan, *Catholic Principles of Politics* (The Macmillan Company, 1960), p. 169.

58. See e.g., O'Brien, "Why Do Catholics Oppose Artificial Birth Control?" *Our Sunday Visitor,* June 15, 1958.

59. Lon L. Fuller, *The Law in Quest of Itself* (Foundation Press, Inc., 1940), pp. 4–6.

60. Cf. Westermarck, *op. cit.,* p. 378.

61. Wiley B. Rutledge, *A Declaration of Legal Faith* (University of Kansas, 1947), p. 6.

62. Holmes, "The Path of Law," 10 *Harv. L. Rev.* 456, 467 (1897).

63. Cf. Bruno Bettelheim, *Love Is Not Enough* (The Free Press of Glencoe, 1950), *passim.*

64. State v. Chandler, 132 Mo. 155, 164, 33 S.W. 797, 799 (1896).

65. *Model Penal Code* § 207.11, comment at 149 (Tent. Draft. No. 9, 1950). But cf. Tinnelly, *Abortion and Penal Law,* 5 Catholic Law. 187 (1959).

66. Edmond Cahn, *The Sense of Injustice* (New York University Press, 1949), p. 31.

67. William Temple, in *Theology,* 8. 17 (1936).

68. This is not quite true any longer. One well-known psychiatrist was quoted as saying, "No human being should ever be blamed for anything he does." *Time,* Sept. 14, 1959, p. 69. This presumably entails a "no praise" clause also. It repudiates ethical judgment altogether.

69. Sylvanus Duvall, *Men, Women and Morals* (Association Press, 1952), p. 285.

70. Patrick Devlin, *The Enforcement of Morals* (1959), p. 15.

71. Lippmann, *op. cit.,* p. 292.

72. Cf. Joseph Fletcher, "A Twentieth-Century Philosophy of Sex," *Ladies' Home Journal,* March, 1959, p. 48.

Chapter VII.   On Fertility Control

1. Having received the commission's report, Pope Paul, in November, 1966, decreed that the prohibition of "artificial" birth control would remain in force for the foreseeable future. It is not clear whether this is natural or positive law!

Chapter VIII.   Ethics and Unmarried Sex

1. Lewis H. Terman, *et al., Psychological Factors in Marital Happiness* (McGraw-Hill Book Company, Inc., 1938).

2. *Sex and the College Student,* Group for the Advancement of Psychiatry, Report 60, 104 E. 25th Street, N.Y., 1965, p. 98.

3. *Newsweek,* April 6, 1964.

4. *Time,* April 18, 1960, p. 48.

5. *Time,* Feb. 13, 1950, p. 57.

6. *Saturday Review,* Dec. 12, 1964, p. 61.

7. *The New York Times,* Sept. 2, 1965, p. 1.

8. *Sex Ethics: A Study By and For Adult Christians,* The Sycamore Community, P.O. Box 72, State College, Pa., 1965.

9. *Christianity Today,* Oct. 8, 1965.

10. Dorothy Sayers, *The Other Six Deadly Sins* (London: Hodder & Stoughton, Ltd., 1961).

11. I Cor. 6:16: "Do you not know that he who joins himself to a prostitute becomes one body with her? For, as it is written, 'The two shall become one.'"

12. See also *Consultation on Sex Ethics,* World Council of Churches, Founex, Switzerland, July 6–10, 1964.

13. See Lester Kirkendall, *Premarital Intercourse and Interpersonal Relations* (Julian Press, Inc., 1961).

14. John Macmurray, *Reason and Emotion* (Barnes & Noble, Inc., 1962), p. 39.

15. Mary Calderone, in *Redbook Magazine,* July, 1965.

16. John Hersey, *Too Far to Walk* (Alfred A. Knopf, Inc., 1966).

17. Quoted in R. F. Hettlinger, *Living with Sex: The Student's Dilemma* (The Seabury Press, Inc., 1966), p. 139.

18. Hugh Hefner, in *Playboy,* December, 1964.

19. See Harvey Cox, *The Secular City* (The Macmillan Company, 1965), p. 212.

20. Joseph Fletcher, "Sex Offenses: An Ethical View," *Law and Contemporary Problems,* Spring, 1960, pp. 244–257.

21. Ruth Adams, in *The New York Times,* March 22, 1966.

Chapter IX.   Euthanasia and Anti-Dysthanasia

1. A Dr. Kildare episode, November 30, 1961, Boston, Channel 4, NBC.

2. Cf. J. J. Shinners, *The Morality of Medical Experimentation* (Catholic University of America Press, 1958), pp. 50–67.

3. Rabbi Immanuel Jakobovits, *Jewish Medical Ethics* (Block Publishing Co., 1962), p. 124.

4. *Acta Apostolicae Sedis,* 49:1027–1033.

5. Gerald A. Kelly, *Medico-Moral Problems* (Dublin: Clonmore & Reynolds, Ltd., 1955), pp. 131–36.

6. Cf. Norman St. John Stevas, *Life, Death and the Law* (Indiana University Press, 1961), p. 271; Glanville Williams, *Sanctity of Life and the Criminal Law* (Alfred A. Knopf, Inc., 1957), p. 336.

7. David Karnofsky, in *Time,* Nov. 3, 1961.

8. *American Church Union News,* January, 1961, p. 21; *Trud* (Moscow), December 18, 1960, p. 3.

Chapter X.   Situation Ethics for Business Management

1. Ernest J. Hodges, in *The Nation,* June 18, 1960, p. 523.

2. Kenneth Boulding, *A Reconstruction of Economics* (John Wiley & Sons, Inc., 1950); Neil W. Chamberlain, *A General Theory of Economic Process* (Harper & Brothers, 1955).

3. *The Episcopalian,* June, 1960, pp. 2–8.

4. See Joseph Fletcher, "The New Look in Christian Ethics," *Harvard Divinity School Bulletin,* October, 1959, pp. 7–18. (Chapter I of this book.)

5. See the warnings in Eph. 6:12; II Cor. 11:4; and the implicit warnings in I Cor. 7:40. Also see I Tim. 4:1.

6. Jean-Paul Sartre, *Age of Reason* (Alfred A. Knopf, Inc., 1947); Simone de Beauvoir, *The Ethics of Ambiguity* (Philosophical Library, Inc., 1948).

7. A fresh and contemporary survey of such approaches is set out in Wayne A. R. Leys, *Ethics for Policy Decisions* (Prentice-Hall, Inc., 1952).

8. See the discussion by Chamberlain of nonpecuniary satisfactions in business behavior, *op. cit.*, p. 161.

9. *Journals of Søren Kierkegaard,* tr. and ed. by Alexander Dru (Oxford University Press, Inc., 1938), p. 317.

10. R. L. Bruckberger, *Image of America* (The Viking Press, Inc., 1959); a shrewd and perceptive diagnosis of America, described as a nonideological, nondoctrinaire, innovative society—a kind of *situationist culture!* Theories of business behavior might get a few clues here.

11. The information used here is drawn from three sources: Donald R. Cressey, *Other People's Money* (The Free Press of Glencoe, 1953); Norman Jaspan and Hillel Black, *The Thief in the White Collar* (J. B. Lippincott Company, 1960); Edwin H. Sutherland, *White Collar Crime* (The Dryden Press, Inc., 1949).

12. Jaspan and Black, *op. cit.*, pp. 61–82.

Chapter XIV.   Moral Responsibility

1. H. Richard Niebuhr, *The Responsible Self* (Harper & Row, Publishers, Inc., 1963).

2. A. C. Ewing, *The Definition of Good* (The Macmillan Company, 1947).

3. Joseph Fletcher, *Situation Ethics* (The Westminster Press, 1966).

4. Nicolas Berdyaev, *Solitude and Society* (Charles Scribner's Sons, 1938).

5. Martin Buber, *I and Thou* (Charles Scribner's Sons, 2d ed., 1958).

6. James Sellers, *Theological Ethics* (The Macmillan Company, 1966).

7. Maurice S. Friedman, *Martin Buber: The Life of Dialogue* (Harper & Row, Publishers, Inc., 1960).

8. Friedrich Gogarten, *Glaube und Wirklichkeit* (Jena: Eugen Diedrichs Verlag, 1928).

9. Karl Heim, *God Transcendent* (Charles Scribner's Sons, 1936).

10. Eberhard Griesbach, *Gegenwart. Eine kritische Ethik* (Halle, 1928).

11. Karl Barth, *Church Dogmatics,* III/2 (Edinburgh: T. & T. Clark, 1960).

12. Emil Brunner, *The Divine Imperative,* tr. by Olive Wyon (The Westminster Press, 1947).

13. Harvey Cox, *God's Revolution and Man's Responsibility* (Judson Press, 1965).

14. John Wild, *The Challenge of Existentialism* (Indiana University Press, 1955).

15. Dietrich Bonhoeffer, *Ethics,* ed. by Eberhard Bethge (SCM Press, Ltd., 1955).

16. Jean-Paul Sartre, *Existentialism* (Philosophical Library, Inc., 1947).

17. Eric Berne, *Games People Play* (Grove Press, Inc., 1964).

18. Helmut Thielicke, *Theological Ethics* (Fortress Press, 1966).

19. Gerhard Ebeling, *The Nature of Faith* (London: William Collins Sons & Co., Ltd., Fontana Library, 1966).

20. Ralph Harper, *Human Love* (The Johns Hopkins Press, 1966).